BY CHARLES DEL TODESCO

PHOTOGRAPHY BY PATRICK JANTET

TRANSLATED BY JOHN O'TOOLE

THE HAVANA CIGAR

CUBA'S FINEST

ABBEVILLE PRESS PUBLISHERS

NEW YORK LONDON PARIS

Sublime tobacco. . . .
Divine in hookas, glorious in a pipe,
When tipp'd with amber, mellow, rich and ripe:
Like other charmers, wooing the caress
More dazzlingly when daring in full dress:
Yet thy true lovers more admire by far
Thy naked beauties—Give me a cigar!

—Byron, *The Island* II, 19.

FRONT COVER: A WOODEN CIGAR MOLD HOLDING TEN "BONCHES,"
EACH ONE THE EVENTUAL CORE OF A HAVANA CIGAR
BACK COVER: THE HISTORIC PARTAGÁS BUILDING IN HAVANA
ENDPAPERS: ASSORTED HAVANA CIGAR BANDS

ENGLISH-LANGUAGE EDITION:
EDITOR: JEFFREY GOLICK
DESIGNER: CELIA FULLER
PRODUCTION MANAGER: DANA COLE

ORIGINALLY PUBLISHED AS HAVANE: CIGARE DE LÉGENDE
COPYRIGHT © 1996 ÉDITIONS ASSOULINE
ENGLISH TRANSLATION COPYRIGHT © 1997 ABBEVILLE PRESS.
ALL RIGHTS RESERVED UNDER INTERNATIONAL COPYRIGHT CONVENTIONS. NO
PART OF THIS BOOK MAY BE REPRODUCED OR UTILIZED IN ANY FORM OR BY ANY
MEANS, ELECTRONIC OR MECHANICAL, INCLUDING PHOTOCOPYING, RECORDING,
OR BY ANY INFORMATION STORAGE AND RETRIEVAL SYSTEM, WITHOUT PERMIS-
SION IN WRITING FROM THE PUBLISHER. INQUIRIES SHOULD BE ADDRESSED TO
ABBEVILLE PUBLISHING GROUP, 488 MADISON AVENUE, NEW YORK, N.Y.
10022. THE TEXT OF THIS BOOK WAS SET IN BULMER, ITC FRANKLIN GOTHIC,
AND DF ORGANICS. PRINTED AND BOUND IN ITALY.

FIRST ENGLISH-LANGUAGE EDITION
2 4 6 8 10 9 7 5 3 1

LIBRARY OF CONGRESS CATALOGING-IN-PUBLICATION DATA
DEL TODESCO, CHARLES.
   [HAVANE. ENGLISH]
   THE HAVANA CIGAR : CUBA'S FINEST / BY CHARLES DEL TODESCO :
PHOTOGRAPHY BY PATRICK JANTET : TRANSLATED BY JOHN O'TOOLE. —
1ST ED.
      P.   CM.
   INCLUDES BIBLIOGRAPHICAL REFERENCES AND INDEX.
   ISBN 07892-0327-8
   1. CIGARS. 2. CIGAR INDUSTRY—CUBA—HISTORY.   I. TITLE.
TS2260.D4513 1997
679'.72'097291—DC21   96-47588

PART ONE

✸

CONTENTS

PART TWO

✸

✸

THE CREATOR OF THE WORLD, ACCORDING TO THE CUBAN writer Fernando Ortiz, after molding the American continent, broke off a few bits of earth which formed a string of islands as they fell into the sea. In this way the Antilles were born. Among these thousands of islands the largest is Cuba, the "Pearl of the Antilles."

Anchored in the Tropic of Cancer, Cuba enjoys fine weather that alternates every six months between trade winds and tropical calm. The island's fertile lands, criss-crossed by innumerable small rivers and streams, and blessed with a moderate climate, are the true kingdom of tobacco.

On October 27, 1492, Christopher Columbus came to the shores of the large island of "Colba." Following a jour-ney that had taken longer than expected, he was nonetheless convinced he had reached Japan. The Genovese navigator had in fact just discovered the Caribbean, gateway to the Americas, which he mistook for Cathay, present-day China.

THE HAVANA: FIVE HUNDRED YEARS OF HISTORY

He dispatched two emissaries, Rodrigo de Xerez and Luis de Torres, to the island's interior to establish the first contact with the king of the lands lying before him. The scouts, however, only found villages of simple huts and half-naked inhabitants, the Taino people. They may have noticed as individuals fashioned strange firebrands from dried leaves, which they kindled at one end while inhaling the smoke from the other.

Blinded by his expected meeting with the emperor of China and his own mission of presenting the powerful ruler with a letter from the king of Spain, Columbus paid no atten-tion to tobacco and its exceptional aroma. Even if he had, Columbus would probably have not recognized its signifi-cance: since time immemorial tobacco had served as the cement binding together pre-Columbian civilizations, an inte-gral part of numerous sacred rites. Priest, doctor, and sooth-sayer, a *behique* would use tobacco to communicate with his idols during the *cohoba* (or *cojoba*) ceremony. After fasting he would inhale powdered tobacco from a smooth wooden plate through a Y-shaped tube, applying the forked ends to his

nostrils and placing the other end close to the powder. The altered state that tobacco produced allowed the *behique* to speak with supernatural spirits capable of answering questions concerning, for instance, the outcome of a battle, the abundance of the coming harvest, the causes of an illness, or the chances of a patient's survival. West Indian families also grew tobacco near their homes simply for the pleasure of smoking *tabaco,* the forerunner of the Havana cigar *(Habano).*

Back in Europe, Catholic priests emphasized tobacco's use in Native religious ceremonies in order to demonstrate—and denounce—more strongly its diabolical character. Legend has it that sometime after his return, Rodrigo de Xerez was caught by his wife smoking at home some of the tobacco he had brought back with him from Cuba. Thinking him possessed by a demon, she denounced de Xerez and had him thrown into the dungeons of the Inquisition. When de Xerez was freed years later—*¡Cielos!* (in other words, *Holy smoke!*)—using tobacco had become commonplace among his fellow countrymen. Indeed, despite religious authorities the world over, who never held the sweet-smelling leaf in good odor, tobacco had no trouble spreading throughout the world, reaching Europe by 1540, and the Far East during the seventeenth century.

The conquest and colonization of Cuba was undertaken by Diego Velázquez in 1511. Sailing from Santo Domingo, he landed on Cuba's southcentral shore, founding first the city of Trinidad; then Sancti Spiritus, further inland; Bayamo, also inland and toward the island's southeastern tip; and Havana (or, in Spanish, Habana, 1514), whose strategic position along the northern coast soon made it an obligatory stop for ships hailing from or setting sail for Spain.

Colonists quickly learned from the local Indians the secret of raising tobacco and the steps for drying and curing it. In the meantime, tobacco had traveled to Spain and Portugal, where the French ambassador to Lisbon, Jean Nicot (hence *nicotine* and tobacco's scientific name: genus *Nicotiana),* raised some of the famous plant and discovered that it possessed curative properties. He even sent a sample of it to Catherine de Médicis, the queen consort and regent of France, and was able to treat one of her pages. This cure earned tobacco the nickname "the queen's herb."

Helped by its favorable reputation as a medicinal, tobacco was introduced into Belgium (1554), Germany (1559), Holland (1561), and England (1570), even making its way around the world to Japan (1605) and China (1638), where it was brought by sailors who had learned to smoke in Havana. In order to meet growing demand, tobacco farming and trade were expanded in Santo Domingo sometime after 1531, Cuba around 1580, Brazil in 1600, Virginia in 1612, and Maryland after 1631, a boom that was naturally stimulated at first by the absence of any specific laws governing such commerce.

TOBACCO TAXONOMY

TOBACCO IS A PLANT THAT HAS LONG BEEN WIDELY CULTIVATED AND JUST AS WIDELY MALIGNED. TOBACCO BELONGS TO THE FAMILY SOLANACEAE, GENUS *NICOTIANA,* THE SCIENTIFIC NAME THAT REFERS TO ONE OF THE FIRST ADVOCATES (FOR HEALTH REASONS!) OF THE "SOT WEED," THE FRENCH AMBASSADOR TO PORTUGAL (1559–61), JEAN NICOT. TOBACCO ALSO BOASTS SEVERAL SURPRISING GENETIC COUSINS, INCLUDING THE POTATO, THE CHICKPEA, THE TOMATO, AND THE PEPPER.

THERE ARE OVER SIXTY RECOGNIZED SPECIES OF *NICOTIANA.* OF THESE, HOWEVER, ONLY TWO—*N. TABACUM* AND *N. RUSTICA*—ARE COMMONLY USED FOR CONSUMPTION.

N. RUSTICA WAS ALREADY GROWN BY NATIVES WHEN COLUMBUS SET FOOT ON AMERICA. IT IS THAT SPECIES, WITH ITS GREENISH YELLOW FLOWERS, THAT WAS BROUGHT TO THE OLD WORLD, WHERE IT HAD NO TROUBLE ADAPTING TO ITS NEW SURROUNDINGS.

N. TABACUM HAS GIVEN RISE TO NUMEROUS VARIETIES, WHICH INCLUDE THE MAJORITY OF TOBACCOS RAISED COMMERCIALLY. IT HAS A DISTINCTIVE PYRAMIDAL SHAPE, WITH THE PLANT'S LARGEST LEAVES GROWING AT ITS BASE NEAR THE GROUND. THE COLOR OF ITS FLOWERS VARIES FROM WHITE TO RED.

A THIRD SPECIES, *N. ALATA,* INCLUDES A PERSIAN VARIETY CALLED *TUMBAK* OR *TUMBAKI,* CULTIVATED IN TURKEY AND IRAN FOR USE IN *NARGHILES,* OR WATERPIPES. OTHER SPECIES, *N. SYLVESTRIS* AND *N. ALATA GRANDIFLORA,* ARE PRIZED AS ORNAMENTAL PLANTS.

Taxonomic Classification of Cuban Tobacco

PHYLUM:	SPERMATOPHYTA
CLASS:	ANGIOSPERMAE
SUBCLASS:	DICOTYLEDONEAE
ORDER:	CAMPANULALES
FAMILY:	SOLANACEAE
GENUS:	*NICOTIANA*
SPECIES:	*TABACUM*

OPPOSITE
Only the name of this bygone manufacturer has held up against the assault of time.
PAGES 10–11
Neither the trademark nor the automobile remains of this once glorious period.

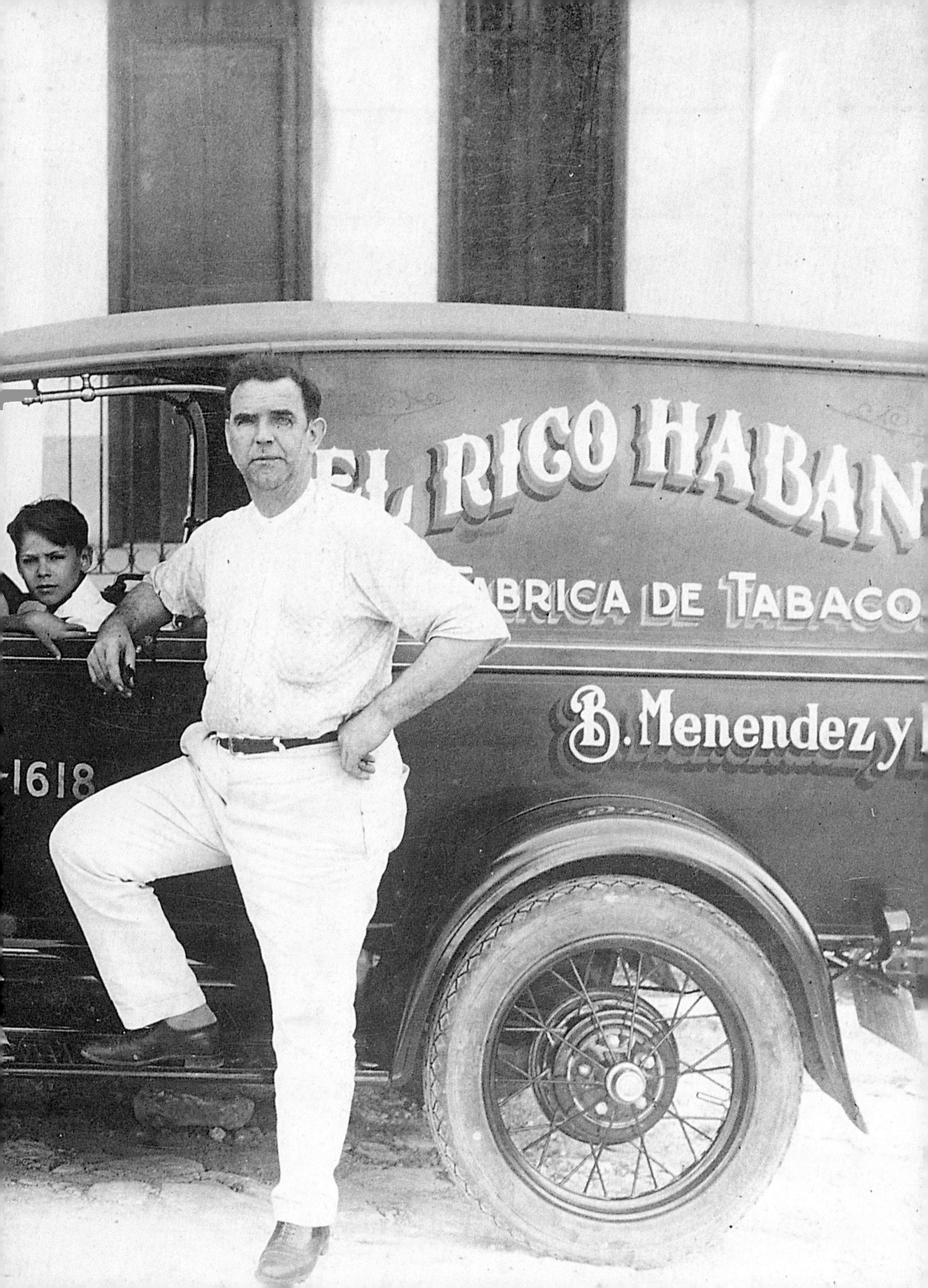

EL RICO HABAN
FABRICA DE TABACO
B. Menendez y
1618

Seated behind anonymous numbers, workers' skillful hands baptize the Havanas.

Cuba's first European tobacco farmers, native Canary Islanders for the most part, bartered their aromatic leaves or rudimentary cigars for food. Some even dealt directly with smugglers. It was only in 1614 that the king of Spain decreed that all tobacco not consumed on the island had to be registered in Seville, while to regulate tobacco farming on the island the Assembly of Havana instituted a license in 1616. The city's leading citizens had complained that lands set aside for raising fruit and vegetables were actually planted with tobacco, and consequently the needs of the people could no longer be met. Furthermore, whole forests were being felled to make room for new plantations, endangering the lumber supply needed for repairing ships in port.

The problems raised by the rapid success of tobacco farming created a rivalry between landowning ranchers *(hacendados)* and tobacco growers *(vegueros),* whose fields bordered the former's estates. Marked by occasional skirmishes, some legal and some lethal, this competition was to last some fifty years.

Trade in the fragrant leaf proved so lucrative that the Spanish Crown, eager to replenish its treasury after the War of Spanish Succession (1701–14), imposed a monopoly in 1717. The tobacco harvest in its entirety filled the holds of ships bound for Seville, then world capital of the cigar. (The

first cigar factories in Havana would be founded only at the close of the eighteenth century.)

The strict rules of the monopoly, along with the greed of merchants and government officials, sparked several revolts by private tobacco growers who were deprived of their share of the profits. Following the bloody suppression of one of these uprisings, rebellious *vegueros,* fearing possible persecution, fled to the western part of the island, where they discovered the soil that was to give the Havana its quintessential aroma. These were the lands of the Vuelta Abajo, where the world's greatest tobacco was to develop.

The turmoil of the early eighteenth century in no way disturbed exports of Cuban tobacco, which was already well known for its superior quality. Enjoyed in the form of a cigar by Spanish and Portuguese nobility, Jean Nicot's leaf was no less prized in France, where it was consumed in English pipes. The queen's herb proved superbly impervious to European conflicts dividing the Continent. Indeed, it was the Napoleonic Wars (1801–15)—especially the Peninsular War—that gave British soldiers, and eventually the British people, their taste for the cigar.

Suspended in 1723 following the last *vegueros* revolt, the tobacco monopoly was reestablished in 1761, a year before the English occupation of Havana. Upon their arrival

12

in 1762 and throughout the same year, the British seized control of all stocks of tobacco, part of which went to supply their colonies in North America.

After the departure of the English in 1763 the official body regulating the tobacco trade took advantage of the confused situation to set quality standards for the tobacco exported to Seville. This commission established the first criteria for categorizing tobacco leaves, which were broken down into five classes according to texture, color, and possible flaws. Supplemented in 1789 by a series of written instructions, this collection of recommendations formed the tobacco grower's first manual, outlining in detail the different steps in cultivating the "sot weed." The improvements introduced by the manual enabled growers to perfect the curing of tobacco and develop the technique of shade-grown wrapper leaves. At the same time, the actual makeup of the cigar was refined: filler leaves, *la tripa,* were rolled in a binder, *la sobretripa,* which was in turn wrapped in a thin, elegant, lighter-colored leaf, *la capa,* or wrapper.

The Casa de Beneficiencia, the first Havana cigar factory under the Tobacco Board's control, began production in 1799, the same year the name "Havana cigar" was made official. The Cuban capital already had a few small clandestine workshops, or *chinchales,* turning out cigars, but it was with the end of the eighteenth century that the Havana would earn its worldwide reputation. Havana the city was replacing Seville as the center of the cigar trade. Times were changing and the Havana's renown justified scrapping the tobacco monopoly in 1817. Cigar manufacturers now enjoyed a veritable boom, with nearly four hundred factories in operation several years later. Because of a labor shortage, the industry resorted to employing prisoners. Nevertheless, factory owners refused to use slaves, for they felt that such work could only be done by freemen for pay. Certain Havanas were thus rolled in prison cellars, which were often compared to the holds of ships. The workshops of the cigar rollers, or *torcedores,* thus came to be known as *galeras,* literally "galleys."

As early as 1825 the name H. de Cabañas y Carbajol figures in Havana's registry of cigar brands; Partagás was added to the rolls in 1827, Por Larrañaga in 1834, Punch in 1840, H. Upmann in 1844, La Corona in 1845, El Rey del Mundo in 1848, and Romeo y Julieta in 1850. In 1861 there existed on the island 1,217 cigar manufacturers, including 516 in Havana whose entire output was reserved for exportation.

In no time the most prestigious makes had set the Old World on fire; in Europe the after-dinner cigar was the rage. Smoking rooms opened in the most select clubs of London and Paris. Railroads installed smoking compartments in their cars. And to avoid the odor of tobacco clinging to their clothes, gentlemen took to wearing a silk vest. Ever since those days, while the Englishman dons his dinner jacket and the American tucks himself into his tuxedo, the French- or Spanish-speaking man of the world invariably slips into his *smoking.*

Though the cigar now primarily symbolized success in high society, tales of tobacco's healing properties still were told. One anecdote relates how in 1881, in Málaga, the distraught parents of an apparently lifeless newborn watched in amazement as the doctor who presided over the childbirth lit a cigar and blew smoke into the face of the infant, who immediately began to cry. Perhaps the blue curls of the cigar had some lasting influence over the child, who was none other than Pablo Picasso.

Although promoted to the ranks of the nobility by the European market, the Havana continued to travel like a commoner. Bound in packets of fifty or a hundred, five to ten

HOW TOBACCO GROWS

N. TABACUM SENDS DOWN A MAIN ROOT THAT RAPIDLY BRANCHES OUT INTO TEN TO FIFTEEN SECONDARY ROOTS. MOST GROW TO A DEPTH OF 12 INCHES (30 CM), ALTHOUGH SOME MAY PLUNGE AS MUCH AS 60 TO 78 INCHES (1.5–2 M) INTO THE EARTH. IT IS THROUGH THE TIP OF EACH OF THESE ROOTS THAT NUTRITIVE ELEMENTS ARE ABSORBED.

THE STEM ITSELF IS SHAPED LIKE A SLIGHTLY TAPERING CYLINDER AND GROWS FROM 60 TO 71 INCHES (1.5–1.8 M) HIGH AND 5/8 INCH TO 1 INCH (1.5–2.5 CM) THICK. IT SPROUTS BUDS ALONG ITS ENTIRE LENGTH (WHICH BECOME THE PLANT'S LEAVES) AND A FINAL BUD AT ITS TIP, THE UPPER PART OF WHICH EVENTUALLY BLOSSOMS.

THE LENGTH OF THE LEAVES DEPENDS UPON THE VARIETY OF TOBACCO PLANT AND CAN MEASURE ANYWHERE FROM 2 TO 39 INCHES (5–100 CM). THE SHAPE, TOO, MAY DIFFER FROM ONE VARIETY TO THE NEXT, APPEARING EITHER OVAL, OBLONG, TAPERING, OR ROUND. THE SURFACE OF THE LEAF CONSISTS OF TWO TYPES OF TISSUE, ONE OF WHICH SECRETES AN OILY FLUID KNOWN AS *MELUZA.* THE QUALITY OF THE TOBACCO HINGES ON THAT ESSENTIAL SECRETION.

THE PLANT PUTS FORTH IN TOTAL FROM FOURTEEN TO EIGHTEEN LEAVES IN GROUPS OF TWO OR THREE AT VARIOUS LEVELS ALONG THE STEM. STARTING FROM THE BASE OF THE PLANT AND MOVING UPWARDS, THESE SETS OF LEAVES ARE CALLED *LIBRE DE PIE, UNO Y MEDIO, CENTRO LIGERO, CENTRO FINO, CENTRO GORDO,* AND *CORONA.*

A FULLY MATURE LEAF, GROWN IN FAVORABLE CONDITIONS, HAS A SURFACE AREA OF 144 TO 224 SQUARE INCHES (0.096 TO 0.144 M²). A SINGLE SPECIMEN OF *N. TABACUM* REPRESENTS SOME 25 SQUARE FEET (2.3 M²) OF USABLE TOBACCO.

THE TOBACCO FLOWER, BORNE IN A PANICLE, PRODUCES A CAPSULE-SHAPED FRUIT THAT IS DIVIDED INTO TWO CAVITIES CONTAINING TWO TO FOUR THOUSAND MINUTE SEEDS.

thousand of these cigars were piled together in crates of very dry pine engraved with the initials or full name of the manufacturer and the cigars' place of origin. Of course the simplicity of the whole method of shipment only encouraged counterfeiting. To prevent such fraudulent practices, cigar manufacturers began to guarantee the origin of their product by reducing the size of their shipping crates. And instead of bundles of cigars, the crates were now to contain cedar boxes decorated on the inside with a lithograph and holding one hundred individual cigars.

In 1845 Ramón Allones ushered in the era of sumptuous cigar boxes when he chose to package his La Eminencia brand in handsome wooden boxes. By 1880 the *habilitación,* the "equipping" or decorating of these boxes, was done by all makers, introducing a whole genre of multicolor labels *(cromos)* of various sizes and shapes. The king of cigars was now adorned with lithographs, veritable masterpieces, which were soon to be complemented by the use of the cigar band.

It is said, probably apocryphally, that eighteenth-century aristocrats had placed a small ring of paper at the head of a cigar to avoid soiling their gloves when handling the especially moist outer leaf. But it was only between 1830 and 1835 that the Dutchman Gustave Anton Block hit upon the idea of systematically attaching a band to his Aguila de Oro cigars. He hoped to set them apart from other brands while making their origin known to the smoker and his guests. Made of fabric and set off with a small ribbon or pearl, these first ornamental rings eventually gave way to paper bands when the *habilitación* of cigar boxes came into widespread use around 1880.

Cigar manufacturers became a pillar of the Cuban economy. With their employees numbering in the tens of thousands, they were sure to have no small influence on their country's future. In 1865, following a campaign launched by the tobacco weekly *L'Aurora* praising the benefits of reading aloud to the workers on the factory floor, the makers of El Fígaro, followed one year later by Partagás, allowed public readers in their workshops. It is certainly no accident that the first work presented in this way was entitled *Las Luchas del siglo* (The Struggles of the Century). In no time readers' lecterns were transformed into vehicles of free thought, thanks to works by Balzac, Zola, Jules Verne, H. G. Wells, and so on. Workers in cigar factories gradually became the "intellectuals of the proletariat." When the fight to abolish slavery and obtain Cuban independence began in 1868 with the Ten Years War, numerous tobacco workers who were persecuted for their libertarian ideals emigrated to Key West in Florida, where a kind of offshoot of the Cuban tobacco industry took root.

Certain entrepreneurs turned those troubled times to their advantage by setting up the first tobacco trusts. The Henry Clay and Block Company Ltd., founded in 1887 by Gustave Block with English financial backing, brought together sixty-six makes of cigar, including Henry Clay's La Flor, El Aguila de Oro, and La Intimidad.

Across the Straits of Florida, Key West cigar workers were throwing all their support behind the Cuban independence movement. On February 24, 1895, José Martí, hero of Cuba's fight for independence, received the call for a revolutionary uprising rolled up in a cigar. This cigar set off a war to free the island from Spanish control. The conflict also dragged in the United States when the battleship *USS Maine* mysteriously exploded in Havana Harbor on February 15, 1898. Although four years of war eventually drove the Spanish out, independence had yet to be won. Three more years were needed before the Americans returned home. The occupation enabled them to found a new tobacco trust, the Havana Commercial Company, popularly called the "American trust." By 1902 there were 291 brands of Havana cigar that belonged to the trusts. Only a few die-hard manufacturers resisted being bought out, the most important being José Gener's La Escepción and José Antonio Bances's Partagás, as well as Romeo y Julieta, H. Upmann, and Por Larrañaga.

To explain this serious struggle to control various brands of Havana we need only look at the extraordinary infatuation the great—and less great—felt for the excep-

Since 1789 the rezagadores *have carried out the painstaking task
of classifying wrapper leaves.*

tional aroma and flavor of these cigars. While Ulysses S. Grant smoked no less than twenty to twenty-five cigars a day, Abraham Lincoln gave up his pipe after tasting a Havana. (By way of an indication of the cigar's popularity in the United States around this time, Cuba was exporting some 360 million Havanas yearly to America before President James Buchanan announced a tariff increase on their importation in 1857.) The Cuban cigar also won the esteem and affection of the composer Richard Wagner, who unhesitatingly named the Havana as his source of inspiration for *Götterdämmerung.* Jean Sibelius and Enrico Caruso were also quite partial to the bouquet of the fragrant Cuban leaves throughout their lives.

Whereas the first World War had only a slightly adverse effect on American sales, the Great Depression of 1929, coming hard upon poor harvests of several years prior, proved disastrous for many manufacturers. The American trust concentrated numerous brands at the Casa de Hierro before letting them disappear from the market altogether. The financial crisis prompted the trust to try to cut workers' salaries by 20 percent; following a very bitter strike, the Havana Commercial Company withdrew from Cuba and was replaced by Tabacalera S.A.

Beginning in the 1930s, Havana was to witness the wildest years of its history, from dictatorship to coup d'état, coup d'état to free elections, then back to dictatorship once again. Fulgencio Batista rose from sergeant to general during these years, and came to directly or indirectly dominate power in Cuba. Yet political turmoil did not stop Havana from becoming the capital of gambling and good times well before Las Vegas. Far from the teetotalery of the United States during Prohibition, Cuba prospered. Gaily gadding about between the hotel casinos of the Deauville, the Capri, and the Riviera, moving in "tight" formation from the Tropicana Cabaret to the bars of the Floridita and the Bodeguita del Medio, celebrities like Marlene Dietrich, Nat King Cole, Errol Flynn, Gary Cooper, Ginger Rogers, Ava Gardner, and Frank Sinatra, mingling with the likes of Lucky Luciano and Meyer Lansky, tasted the madness of Havana nightlife. Bodies swayed to the salsa beat, hearts filled with good cheer and *añejo* rum, and minds were spellbound by the Havana cigar's heady aroma. It is said that only Ernest Hemingway, who was exclusively devoted to daiquiris at the Floridita and *mojitos* at the Bodeguita, resisted the Havana's charms.

The 1930s also saw one of Havana's most reputable brands of cigar, the Montecristo, come into its own. Legend

In meditative silence the despalilladores
skillfully remove the leaf's midrib.

has it that the brand took its name from the hero of Aléxandre Dumas's novel *The Count of Monte Cristo,* made popular by public readings in cigar factories. However Doña Dina Menéndez, the daughter of the man who created the brand, tells a different version, one that is less literary, but perhaps slightly more truthful. Menéndez and some of his friends were in a restaurant making preparations for an ascent of Monte Altube when the waiter served them a bottle of Lacrima Cristi. The pleasing harmony of the words delighted Menéndez and, just as one sound leads to another, he joined them to coin Monte Cristi, which Dumas had already transformed into Monte Cristo years before.

Popularized by Sir Winston Churchill, who liked to quip that Cuba was always on his lips, the Havana became the comrade of revolutionary firebrands. Just like Fidel Castro, Ernesto "Che" Guevara was an aficionado, and both men enjoyed savoring a good cigar after a hard day of class struggle and guerrilla fighting in the Sierra Maestra. Che liked pointing out that the cigar was the only original Cuban product.

The Havana, which had linked Martí and the island in the last century, was now pressed into service once again for the Cuban revolutionary cause. While in prison, Castro was passed messages from the outside world hidden in cigars. Later, as victor of the revolution, the new head of Cuba put an end to any and all foreign hold over the island's tobacco. As the story goes, President John F. Kennedy had the White House cellar filled with Havana cigars on the eve of declaring a total embargo against Cuba. Private pleasure, it seems, occasionally gets the better of public policy. (And of course the $574,500 that JFK's walnut humidor fetched at the 1996 Sotheby's auction only adds to the aura of the cigar and Kennedy's fondness for it.) Under socialism, Cuban cigar manufacturers were nationalized, while 80 percent of the plantations remained the property of the *vegueros* who worked them—"property" being a relative term here since their output has to fall in line with state planning.

One of the *líder máximo's* first wishes was to bring together all makes of Havana cigars under one brand, a plan that Guevara immediately opposed. It was the latter's point of view that won out in the end, although Che failed to save a number of celebrated brands from the dustbin of history: Cabañas y Carbajol, Murias, Henry Clay, Farach, and Villar y Villar. The early years of the revolution greatly added to the difficulties Castro was facing; it seemed that only the Havana's bluish wisps of smoke occasionally afforded him a

few minutes of repose. One day Castro was taken by the aroma of the long cigar his bodyguard, Chicho Pérez, was smoking and asked to sample it. It was a Havana produced by one of Chicho's friends in the "galleys" of La Corona. A short while later twenty-three-year-old Eduardo Rivero became Fidel's secret supplier, a necessary post, for a doctored cigar would have been one of the surest ways of trying to eliminate the Communist leader. That particular make became the Lancero de Cohiba, Castro's cigar of choice and one of the most sought-after brands by cigar lovers before it was officially marketed to the world at large in 1983. The Cohiba came to be the symbol of Cuban political power, proof that the socialist government was capable of creating a brand superior to all those inherited from the capitalist system. The emblem chosen by Fidel is significant. It represents Hatuey, a valiant Taino warrior, a true Cuban born well before colonialism, a native of unquestionable birth.

The revolution opened the tobacco industry to women, who eventually accounted for 70 percent of the workforce at some manufacturers. El Laguito, for example, makers of the Cohiba, even became a kind of Magdalen house, enabling former prostitutes to quite literally turn over a new leaf.

The U.S. embargo forced Cubans to prospect for new markets. Because the Soviet Union represented little potential, Cuba turned to Europe. Spain, historically a privileged trading partner with the island, absorbed nearly half of Cuba's output and became one of the Havana cigar manufacturers' biggest clients. That opening was not enough, however. What was needed was a goodwill ambassador, a "smokesman" for the Cuban cigar, a well-known aficionado who possessed the right business acumen for marketing the Havana. Contacted in 1967, legendary Swiss tobacconist Zino Davidoff went to Havana to talk with the Cuban tobacco authorities, including the now well-established Eduardo Rivero. Well aware of the chance he was being handed, Davidoff offered to buy out the El Laguito factory and its Cohiba cigars. Although quite willing to part with their cigars for a price, the Cubans did not wish to sell off the manufacturer. And so it was under the name Davidoff that the first Cohibas delighted the palates of smokers abroad. These cigars quickly became a success for they were indeed exceptional. This Cubano-Swiss marriage of convenience lasted until 1983 when Cubatabaco, Davidoff's official partner, decided to put the Cohiba directly on the market. The dispute that ensued would lead the two associates to part company definitively in 1988. Davidoff cigars would no longer be Havanas. Yet Zino had played his part as champion of the Havana with great brio.

To promote the Havana cigar there remained, until he recently quit smoking, Fidel Castro. Emblem of the capitalist businessman, the Havana, produced by women for the most part, has long been the calling card of the Castro regime. It has been offered to many of the political leaders marking this century, from Churchill and Charles de Gaulle to Nikita Khrushchev and Mao Zedong. For smokers today, the Havana cigar is a symbol of their having made the grade. If, as Rudyard Kipling wrote, a "cigar is a Smoke," the Havana is by all means the Smoke of Smokes.

OVER THE CENTURIES, THE ISLAND OF CUBA HAS BEEN divided into five agricultural areas. At the far eastern end of the island lies the aptly named Oriente. It is here that Rodrigo de Xerez and Luis de Torres first caught sight of Taino Indians smoking cigars. In the center Remedios, or Vuelta Arriba, stretches over the provinces of Las Villas and Camagüey. Partidos is situated in the province of La Habana, while Semi Vuelta covers the central part of Pinar del Río, a province made up of pine lands in western Cuba.

The area of Vuelta Abajo, Cuba's fifth agricultural zone, is where Havana cigars are born, on the outskirts of the town of Pinar del Río. The unique fragrance of the leaves grown in this zone makes Vuelta Abajo the sole supplier of the capital's cigar manufacturers. Vuelta Abajo is subdivided into seven districts, El Llano (between San Luis and San Juan y Martínez), Lomas, Remates, Guane, Mantua, Costa Sur, and Costa Norte. The best plantations, which are called

CULTIVATING A SINGULAR TOBACCO

vegas finas, lie between the communes of San Luis and San Juan y Martínez.

Over the reddish soil of the plains numerous streams have patiently deposited a layer of fertile silt. This sandy earth has been blended underground in a way that is unique to Cuba, perhaps the world. The soil's influence is such that each *vega* produces a different "vintage" tobacco, just as individual vineyards in France's Bordeaux region claim that each of their wines is absolutely unique. The Havana's excellence depends above all on the particular selection of vegas and the care taken by the *veguero,* or grower.

The quality of the seed used for planting tobacco is of capital importance in Cuba since its production and distribution are centralized and controlled by the state. Tobacco-growing enterprises hand over the whole of their output to seed banks that redistribute the seed free to the vegueros in order to preserve the uniqueness of each variety of tobacco. Seed is divided into four categories according to developmental phases of the different generations.

OPPOSITE
Accepting the hard task at hand, the veguero *plants the seedlings one after another in the nourishing earth.*

Semilla original (original seed) is obtained by a geneticist, who carefully maintains its quality. It is inoculated with diseases like the mosaic virus to verify the plants' resistance.

From the most resistant of these plants comes *semilla básica* (base seed), which must guarantee the highest degree of genetic identity and purity. The tobacco plants grown from these two categories are raised in research centers. If any individual plants sown from semilla básica show characteristics that differ from those of the original strain, they are subjected to tests to determine whether the changes are hereditary or merely circumstantial. The next generation, *semilla registrada 1 y 2* (registered seed one and two), is produced from growths of base seed raised in special centers. Semilla registrada enables experts to ensure that the offspring's genetic identity corresponds to prevailing standards. The fields where this seed is grown must lie a minimum of 984 feet (300 m) from other plantings of tobacco.

Finally *semilla certificada* (certified seed) is used in actual tobacco production. It comes from growths of registered seed and corresponds to standards set for its category. Specialists raise this seed under the supervision of research center technicians, and only state agricultural enterprises are

COROJO AND CRIOLLO TOBACCO

A HAVANA CIGAR CONTAINS TWO VARIETIES OF *N. TABACUM*: *COROJO* FOR THE WRAPPER LEAVES AND *CRIOLLO* FOR THE BINDER AND FILLER LEAVES.

Corojo Tobacco Characteristics

HEIGHT WITH FLOWER	82 IN. (207 CM)
NUMBER OF LEAVES	16–18
COLOR	LIGHT GREEN
LENGTH AND WIDTH OF CENTRAL LEAVES	19 X 11 IN. (48.5 X 27.9 CM)
DISTANCE BETWEEN KNOTS IN THE STEM	4 IN. (9.9 CM)
DEVELOPMENT OF SECONDARY SUCKERS	ABUNDANT
TIME BETWEEN TRANSPLANTING AND FLOWERING	61.9 DAYS

THE BEST WRAPPERS COME FROM *UNO Y MEDIO, CENTRO LIGERO,* AND *CENTRO FINO* LEAVES. *LIBRE DE PIE, CENTRO GORDO,* AND *CORONA* LEAVES ARE USED FOR CONSUMPTION WITHIN CUBA.

Criollo Tobacco Characteristics

HEIGHT WITH FLOWER	69 IN. (174 CM)
NUMBER OF LEAVES	14–16
COLOR	VERY DARK GREEN
LENGTH AND WIDTH OF CENTRAL LEAVE	17 X 10 IN. (42.8 X 26.5 CM)
DISTANCE BETWEEN KNOTS IN THE STEM	2⅞ IN. (7.2 CM)
DEVELOPMENT OF SECONDARY SUCKERS	ABUNDANT
TIME BETWEEN TRANSPLANTING AND FLOWERING	56.1 DAYS

PAGES 26–27
*With one last bow the vegueros delicately
pull up the tobacco seedlings.*
OPPOSITE
*The supreme reward: after a day of hard work in the fields,
a veguero savors the subtle flavors of a Havana cigar.*

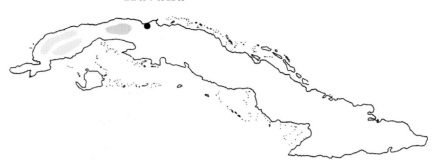

Havana

Production Regions for Havana Cigars
⬤ : Vuelta Abajo
⬤ : Partidos

authorized to grow it. The lands used to cultivate this seed have to ensure its genetic purity: they must be situated near a source of pure water, have lain fallow for five years and have been decontaminated before planting. They may be located between stands of the same variety of tobacco, but are adjacent in that case to avoid any risk of recontamination from the passage of animals, humans, or any matter foreign to tobacco production.

Once the desired variety of tobacco is developed, semilla registrada is no longer grown and semilla certificada is obtained directly from semilla básica. The original seed is

TOBACCO RESEARCH

THE TOBACCO PLANT IS TO THE CIGAR WHAT THE GRAPEVINE IS TO WINE. IT IS THE PLANT'S PERFECT HARMONY WITH THE SOIL IN WHICH IT IS GROWN THAT GIVES A TOBACCO ITS UNIQUE AROMA. YEAR AFTER YEAR IN TOBACCO RESEARCH LABORATORIES, SPECIALISTS STRIVE TO IMPROVE THE PLANT IN ORDER TO OBTAIN A BETTER YIELD, BUT ESPECIALLY TO RENDER THE PLANT MORE RESISTANT TO VARIOUS DISEASES. THE LATTER AIM IS INDEED A PRIORITY, SINCE DISEASE DRASTICALLY REDUCES THE PLANT'S YIELD.

TOBACCO IS IMPROVED THROUGH CROSSBREEDING AND NATURAL OR ARTIFICIAL SELECTION. NATURAL SELECTION IS FUNDAMENTAL TO THE EVOLUTION OF TOBACCO PLANTS BECAUSE IT ALLOWS THE SPECIES TO CONSERVE AND REPRODUCE ITS FINEST SPECIMENS. ARTIFICIAL SELECTION, THE RESULT OF HUMAN INTERVENTION, DEPENDS ABOVE ALL ON THE GROWER'S EXPERIENCE. IT IS UNDERTAKEN WITH THE FIRST GENERATION OF A HYBRID WHEN THE DESIRED CHARACTERISTICS ARE MORE EASILY VISIBLE THAN IN SUCCEEDING GENERATIONS.

PREGERMINATION

PREGERMINATION OF THE TOBACCO SEED, PRACTICED BY MOST *VEGUEROS*, IS THE LAST STEP BEFORE SOWING. THIS TECHNIQUE LESSENS THE TIME IT TAKES THE *SEMILLA* TO GERMINATE IN THE EARTH AND GUARANTEES THAT ALL THE SEEDLINGS OF THE SAME *CANTERO* WILL BE UNIFORM.

TO PREGERMINATE TOBACCO, CLEAN SEMILLA IS PLACED IN SMALL CLOTH BAGS CONTAINING ABOUT FOUR POUNDS (2 KG) OF SEED. THESE ARE SOAKED IN CLEAN WATER FOR TWENTY-FOUR TO FORTY-EIGHT HOURS. THE SEED IS THEN SPREAD OUT ON LONG, WIDE TRAYS THAT ARE RELATIVELY SHALLOW—ABOUT ¾ IN. (2 CM) DEEP—AND LEFT THERE FOR ANOTHER TWENTY-FOUR HOURS. SOWING BEGINS SEVENTY-TWO HOURS LATER. FOR THE BEST RESULTS, PREGERMINATION HAS TO BE DONE TO BETWEEN 80 AND 89 PERCENT OF THE SEEDS (BELOW 70 PERCENT, THE AMOUNT OF SEED SOWN PER SQUARE FOOT MUST BE INCREASED).

taken from thirty plants selected for their genetic characteristics. Seed banks keep three years of production safely stored in refrigerated rooms in the event that one year's harvest is destroyed.

Each tobacco plant naturally develops between 150 and 250 flowers, depending on the variety. Not all of these blossoms produce useful capsules—seed-bearing blossoms yielding the best biological specimens. Thus the blossoming plants are disbudded, tobacco workers nipping off all but the central flower and the two buds closest to it. This process is done at some three inches (8 cm) down the plant's stem; any longer and the biological quality of the seed would be affected. Constant checking of the young plants eliminates any harmful contamination of the blossoms and the subsequent production of seed. It also allows the tobacco growers to single out and destroy any sick or abnormal plants in order to maintain established quality standards.

From the three flowers that have been allowed to further develop on each plant the *vegueros* gather seed for future crops. This operation takes place early in the morning with relative humidity at no more than 85 percent. The mature flowers are cut so as to leave a four- to six-inch (10–15 cm) stem. Gathered into bouquets of ten flowers each and bound with vegetable fiber, the flowers are then suspended from *cujes*—tobacco drying poles—and transported to disinfected curing barns, where they are set on supports situated a minimum of six and a half feet (2 m) from the roof and walls. Only flowers of the same variety of tobacco are dried in the same curing barn. Relative humidity is maintained at 70 percent by opening or closing windows in the curing barn.

After drying (to a moisture content of 5 percent at most), the seeds are separated from their capsule by threshing *(trilla)* either by machine or by hand, in which case

The ox has always been the veguero's *most faithful co-worker.*

crouching men beat the capsules with wooden bats. At each blow a little more of the golden brown grain flies out of the burst capsules. Once in a while, the ground is lightly fanned to separate the seeds from their husks, which float off. The extremely fine grain, now freed of all chaff, is loaded into cloth sacks and transferred to a cleaning center where relative humidity is kept below 85 percent.

Within twenty-four hours the seed has been poured into different sacks holding fifteen pounds (6.85 kg) of the grain. Before closing them, workers prepare two labels, one to go inside and one for the outside of the sack, indicating the variety of the tobacco seed, its origin, the year of its production, and the number of its lot. Within seventy-two hours the sacks have been stored in the seed bank's refrigerated storerooms. Clearly, the *veguero* is no simple farmer.

The long process leading up to the Havana cigar begins far from the actual *vegas* when the first rays of the mid-September sun gently illuminate the nursery beds that patient summer tilling has prepared for the precious seed. Tobacco is not sown directly in the fields where the plants are raised to maturity, but rather in plots specially prepared for growing seedlings. These are the *semilleros*

(seedbeds), which are divided into *canteros* (strips of land). During germination, great care must be taken with the small tobacco seed, which is the size of ground coffee. By confining the seed to relatively small plots that are easier to tend, these nursery beds serve as tobacco's cradle until the young plants are strong enough to survive natural conditions.

The future seedbeds have already been selected in the first half of April. The choice of sites here is crucial for although this phase of tobacco growing represents but 5 percent of the total cost of making a cigar, failure to choose correctly would jeopardize the entire output of tobacco leaves. A commission made up of technicians from the Provincial Department of Tobacco, Plant Hygiene, Soil and Irrigation, and the Territorial Station for Plant Protection verifies that the selected areas and soils correspond to accepted standards of nutritive elements, absence of parasites, pH level, and exposure to the sun. The development of *Nicotiana tabacum* depends of course on the quantity of water and mineral elements that the plant absorbs through its roots, as well as the carbon monoxide and sunlight that its leaves are able to capture. The combination of those various elements produces a leaf whose chemical composition is strictly defined, one that is capable of satisfying the most rigorous quality standards.

The *semilleros* also have a special irrigation system with channels situated in such a way as to water the entire bed uniformly. Laid out according to the site's topography and the position of the main irrigation channels, the *canteros* measure fifty-nine feet (18 m) long, making movement and work within the nursery beds easier while affording the best use of available lands. They are about three feet (1 m) wide so that workers can pull up the seedlings without stepping on them; and ten to twelve inches (25–30 cm) deep to ensure good aeration of the soil. finally, there is a sixteen-inch (40-cm) strip of land running between each of the canteros. The surface must be smooth and free of debris so that accumulations of rain or irrigation water do not promote disease.

Two to three days before sowing the tobacco the canteros have been fertilized, raked, and lightly watered. Watering helps fertilizers dissolve into the soil and hinders recontamination of the seed, which has already been disinfected in a solution of silver nitrate and distilled water. The soil is fertilized a second and third time twenty and thirty days after planting.

The semilleros of Vuelta Abajo are located far from the fields in which tobacco is raised to maturity, although they have practicable entries. The risk of contaminating the tobacco plants gives rise to constant safeguards. At the entrance to each zone there are three basins containing a formaldehyde solution, two of which are located well above the ground for disinfecting workers' and visitors' hands every time they pass, and one at their feet to clean their shoes; likewise, any building within these areas is sterilized and—irony of tobacco farming—smoking is forbidden. The are cultivated for a maximum of two consecutive years, after which tobacco seedlings are no longer grown on them for a minimum of five years.

It begins in September. The *veguero's* hands painstakingly loosen the tie holding the tobacco seed in its gunnysack. Once open, the sack reveals a handwritten label identifying the seed as either *corojo* or *criollo*. The former will produce

With his Socialist revolution in place, Fidel Castro nevertheless refused to nationalize the tobacco plantations of Vuelta Abajo, returning them to the vegueros who worked their fields.

wrapper leaves, the latter binder and filler leaves. The worker plunges a small gauge into the sack and draws out .2 ounces (5 g) of seed. He drops them into twenty-two quarts (20 l) of water in a watering can and stirs the whole solution. The veguero is now ready; ahead stretch seven months of nearly endless toil. The tobacco plant is fragile and will, without constant attention, quickly wither.

With a quick movement the veguero lifts the watering can and pours the fertile liquid over the *cantero;* ten to twenty of his fellow workers follow his example. Over the next few days—sowings are staggered in order to spread out the future harvest—all of the canteros making up the nursery will be seeded in this manner.

The tiny tobacco seed disappears into the wet earth. Yet the *semilla* is no less vulnerable for being hidden to the naked eye. The tobacco growers cover the canteros with straw to protect the developing seed from the harmful rays of the sun and the devastating effect of rain. As the nursery

GROWING CONDITIONS

AS A SPECIES TOBACCO IS PARTICULARLY SENSITIVE TO ENVIRONMENTAL FACTORS, TEMPERATURE, AMOUNT OF SUNLIGHT, HUMIDITY, AND SO ON. THE IDEAL TEMPERATURE FOR GROWING TOBACCO VARIES BETWEEN 68 AND 81°F (20–27°C). A TEMPERATURE BELOW 57°F (14°C) SLOWS ITS DEVELOPMENT, WHICH IS GREATLY AFFECTED BY FROSTS EVEN THOUGH THE PLANT CAN SURVIVE FOR A SHORT PERIOD AT TEMPERATURES OF 27°F (–3°C). ABOVE 104°F (40°C) THE LEAVES OF THE PLANT BURN UP. THE ADVERSE EFFECTS OF HEAT ARE MOREOVER HEIGHTENED BY WIND.

SUNLIGHT OF COURSE INFLUENCES PHOTOSYNTHESIS (THE CREATION OF SUGAR AND STARCH WITH THE AID OF CHLOROPHYLL), ON WHICH THE LEAF'S TEXTURE, SIZE, AND NICOTINE CONTENT LARGELY DEPEND. WHEN TOBACCO IS RAISED UNDER CHEESECLOTH COVERS, THE LEAVES' SURFACE AREA IS INCREASED BY 40 PERCENT, WHILE THE LEAVES THEMSELVES ARE THINNER, MORE FLEXIBLE, AND THEIR NICOTINE CONTENT IS LOWER.

N. TABACUM CAN WITHSTAND RELATIVELY BRIEF SPATES OF DRY WEATHER; A SOIL THAT IS NOT OVERLY WET IS GENERALLY PREFERRED. AS SOON AS WATER SATURATES THE GROUND, IT HINDERS THE PLANT'S ROOTS FROM DRAWING IN OXYGEN. THE LEAVES BECOME THIN WHILE THEIR SUGAR CONTENT SOARS, BUT THEY WILL ALSO CONTAIN TOO FEW NITRATES. ON THE OTHER HAND, A LACK OF WATER PRODUCES A THICK LEAF WITH A COARSER TEXTURE AND LARGER VEINS. IN THIS CASE, THE LEAF HAS A HIGHER THAN NORMAL CONCENTRATION OF NITROGENOUS ELEMENTS.

FINALLY, RELATIVE HUMIDITY PLAYS A PREPONDERANT ROLE IN THE QUALITY OF TOBACCO. AIR THAT IS TOO DRY PROMOTES EVAPORATION OF THE WATER IN THE SOIL AND LOSS OF MOISTURE FROM THE SURFACE OF THE LEAVES. THIS LEADS TO EXCESSIVE DEVELOPMENT OF VEINS AND LIGNIFICATION OF THE LEAF TISSUE ITSELF, DIMINISHING THE CALIBER OF THE TOBACCO.

OPPOSITE
Gathered into mazos *of one hundred seedlings, the young tobacco sets are readied for transporting to the* vegas.
PAGES 36–37
A sanctuary to the development of tobacco in Vuelta Abajo.

beds are gradually dressed in bands of gold, the work cycle takes shape. Some vegueros seed, others lay down hay, and still others remove this protective cover little by little after ten or so days have passed, the time it takes for the seed to germinate. first half, then three quarters and finally all of the hay is taken off. Now the tobacco seedlings are strong enough to resist changes in the weather.

Women are as much a part of this precise work as men. Every day brings a host of problems, for tobacco requires painstaking attention. The seedlings have to be fumigated, their beds fertilized, aerated, and freed of weeds that could otherwise spoil the tobacco's flavor, which the plant absorbs through contact with the nourishing earth. The seedlings' leaves are protected from insect pests, and the plants' overall health is carefully looked after.

The nursery changes colors over the succeeding days, from the light brown of the tilled earth, to the pale blond of the straw mulch, to the rich green of the developing plants. And that green is itself transformed as the plants mature, slowly taking on a deeper hue as they approach the crucial period of transplantation. While up to this point the task of tending the seedlings required time and patience, suddenly it demands utmost speed. The young tobacco plants, *posturas,* which stand about six inches (15 cm) high, must be quickly moved to the field where they will grow to maturity. About thirty-five days after they began, the vegueros make one last bow, bending over to pull up the sets gently and gather them in bunches of one hundred, which they tie together with palm leaves called *coyo de palma.*

Only two hours are needed for the posturas to reach the *vegas,* where they are disinfected and placed in baskets; now they can be replanted in fields that months of work have readied for the still quite fragile sets. The nursery beds, like the good wetnurses that they are, have fulfilled their task and transmitted their strength to the plants. Now they pass on to the vegas the role of infusing the tobacco with the force and flavor that will guarantee its integrity and individuality.

Fifty-one vegas are laid out on the land stretching between San Luis and San Juan y Martínez. These are the estates, as it were, where "vintage" Havanas are grown. Twelve are reserved for the shade-grown *corojo* tobacco. Practically all of the vegas belong to the vegueros who farm them, although the revolution seriously changed the rules governing their business.

Previously, for example, each brand of cigar was supplied by a particular vega whose harvest of either wrapper leaves or binder and filler leaves corresponded exactly to the desired taste. Nowadays, that freedom is only partly respected. Only the best-known brands enjoy the right of selecting their vegas. The Cubatabaco monopoly has made the central administration arbiter over the distribution of tobacco, its price, and the terms of payment. Rare (and happy) is the manufacturer who can still choose the five best plantations to supply the right amounts of the five types of leaves that make up a Havana cigar.

The vega's reddish earth has been carefully prepared before replanting. Between April and May its chemical composition is analyzed to determine precisely what the soil lacks in mineral elements like nitrogen, phosphorus, potassium,

DIFFERENT WAYS OF GROWING TOBACCO

IN CUBA THERE EXIST FOUR DIFFERENT METHODS FOR GROWING TOBACCO, DEPENDING ON THE VARIETY OF TOBACCO AND ITS USE:

TAPADO PARA CAPAS NATURALES (COVERED FOR NATURAL WRAPPERS): THIS TOBACCO IS RAISED BENEATH A CHEESECLOTH COVER TO DIMINISH THE SUN'S IMPACT, TO WARD OFF HARMFUL INSECTS, AND TO SHELTER THE PLANTS FROM THE WIND, THUS ENSURING THAT THE LEAVES RECEIVE SPECIAL CARE. AS IN THE FOLLOWING METHODS, THESE LEAVES ARE HARVESTED INDIVIDUALLY (FOR WHAT IS CALLED "PRIMED" TOBACCO).

TABACO DE SOL ENSARTADO (BOUND SUN-GROWN TOBACCO): THIS TOBACCO IS RAISED IN DIRECT SUNLIGHT AND THE LEAVES, HARVESTED INDIVIDUALLY, ARE STRUNG TOGETHER AND HUNG FROM WOODEN TOBACCO POLES TO DRY NATURALLY.

TABACO DE SOL EN PALO (SUN-GROWN TOBACCO ON THE TRUNK): THIS TOBACCO IS RAISED IN DIRECT SUNLIGHT AND THE LEAVES ARE HARVESTED TWO, SOMETIMES THREE, LEAVES AT A TIME WITH A SHORT PIECE OF THEIR STALK ATTACHED.

TABACO RUBIO (LIGHT TOBACCO): TOBACCO THAT IS DRIED ARTIFICIALLY.

THE HAVANA CIGAR USES ONLY PRIMED TOBACCO, *TAPADO* LEAVES, FOR THE WRAPPER AND *SOL ENSARTADO* LEAVES FOR THE BINDER AND FILLER.

OPPOSITE
*A touch of the cigar's glowing tip and
the tobacco leaf slowly burns.*
PAGES 40–41
Behind a cloth veil the flowers are sheltered from contamination.

calcium, or magnesium, to mention only the most essential nutrients. There is rarely a deficiency of calcium and magnesium, for instance, since these elements are already found in adequate amounts in the fertilizer used to regulate levels of nitrogen, phosphate, and potassium in the soil. All of the other elements are classified as secondary nutrients.

With a precision that has been transmitted over many generations, the vegueros have tilled the land in several stages, each time plowing a little deeper according to the soil's makeup, while taking care not to mix the sandy topsoil with the clayey subsoil. To destroy parasites, insect pests, and weeds, these seasoned workers apply various disinfectants like methyl bromide, Vapam, Diazinon, and Trizilin to the moist, though not wet earth.

In general the vegueros are a prudent lot and plant 30 percent more tobacco than what is called for; indeed, a vega that is unable to produce enough leaf because of an insufficient number of tobacco sets would represent considerable financial loss for the industry.

A tedious, backbreaking task, replanting the sets at regular distances is done with the help of a knotted rope which measures, along each furrow, the requisite twelve-inch (30-cm) interval between seedlings. Sporting a simple straw hat, the veguero bends to replant the young tobacco shoots one by one in the nourishing earth. The fields, combed into neat furrows, start to take on a different color. Straight-as-an-arrow, evenly spaced lines of pale green appear, growing day after day until they conceal the burnt sienna of the soil entirely—except for fields of shade tobacco, whose white cheesecloth sun-screens set them off from neighboring vegas.

For the first few days the tobacco seedling seems exhausted, its leaves drooping lifelessly and head sinking toward the ground. Soon, however, the shoot revives and proudly straightens up as it shakes off the effects of replanting. The veguero helps the tobacco sets along, nurses and feeds them, keeps a watchful eye over them. Seedlings that do not survive transplanting are immediately pulled up and replaced. Not one useful part of the field is left empty.

As dictated by the island's climate, the timetable in these early stages is strict: day three, first watering; day ten, shoring up each plant with additional soil; day twelve,

deploying the cheesecloth screening above shade tobacco; day twenty-five, staking out the stalks of young shade tobacco; day thirty-five, pinching off suckers and shoots. And all the while, the vegueros continue to fertilize, fumigate, water, and patiently tend their still-young tobacco plants.

The process of disbudding the tobacco plants comprises two distinct stages, which the vegueros call *desbotonado* (topping the plant) and *deshije* (removing shoots and suckers). During the former, workers relieve the plant of its extraneous blossoms, while in the latter they eliminate the shoots and suckers that naturally sprout following the initial loss of the flowers as the plant continues to try to reproduce itself. These operations are carried out to concentrate the plant's nutritive elements in its leaves, enabling them to give off their exquisite aroma after curing.

Lost in a sea of green leaves, the vegueros examine the plants one at a time in search of secondary shoots that feed on the mother plant. These suckers and shoots never tire of sprouting, and the tobacco growers labor constantly to prune them back.

HARVESTING THE LEAVES

PRIMED TOBACCO IS HARVESTED IN SEVERAL STAGES CALLED CUTTINGS (*CORTES*), WITH ABOUT A WEEK INTERVAL BETWEEN EACH CUTTING, DEPENDING ON WEATHER CONDITIONS. THIS METHOD ALLOWS THE LEAVES GROWING AT DIFFERENT LEVELS ALONG THE PLANT TO REACH FULL MATURITY. *VEGUEROS* BEGIN AT THE BOTTOM OF THE PLANT BY HARVESTING THE *LIBRE DE PIE* AND *UNO Y MEDIO* LEAVES. THE TIMETABLE GIVEN BELOW IS ONLY AN APPROXIMATION, SINCE A NUMBER OF OTHER VARIABLES HAVE TO BE TAKEN INTO ACCOUNT.

TAPADO TOBACCO FOR THE WRAPPERS (*COROJO*)

Leaf type (bottom to top)	Days from transplant to harvest	Number of leaves harvested
LIBRE DE PIE	47–50	2–4
UNO Y MEDIO	51–53	3
CENTRO LIGERO	60–66	3
CENTRO FINO	71–75	3
CENTRO GORDO	78–80	2–3
CORONA	82–85	2

SOL ENSARTADO TOBACCO FOR THE BINDER AND FILLER (*CRIOLLO*)

Leaf type (bottom to top)	Days from transplant to harvest	Number of leaves harvested
LIBRE DE PIE	48–50	2–3
UNO Y MEDIO	52–55	3
CENTRO LIGERO	58–66	3
CENTRO FINO	72–75	2
CENTRO GORDO	78–80	2
CORONA	82–85	2

OPPOSITE

The fragile tobacco flower demands great care and attention.

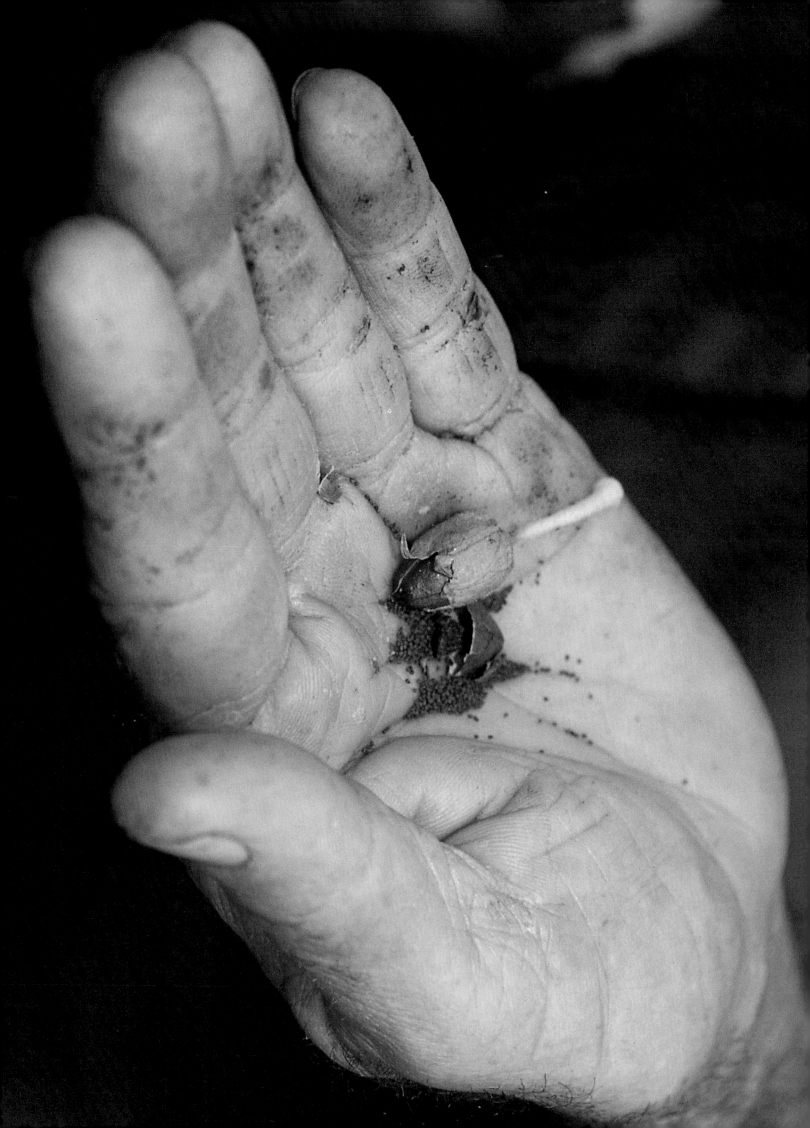

Within three months a seed measuring ⅟₄₈ in. is transformed into a plant standing nearly six feet and yielding close to twenty-five square feet of tobacco leaf.

Starting in mid-January the *vegueros* turn their attention to harvesting the leaf. Some forty days have passed since the seedlings were transplanted and the stands of tobacco seem almost to beckon to their protectors. The deep green plant has taken on lighter hues, while its leaves have become more glossy and now brightly shine in the sunlight.

A single tobacco plant generates from sixteen to eighteen leaves, growing in groups of two to three leaves at six levels along the plant stem. In the terminology of Cuban tobacco growers these are called, beginning with the base of the plant and moving upward, *libre de pie* (base), *uno y medio* (one and a half), *centro ligero* (light center), *centro fino* (thin center), *centro gordo* (thick center), and *corona* (top). Generally tobacco is harvested in two ways, either cutting down the entire plant (stalking) or removing the individual leaves by stages (priming). Havana cigars use only the latter. The leaves are collected one level at a time with one week between each harvest, starting at the *libre de pie* leaves and working up to the *corona*. The week-long interval allows each level to mature fully.

When a level (*libre de pie, uno y medio,* etc.) has reached maturity, the *recolector* gently detaches the individual leaves and lays them on a sort of tray. They are covered with a piece of cloth and the *sacador* transports them to the *llenador de cesto*. The quality of the leaves is checked, then they are placed in baskets that the *cestero* will send to the curing barns. After forty-two days sporting lush green leaves, the bare fields, bristling with row upon row of forlorn stalks, appear to have been set upon by locusts.

OPPOSITE
*Each of these seeds will yield a plant that
stands nearly six feet high.*

PAGES 46–47
In the half-light the veguero *separates the seed from the husks using the same gestures
practiced by the native islanders over five hundred years ago.*

PAGES 48–49
Cuba's brown gold: the seed and leaf of the tobacco plant.

THE "CASA DE TABACO," LITERALLY THE TOBACCO HOUSE, is a curing barn, a wooden cocoon in which the freshly harvested tobacco, having neither odor nor taste, is progressively transformed into a fragrant and savory leaf. Located not far from the *vegas,* the *casa de tabaco* runs east to west, parallel to the path of the sun whose rays are meant to heat only the building's front and back openings. Indeed, what determines a good curing barn is its temperature (72°F/ 22°C) and relative humidity (65–75 percent).

The layout inside a curing barn has changed little over the centuries. The *casa's* bare walls are made of wood while the roof might still be fashioned from *guano* (the local word for the dried leaves of the Cuban royal palm used as thatching and covering for bales of dried tobacco leaves), although nowadays stronger fibrocement or galvanized iron are more commonly used. Inside the curing barn stand several rows of posts, or *puntales.* Planted every seven feet (2 m) or so, these upright timbers bear short horizontal lengths of wood called

CURING IN THE CASA DE TABACO

barrederas, the tiers on which the ends of the tobacco poles *(cujes)* rest. The tobacco leaves, attached with needle and thread, are hung from these *cujes.* The casa is divided into four to six sections called *aposentos,* each of which is the length of one of the drying bars, that is, about thirteen feet (4 m) long, and can hold some fifteen hundred bars in toto. Finally, between sections runs a narrow passageway known as a *falso* (literally, a "false").

Controlling moisture is essential. If a curing barn is too humid, there is a danger that the tobacco leaf will become mottled or will rot before drying. On the other hand, overly dry air inhibits the chemical transformations that are necessary for the tobacco to dry properly, leaving green traces of chlorophyll on the leaf. For those reasons, the *veguero* must open or close the casa's doors accordingly, carefully maintaining a constant temperature and relative humidity inside. Generally, these doors are left open during the day and closed

OPPOSITE
In their wooden shelter the tobacco leaves dry naturally.
PAGES 52–53
Once thoroughly dried, the leaves take on the same colors as the wooden poles supporting them.

at night. During a spate of dry weather, the doors will only be opened in the early morning and evening to allow the required amount of humidity to penetrate the leaf and preserve its suppleness. In rainy weather, the curing barn's natural humidity is enough and airing the building is unnecessary.

When conditions require that the veguero maintain the highest possible relative humidity, the curing barn is hermetically sealed and the drying bars are raised to the upper reaches of the *aposentos* and carefully shaken. On the other hand, relative humidity can be lowered, if need be, by vegetable-charcoal heaters set up in the *falsos*. In the past quicklime, spread out on platters set near the casa's openings, was used to absorb water vapor.

The number of curing barns depends upon the size of the *vegas*. A *casa de tabaco* containing six *aposentos* can hold the equivalent of 1.7 acres (.69 ha) of shade tobacco, or 3.2 acres (1.3 ha) of tobacco grown normally.

As soon as the freshly harvested leaf arrives at the casa de tabaco, the *descargador* (unloader) carefully sets the baskets of tobacco on a table. It is now the *ensartadores'* turn to get down to work. Using a special needle, they attach the leaves to *cujes*, passing a cotton thread through the midrib about a half inch (1 cm) from the base. The ensartadores then suspend the leaves back to back from the drying bar, allowing a minimum distance between leaves to avoid their sticking together and causing *sahorno*, a swelling of the cold, moist leaf. To remedy this, the leaves are exposed to the sun when there is no risk of rain. A good ensartador can complete about one hundred bars in a day.

Next the drying bars are hung in the various sections of the casa, starting at the top and working down. It is important to maintain a minimum distance of four to five inches (10–12 cm) between the bars because the leaves must never touch. By the same token, they are suspended no less than three inches (8 cm) from the *barrederas*, again to avoid contact with the wooden support that might cause the leaf to deteriorate. In certain *vegas* the tobacco poles holding *sol ensartado* (sun-grown) leaf are replaced by metal ones, or *portahilos*, fitted with hooks for attaching them to the tier poles and strung with cotton thread from which the leaves

are hung. Each bar has some twenty holes to which the strands of threaded leaf are attached.

In the shelter of their wooden refuge the tobacco leaves slowly dry. It takes about six weeks to eliminate all the moisture from the leaf (about 85 percent of a green leaf's weight). This process is only complete when the midrib itself is thoroughly dry. In the past Havana manufacturers themselves used to come and watch the leaf mature, and from that moment would know that their future cigars were indeed going to live up to their promise. Today the vegueros alone are present at this important stage of cigar production. Every day they return to the silence of their *casa de tabaco,* watching as little by little the leaves turn from green, to yellow, and finally to dark brown, until they seem to blend in with the wooden poles that hold them.

The vegueros must now handle the leaves with absolute precision, preferably in the morning when relative humidity is highest, thus lending a certain suppleness to the tobacco. As the leaves yellow, the lower bars of one section are raised toward the casa's roof, while the minimal distance between bars is maintained. A single *aposento* may only contain leaves that have reached the same degree in the drying process, since the humidity lost by greener tobacco would be absorbed by drier leaves, which run the risk of becoming moldy or mottled.

If, however, there is not enough room to observe the above rule, bars holding the driest leaves are mounted at the very top of the *aposentos*, where they are spaced widely apart so that their tobacco will not be affected by evaporation from leaves that are still green.

After twenty-five to thirty days, the whole of the tobacco leaf is dry except for the midrib. About forty days after entering

DRYING TOBACCO LEAVES

THE NUMBER OF LEAVES A DRYING BAR CAN HOLD VARIES ACCORDING TO THE TYPE OF LEAF:

Leaf type (bottom to top)	Leaves per drying bar
LIBRE DE PIE	140
UNO Y MEDIO	110
CENTRO LIGERO AND CENTRO FINO	100
CENTRO GORDO	120
CORONA	140

PAGES 54–55
After fermenting a second time, the leaves give off their ammonia-rich fragrance.

OPPOSITE
Forty leaves, two hands: a gavilla, *or sheaf of tobacco.*

Harvesting, fermenting, aging—creating cigars has often been likened to producing a vintage wine.

the casa the leaves are completely dry, but have yet to acquire their distinctive fragrance. They are like must, the pressed juice of grapes that is imbued with the color of the fruit but is still not wine. Just like must, the tobacco has to ferment.

The *cujes* are now brought down, the leaves detached from the bars and gathered into sheaves, which are sent to a secluded, dimly lit building with low humidity. Arranged in stacks, or *pilones,* the leaves remain there from twenty to fifty days. For added protection, each *pilón* is placed on a wooden platform twelve to sixteen (30–40 cm) high. And then a minor miracle occurs. In the building's half-light, the tobacco leaf is transformed and starts to give off the first faint hints of ammonia that make up its bouquet. Day after day the leaf's fragrance grows more pronounced, refined, full-bodied.

Once the curing process is complete, *tapado* (covered, or shade-grown) tobacco is packed in wooden crates or strong cardboard boxes (maximum one hundred pounds [50 kg]), while *sol* (sun-grown) tobacco is stocked in *yagua* bales or gunnysacks (one hundred sheaves of *libre de pie* [inferior] leaves or eighty sheaves of *centro* [superior] leaves). They are then transferred to the *casa de escogida,* the grading house. In certain *vegas,* curing and grading the leaves are done under the same roof.

The now fragrant leaves are put to different uses according to their nature. Following a number of extraordinarily complex manipulations, they will be grouped into "families," or *tiempos* in the jargon of Cuban cigar manufac-

FERMENTATION

GENERALLY, THE STACKS FOR FERMENTING TOBACCO LEAVES MEASURE ABOUT THIRTEEN FEET (4 M) LONG, WITH A WIDTH OF FOUR BUNCHES OF LEAVES JUXTAPOSED STALK TO STALK, AT A HEIGHT OF THIRTY-NINE INCHES (1 M). A GREATER HEIGHT WOULD HINDER THE FERMENTATION PROCESS.

A *PILERA* ONLY CONTAINS LEAVES FROM THE SAME HARVEST SINCE FERMENTATION TIME VARIES WITH THE DIFFERENT TYPES OF LEAVES:

Leaf	Fermentation time
LIBRE DE PIE	20–25 DAYS
UNO Y MEDIO	30–35 DAYS
CENTRO	35–40 DAYS
CENTRO GORDO AND *CORONA*	50 DAYS

FERMENTATION TIME ALSO VARIES ACCORDING TO THE QUALITY AND TYPE OF LEAF HARVESTED. A THERMOMETER PLACED MIDWAY UP A *PILERA* INDICATES THE TEMPERATURE INSIDE THE STACK DURING FERMENTATION. TEMPERATURE SHOULD NOT EXCEED 108°F (42°C) AND, AGAIN, VARIES ACCORDING TO THE LEAF HARVESTED:

Leaf	Fermentation temperature
LIBRE DE PIE	90°F (32°C)
UNO Y MEDIO	93°F (34°C)
CENTRO LIGERO	93°F (34°C)
CENTRO FINO	100°F (38°C)
CENTRO GORDO AND *CORONA*	104–108°F (40–42°C)

turers. The deciding factor in sorting out the leaves is their *jugosidad,* literally their "juiciness," or "succulence," or in other words, their texture and oily content, their strength and gumminess. Wrapper leaves are further classified by color.

Rigorous selection is one of the secrets of the Havana's quality. Classifying tobacco by its characteristics enables manufacturers to assign a specific function to each leaf in creating the aroma, savor, and combustibility of their unique brands.

The steps in sorting out the leaves also differ according to the tobacco's origin. A distinction is made between

TAPADO CLASSIFICATION

TAPADO TOBACCO, WHICH PROVIDES WRAPPER LEAVES, IS BROKEN DOWN INTO FOUR *TIEMPOS: LIGERO* (L), *LIGERO SECO* (LS), *VISO SECO* (VS), AND *VISO CLARO* (VC); AND INTO FOUR SUB-*TIEMPOS: SECO, VISO, QUEBRADO,* AND *AMARILLO.* THESE SUBGROUPS ARE NOT FOR EXPORTATION.

A LEAF'S SIZE AND THE FLAWS IT REVEALS DICTATE WHICH *TIEMPO* IT IS ASSIGNED TO. THE *TIEMPOS* ARE SEPARATED INTO TWO MAIN CLASSES. THE *ABERTURA* CLASS BRINGS TOGETHER THE SMALLEST OR MOST DAMAGED LEAVES, WHICH HAVE BEEN LEFT OPEN DURING THE FIRST CLASSIFICATION; THE *REZAGO* CLASS REFERS TO LARGER LEAVES WHICH ARE GIVEN A SECOND CLASSIFICATION AFTER THE ABERTURA. REZAGO LEAVES ARE DOUBLED OVER ALONG THEIR MIDRIB.

REZAGO LEAVES ARE GRADED ON A SCALE BETWEEN 10 AND 20. LEAVES WITH A GRADE BETWEEN 10 AND 17 ARE USED AS WRAPPERS; REZAGOS BETWEEN 18 AND 20 ARE SET ASIDE FOR THE FILLER. IF THE LEAVES SHOW NO FLAWS (THAT IS, ARE RATED *PUNTA, ORILLA, Y FONDO LIMPIO:* CLEAN POINT, EDGE, AND CENTER), THEY ARE ASSIGNED AN ODD NUMBER BETWEEN 11 AND 17, STARTING WITH THE LARGEST LEAVES AND GOING TO THE SMALLEST. ON THE OTHER HAND, IF THEY SHOW FLAWS OR STAINS, THEY ARE GIVEN AN EVEN NUMBER BETWEEN 10 AND 16, WITH THE LOWEST NUMBER INDICATING A SINGLE IMPERFECTION.

SOL ENSARTADO CLASSIFICATION

SOL ENSARTADO TOBACCO, USED AS BINDER AND FILLER LEAVES, IS BROKEN DOWN INTO FOUR *TIEMPOS. LIBRE DE PIE* AND *UNO Y MEDIO* LEAVES ARE CLASSIFIED AS *VOLADO* (V OR *FORTALEZA* NO. 1, SINCE THEY CONTAIN LESS THAN 1 PERCENT OF NICOTINE). THESE LEAVES AFFECT BOTH THE CIGAR'S AROMA AND COMBUSTIBILITY. THEY DISPLAY A SMOOTH TEXTURE WITH A LIGHT-COLORED, GENERALLY MOTTLED SURFACE, AND HAVE NO ELASTICITY AND NO OILY SUBSTANCES. BINDER LEAVES COME EXCLUSIVELY FROM *VOLADO* TOBACCO AND ARE BROKEN DOWN INTO FIVE CATEGORIES ACCORDING TO SIZE: *CAPOTE ESPECIAL* (8½ X 11 IN. [21.5 X 28 CM]), AND NUMBERS ONE (7½ X 13⅞ IN. [19 X 35 CM]), TWO (6¾ X 13 IN. [17 X 33 CM]), THREE (6 X 11⅞ IN. [15 X 30 CM]), AND FOUR (5⅛ X 6¾ IN. [13 X 17 CM]); FOR CIGARS SOLD ONLY IN CUBA, *VOLADO* LEAVES ARE CLASSIFIED AS *GRANDE, MEDIANO,* AND *CHICO* (LARGE, MEDIUM, AND SMALL).

CENTRO LIGERO AND *CENTRO FINO* LEAVES ARE CLASSIFIED AS *SECO* (S OR *FORTALEZA* NO. 2). THEY BEAR ON THE CIGAR'S FLAVOR AND AROMA, BUT NOT ITS COMBUSTIBILITY. SECO LEAVES HAVE LITTLE FLEXIBILITY, ARE LOW IN OILY SUBSTANCES, AND DISPLAY A DULL, DEEPLY HUED COLOR.

CENTRO GORDO AND *CORONA* LEAVES ARE CLASSIFIED AS EITHER *LIGERO* OR *MEDIO TIEMPO* (L OR MT, OR *FORTALEZA* NOS. 3 AND 4). LIGERO LEAVES AFFECT THE CIGAR'S STRENGTH AND FLAVOR. OF AVERAGE THICKNESS, THESE LEAVES ARE FLEXIBLE AND HIGH IN OILY SUBSTANCES, DISPLAYING A COLOR THAT RUNS FROM DARK BROWN TO CHESTNUT. MEDIO TIEMPO LEAVES HELP ONLY TO DEFINE THE CIGAR'S STRENGTH. RATHER THICK AND QUITE FLEXIBLE, THEY ARE RICH IN OILS AND HAVE A DEEP CHESTNUT COLOR. LIGERO AND MEDIO TIEMPO LEAVES ARE CLASSIFIED TOGETHER IN THE SAME CATEGORY. ONE OR MORE OF SECO, LIGERO, AND MEDIO TIEMPO LEAVES ARE USED IN THE FILLER, DEPENDING ON THE *VITOLAS* PRODUCED.

tapado tobacco which is used as wrapper leaf, and *sol ensartado,* which serves as binder and filler leaf. These two types of tobacco are sorted out and graded in separate *casas.*

Corojo tobacco leaf, a shade tobacco used for wrappers, is thin and fragile. It is handled with the greatest care since an imperfect wrapper would detract from a Havana's overall elegance. The nimble fingers of the *zafador* ("loosener") undo the sheaves of leaves, which are then moistened, a process known as *moja,* to prevent cracking and breaking when handled. Next they are allowed to air *(oreo)* to ensure that all the leaves have the same moisture content. They are detached *(deshiladas),* sorted a first time to remove leaves that are too small or broken, and classified *(escogidas),* an extremely complex process that requires long experience, great rigor, a sharp eye, and a keen sense of touch. The *rezagadoras,* the women who perform this demanding task, take only a few tenths of a second to classify a leaf and stack it with its kind on the floor, covering the ground at their feet with a sweet-smelling bed of golden brown. And to make absolutely certain the leaves meet cigar manufacturers' standards of quality, a *revisadora* oversees her colleagues' work. She walks among the rows of chairs around which the sorted leaves are stacked to give them one final look, verifying that they have been properly grouped with respect to size, texture, and color. The classification of the wrapper leaves that go into Havana cigars is probably the most thorough and discriminating in the world. No less than forty-seven types of leaves are thus identified and set apart.

The leaves are now transported to a *picadero,* a wooden structure where they are stocked in bulk in their respective groups, to be gathered the following day into sheaves *(gavillas)* of forty to sixty leaves, then into hands *(manojos)* of four gavillas each. These are put in bales *(tercios)* and sent to a warehouse *(almacén)* where they must repose before continuing their way to the cigar manufacturers of Havana.

On the other hand, *criollo* tobacco, for binders and filler, is subjected to a somewhat less complicated treatment in the *casa de escogida.* The leaves are detached from their bundles, moistened directly on the ground, and stacked in heaps for fermenting. The following day the tobacco workers proceed with the *abertura,* the opening (that is, the unfolding) of the leaves. They are then arranged into different grades and placed in the appropriate pile. Sorting these leaves is nearly as complicated as classifying wrapper leaves and demands just as much experience and skill.

Bound together in sheaves of a fixed weight, then assembled into hands, *crillo* tobacco is finally put into burlap-covered bales and transported to warehouses, an intermediary step before being sent on to the center where the leaf is stemmed.

The process of stemming tobacco consists of separating the leaf from part or all of its midrib, an exacting, methodical task that is carried out by women only. Before stemming, *sol ensartado* leaves (*tapado* tobacco for wrappers is treated differently) must be specially prepared as follows.

The tobacco is dampened before being removed from the bales and spread out directly on the floor near a large tub, or *cantero*. A *zafador* peels off all the leaves and places them layer upon layer in the tub where they are moistened a second time, their fine earthy fragrance mingling with the smell of the surrounding wood. Filled to the brim of the tub, the leaves are allowed to stand for two to three hours before being stirred to make sure they are all equally damp. Now the process of prefermentation can begin.

Stacked and set out to dry, finer *volado* tobacco is allowed seventy-two hours of prefermentation; *seco,* fifteen days; *ligero* and *medio tiempo,* twenty-five days. When the correct fermentation temperature is reached—113°F (45°C) for seco, 118–122°F (48–50°C) for ligero and medio tiempo—the leaves lying in the upper part of the rack are shifted down to the bottom and replaced by the lower-lying leaves, a process called *virado.* Seco leaves go through this process twice; ligero and medio tiempo, three times. And each time the tobacco exhales its unmistakable ammonia scent. When the process of prefermentation is complete, the leaves are put in nylon bundles, each holding ten pounds (5 kg) of tobacco, and sent to the processing center where they will be stripped of their midrib.

Beneath fluorescent lights the *despalilladoras,* women

An experienced rezagadora *is capable of recognizing over forty different classes of tobacco leaf at a glance.*

specialized in stripping tobacco, plunge their hands into the warm mass of leaves. These specialists grasp one bunch of tobacco leaves after another and, with a delicate flick of the wrist, remove part of the midrib. They then return the leaves to their appropriate pile, respecting the various families and groups of tobacco.

Hour after hour, on the simple school desks before them the women slowly raise low ramparts of tobacco leaves arranged by size, texture, and thickness. This highly skilled women's work is often watched by young apprentices.

The leaves are pressed down for an entire day to flatten them out, after which they are placed in hogsheads. The largest leaves, however, are stacked once again in *pilones*. Both the wooden barrels and the pilones are used here to round out the leaves' aroma with a second fermentation. When the temperature reaches the maximum required for proper fermentation—108°F (42°C) for volado, 113°F (45°C) for seco, and 122°F (50°C) for ligero and medio tiempo—the contents of the barrels and *pilones* are shifted about; the leaves of one hogshead are now transferred to another, one *pilón* giving rise to a second, and so on. Volado tobacco is subjected to this process once; seco, ligero, and medio tiempo, twice.

When the director who oversees this operation is certain that the right moment has come, the pilones are taken down and the leaves are laid out on large sliding wooden shelves known as *parilleros*.

The leaves remain there drying for about seventy-two hours, until their moisture content stands at 14–15 percent for filler leaf *(tripa)* and 15–16 percent for binder leaf *(sobretripa)*. An instrument can of course give a precise reading of the tobacco's moisture, but most of the time skilled tobacco workers know simply by feeling the leaves. It is especially important to avoid uncontrolled fermentation once the bales of tobacco have been packed, which would greatly alter the tobacco's quality.

Stripped of their midrib, classified, fermented, and now dried, the leaves are rolled up in *pacas* (bales) made of *arpillera* (burlap). Body and soul *and* soil, they are ready to become Havana cigars.

THE OLD HOUSES OF HAVANA TELL PASSERSBY OF ITS former splendor. The city's maze of streets and alleys offers a glimpse of a time of now-faded glory. Yet the Cuban capital is starting to spring back to life. Havana's historic neighborhoods have been declared part of the world's cultural heritage and are gradually recovering the grandeur of bygone days.

Of the forty magnificent prewar residences whose façades once proudly displayed prestigious names like Romeo y Julieta, Fonseca, Cabaña, Por Larrañaga, La Legimidad, and Calixto López, only nine cigar manufacturers remain, perpetuating the names of brands like Montecristo, Romeo y Julieta, Punch, Bolívar, Hoyo de Monterrey, and Partagás. These nine *fábricas de tabacos* hold out to us a way of traveling back in time.

One hundred and fifty years of tradition are sheltered behind the walls of the Partagás building. Here, as in the other *fábricas de tabacos,* the tobacco leaves begin the last

CREATING A CIGAR

leg of their journey, their final metamorphosis into the Havana cigar. Wrapper, binder, and filler—once again each type of leaf will be put through a distinct set of steps on the way to becoming a cigar. The first stop is down in the building's storerooms, perfumed cellars that are the refuge of the world's greatest tobacco.

At 7 A.M. the *zafador,* seated on a wooden chair, a basket by his side, selects a hand of wrapper leaves and deftly unties the sheaves. Cautiously he separates the clusters, holding the tobacco leaves with their tips pointing down to avoid breaking or tearing those at the center. Next, to undo the individual sheaves, he places a hand on either side of a cluster and squeezes it lightly, then gently shakes it, and, with the base of the leaves held between his legs, peels them apart without opening the individual leaves. finally he arranges the now unbound sheaves in a circle around his

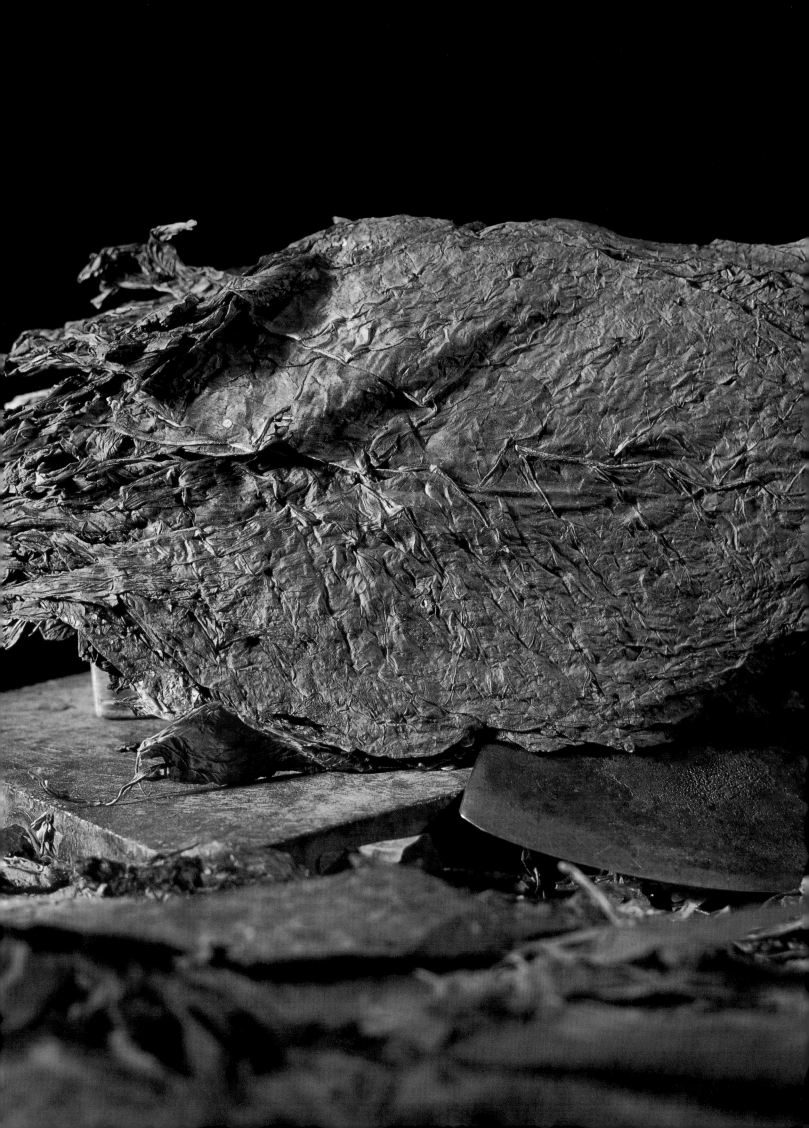

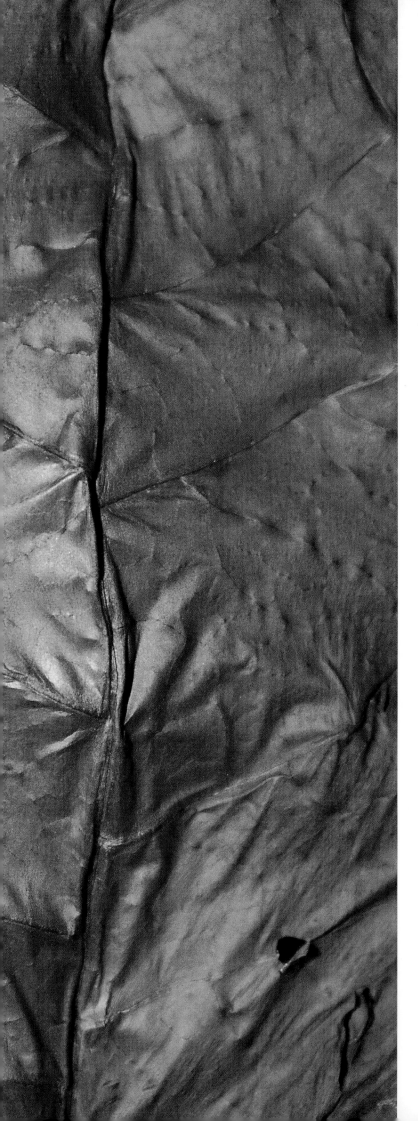

For nearly two hundred years Havana manufacturers have carried on the tradition of the cigar totalmente hecho a mano, *that is, made entirely by hand.*

basket with the tips of the leaves pointing in toward the center. Without a word the *zafador* tirelessly repeats the same gestures. Filling the basket, he records the type and number of sheaves on a scrap of paper and covers the tobacco with a piece of dry cloth.

These sheaves are then immediately moistened to restore elasticity and humidity, enabling workers to handle the leaves without breaking or tearing them. Wearing a protective garment of oilcloth, the *mojador* (dampener) picks up four *gavillas* by the base, holding them vertically with the tips of the leaves pointing down. He then dips the leaves into clean water to a depth of 1 to 1½ inches (3–4 cm) and rapidly pulls them out and turns them over as if he were putting together a bouquet of tobacco. Each cluster then passes through a fine mist sprayed by a water vaporizer. Slowly turning the bunch of fragrant leaves the mojador makes sure the leaves are equally moistened before laying them on metal grills.

The *sacudidor* (literally the "shaker") now removes excess droplets of water that could stain the leaves, holding two bunches in each hand and waving them up and down. The sheaves of tobacco are then hung from a movable frame and transferred to a dark, humid room. As the wrapper is aired moisture spreads evenly throughout the leaf.

When the above operation is completed, the leaves are laid out in wooden crates covered with zinc and protected by plastic sheets, where they will remain undisturbed from ten to seventy-two hours. Indeed, the leaf has been exhausted in the process of regaining its former elasticity. After this short period, the leaves' moisture content stands at 28–38 percent. They are sent on their way to the stripping or stemming *(despalillo)* department.

The now shiny and supple wrapper leaves are no longer in danger of breaking when handled. The *despalillo,* which is staffed by women alone because of their superior dexterity, is where the wrapper leaf will be stemmed. What seems like easy work actually requires long practice. An inexperienced worker, for example, will often damage the wrapper, making it unsuitable for use in a Havana cigar.

In a naturally lit room, comfortably seated on a chair, the tobacco stripper takes a sheaf of tobacco and frees the individual leaves. Carefully she lays them with their tips pointing toward her on a piece of cloth covering her lap, smoothing the leaves out with her hand to soften them. She picks up a single leaf and delicately "opens" it from the base to the tip as if it were made of fine silk. Holding the tip in one hand, with the thumb and index of the other she gently detaches the central vein up to the middle of the leaf. Then, with a quick flick of the wrist, she coils the second half around her fist. The pliable midrib easily comes away from the leaf. She flattens out each strip of tobacco and lays it with both hands along the edge of a semicircular wooden stand placed in front of her.

All of the half-leaves of a single sheaf of tobacco are stacked one atop the other so that their points and outer edges are perfectly aligned. Next the specialist rolls the stripped half-leaves into a kind of scroll, folding the two ends toward the center and doubling the stack in the middle. She then covers this roll of half-leaves with a sheet of plastic which provides momentary protection for the short trip to the *rezagado.*

The day-to-day work of the manufacturer's *rezagadora* consists of sorting the wrapper leaves by size and color. This classification depends upon the number of types of cigar produced by a particular brand. Seated in the middle of a U-shaped shelf, the rezagadora places two of the sheaves of half-leaves prepared by the tobacco stripper on a piece of cloth on her lap. She pulls the half-leaves open one by one to spot any flaws. Then, in a fraction of a second she determines the type of leaf and places it on the appropriate pile, composing before her with astounding agility and precision a palette of tans and browns. At her feet, a bucket of clean water and a sponge stand ready for moistening leaves that are too dry.

Stacks of twenty-five half-leaves, now properly sorted out, are folded once again following the method used when they were first stripped. They are arranged in wooden drawers, each drawer corresponding to a specific type of cigar or *vitola* (corona, panatela, etc.) produced by the brand. Wrapper leaves continue on their way to the "galley."

Meanwhile, binder and filler leaves have been given a different treatment. Packed in protective burlap bales after fermenting, the hands of tobacco are carefully removed to avoid confusing the different types of leaves. The *barbacoa,* the workroom where filler leaf is readied for use, is suddenly filled with a variety of brown hues and complex fragrances.

Before assembling the leaves into the core of the cigar, experts check the tobacco's quality and the accuracy of the labels attached to the bales. The leaves are weighed and counted in accordance with the industry standards specifying the quantity of leaves per half-pound; if need be, leaves are added or subtracted to make up the prescribed weight. This indispensable readjustment determines the number of units the cigar roller must produce with his or her given weight of tobacco leaves at a set degree of moisture content.

If the leaves prove to be too moist, they are laid out on the shelves of a dehumidifying room; too dry, they are moistened directly with water or, in the best manufacturers, placed on wooden shelves in a humidor. Either way, in no time they recapture the many nuances that make up their fragrance. Normally, however, the traditional "aging" in wooden crates evens out the degree of moisture in all the leaves. Twenty-four to seventy-two hours later, the leaves are weighed once again and stocked in barrels. They are now ready to be rolled into *ligas* (blends).

Each brand, each *vitola* has a distinctive taste. The *liga,* the sacrosanct secret of the Havana cigar, is the combination of different *tiempos* and classes of tobacco leaf making up the core of the cigar. It is that masterly blend of leaves that creates the savor and aroma of the vitola and contributes to its strength. Hanging from one of the *barbacoa's* walls, a banal sheet of paper reveals the secret of the particular ligas used by the manufacturer.

Standing or seated in front of a scale, the *ligadora* prepares the *ligada,* that is, the amount of *volado, seco,* and *ligero* leaves needed to produce forty-five to fifty cigars. That quantity of tobacco naturally varies according to the size of the leaves. The different classes of leaves are not mixed, but rather parceled out according to the ligas into distinct stacks whose weights correspond to their proportion in the finished cigar.

Stocked in wooden crates, the ligadas are sent to the "galley" at the production manager's request. The leaves' moisture content is checked one last time, for if the tobacco proved to be too dry the *torcedor,* the trained worker who rolls the cigar, would be unable to produce the required number of cigars at the fixed weight

The *galera* is the Havana cigar's true birthplace, the very heart of the cigar factory. It is here that the torcedor's nimble fingers assemble the tobacco leaves into a harmonious blend.

The cigar roller's experienced hands are assisted by a few simple tools that have remained practically unchanged for over a century. There is the *tabla,* a small wooden board that is placed on the table before the torcedor; the *chaveta,* a broad handleless knife for cutting the leaves and working the cigar roll; the *guillotina,* a standard guillotine for trimming the cigars to the correct length of the *vitola* being produced; the *cepo,* a gauge for measuring the length and diameter of the cigar; a cigar press and five or six cigar molds; the *goma,* a pot of mucilage (usually gum tragacanth) for pasting the head of the cigar; and finally the *toalla,* a wet towel for maintaining the wrapper leaves' suppleness and elasticity.

The cigar is made up of the *capa,* or wrapper leaf (the cigar's envelope), and the *bonche,* the core or body of the cigar, that is, filler leaf (*volado, seco,* and *ligero*) rolled in the binder, or *capote.* The depth and complexity of the leaves' aroma and the torcedor's deft craftsmanship will give the Havana an even color and elegant shape that is firm to the touch and delicious to the tongue.

Just as the painter prepares his or her palette of colors, the torcedor arranges on the smooth tabla in front of him the five classes of tobacco leaf: *capa, capote, volado, seco,* and *ligero.* His cigar mold leans against a small shelf.

While listening to the *lector,* the galley's traditional reader, the torcedor begins to put together the core of the cigar. He selects a binder leaf and removes its midrib, separating it into two strips of tobacco. He will use either one or two strips depending on the cigar's size. The halves of the binder are laid on the table so that their longest edge is positioned horizontally, with the smooth edge of the leaf toward the torcedor. This allows him to conceal the leaf's veins by rolling them in what is to become the very center

PAGES 89-97
Forgetting his day-to-day worries, the craftsman becomes
a master cigar maker as the leaves become a Havana cigar.

The driving force behind Cuba's wars of independence and struggles for social justice, Cuban cigar rollers were dubbed the "intellectuals of the proletariat."

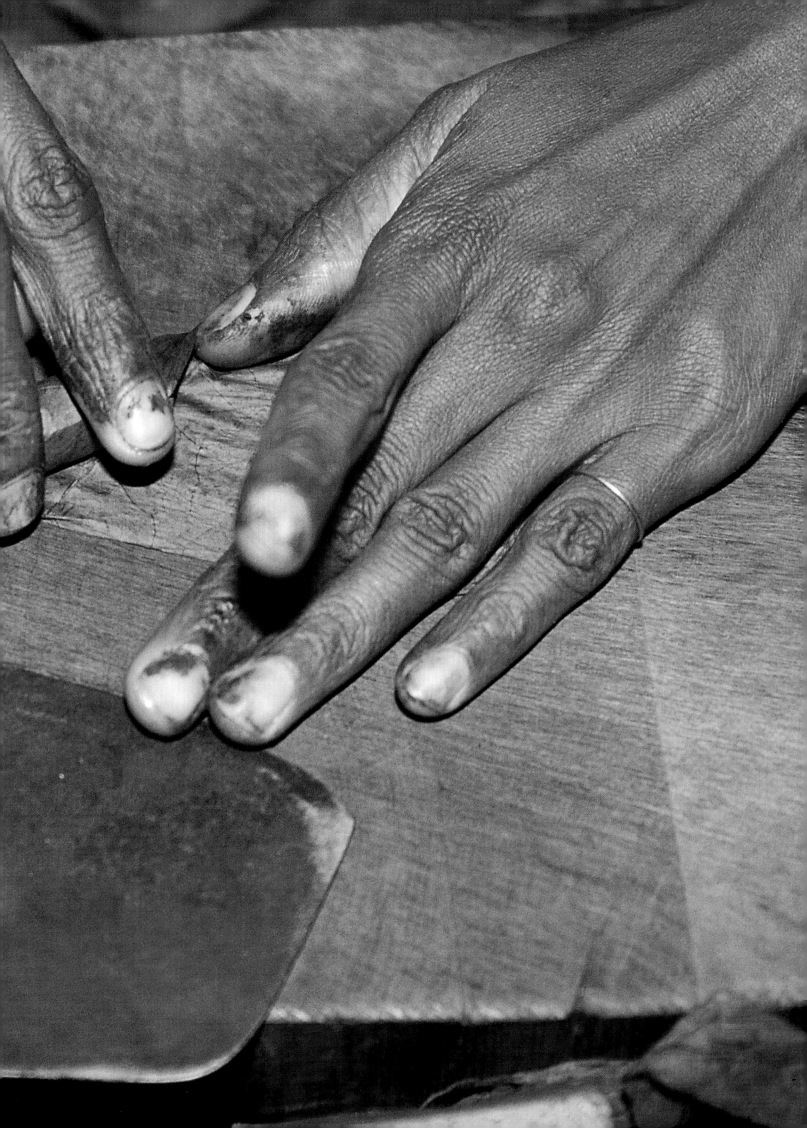

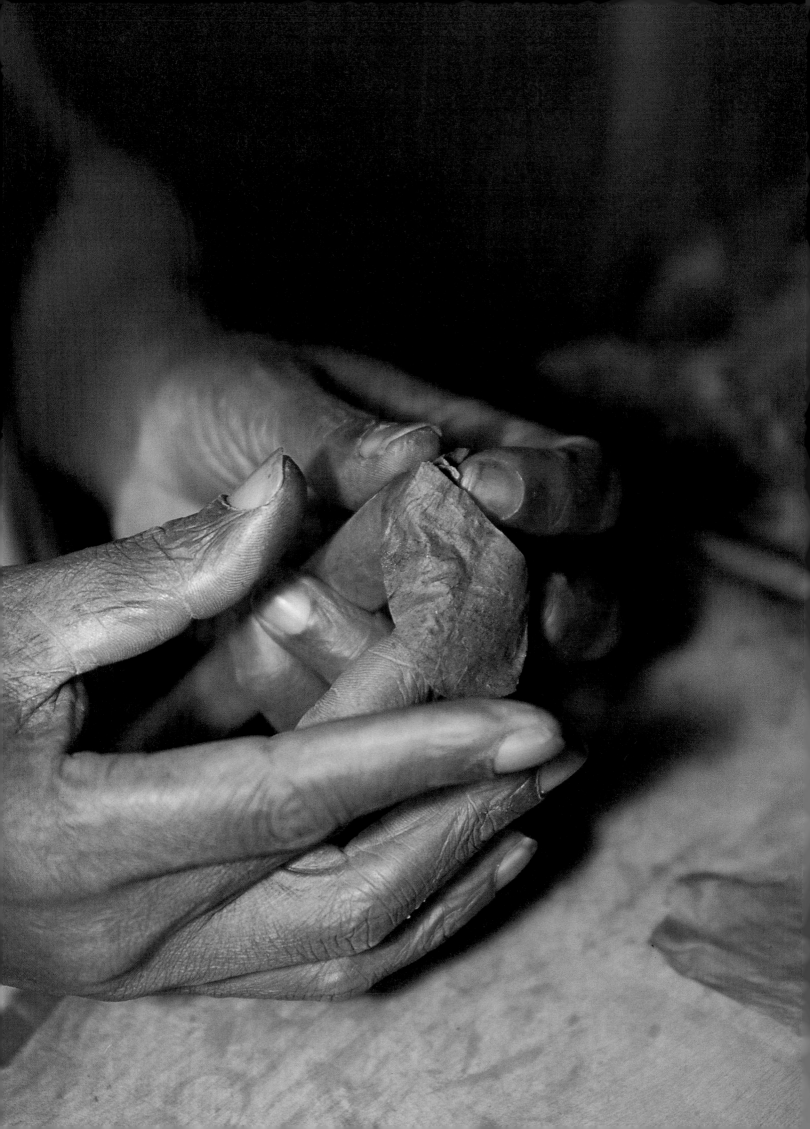

of the cigar. The tip of the leaves, pointing either to the right or to the left, distinguish a right-hand *bonche* from a left-hand one.

In the hollow of his hand the torcedor lays the appropriate leaves for the type of cigar he is creating, placing the *ligero* leaf at the center and wrapping it first in *seco,* then *volado* leaves. Only this order ensures that the cigar will burn evenly. With a sharp twist of one hand he tears off the base of the leaves that extend too far, adding them if necessary to the filler in order to obtain an even density and diameter. In a spiral around this filler he wraps half binder leaves, the tips of both elements now pointing in the same direction, either right or left.

Once the core is assembled, the torcedor takes his knife and trims the head of the nascent cigar (that is, the *perilla,* the end that goes in the mouth), removes any veins that are showing, and puts the compact roll of leaves in a wooden mold that holds ten such *bonches.* Once the mold has been filled to capacity, he closes it and places it in a press from fifteen to forty-five minutes. To avoid leaving lateral marks on the bonches, halfway through this process he opens the mold and gives the rolls of tobacco a quarter turn each. When these bonches have passed the required time in the press, the torcedor slices off the leaves sticking out of the closed mold.

All that remains to transform a bonche into a true Havana cigar is to roll it in its thin silky brown wrapper leaf. Taking a half wrapper leaf, the torcedor smoothes it out on his *tabla,* positioning it in the same way as the binder leaves. With sure, precise strokes of his *chaveta,* the cigar craftsman trims the half-leaf as closely as possible to its upper edge, removing as much of the thickest part of the leaf as he can. He takes a bonche—a left- or right-hand one depending on how the tip of the wrapper leaf is pointing—from the mold and rolls it in the wrapper, starting at the tuck, in other words, the end of the cigar that is lighted, known in the Cuban trade as the *boquilla.* The torcedor rolls it in a spiral with one hand while the other carefully pulls this envelope taut from one vein to the next, eliminating any flaw in the cigar's appearance. Perfectly fitted to the core of the Havana, the wrapper reveals not the slightest wrinkle. When he reaches the *perilla,* he glues the wrapper in place with a dab of mucilage. For the final touches, the torcedor trims the

Havana to the required length in his cigar guillotine and checks its diameter with his *cepo.* A cigar rolled to the right is called a *derecho,* to the left a *zurdo.*

The torcedor's daily output must meet industry norms. According to his category, he has to turn out a certain minimum number of cigars for the type of cigar in question, his category depending upon his experience and skill in producing a perfect cigar. A level-five torcedor, for instance, is limited to the small cigars that are relatively easy to roll, like the demitasse, while a level-seven craftsman creates the large cigars, the prominentes or the pirámides, which demand true expertise.

Tied together in a *media rueda* (literally, a "half wheel"—a *rueda* is a bunch of one hundred cigars; a *media rueda,* fifty), the Havanas are labeled with a tag indicating the torcedor who rolled them and the date they were produced. They are inspected by a quality control department that subjects them to a stringent evaluation of their fragrance, taste, and physical appearance. A Havana cigar must meet every standard or be discarded.

At 8 A.M. the cigar tasters, workers from various other departments who are chosen for their proven sense of taste

THE *VITOLA*

THE SPANISH WORD *VITOLA* IS A CURIOUS TERM, SUGGESTIVE IN MANY WAYS OF THE RICH HISTORY AND TRADITION OF CIGAR CULTURE. ACCORDING TO SPANISH DICTIONARIES, THE WORD SPRANG UP NOT IN A WARM LATIN CLIMATE, BUT IN THE NORTH AMONG THE ANGLO-SAXONS, AS *WITTOL,* WHICH MEANT A KNOWLEDGEABLE PERSON, I.E., ONE WITH WIT. OF COURSE AN ENGLISH WITTOL WOULD NEED, IF NOT WIT, THEN A GOOD SENSE OF HUMOR: IN MIDDLE ENGLISH THE TERM MEANT A COMPLACENT CUCKOLD.

REFLECTING CUBA'S AND CUBAN TOBACCO'S OFTEN VIOLENT PAST, *VITOLA* FIRST MEANT A KIND OF GAUGE, CALIPERS FOR MEASURING BULLETS, BEFORE INDICATING A MEASURE OF CIGAR SIZE AND SHAPE. (APROPOS WITTOLS AND VITOLAS, IT IS TELLING THAT TWENTIETH-CENTURY LITERATURE'S GREATEST WITTOL, LEOPOLD BLOOM OF JOYCE'S *ULYSSES,* PRAISES THE SOOTHING EFFECTS OF THE CIGAR WHILE ON ANOTHER POLITICALLY EXPLOSIVE, MILITARILY OCCUPIED ISLAND WITH A VIOLENT PAST.) IN SPANISH *VITOLA* CAME TO MEAN THE CIGAR BAND ITSELF, AND, GENERALLY, "APPEARANCE" OR "MIEN." (*VITOLFILIA* IS A SPANISH SPEAKER'S PASSION FOR COLLECTING CIGAR BANDS, WHAT IS CALLED IN ENGLISH "CIGRINOPHILY" OR "BRANDOPHILY.") PERHAPS THE CLOSEST ENGLISH TRANSLATION FOR *VITOLA* AS IT IS UNDERSTOOD TODAY IS SIMPLY "TYPE."

BUT VITOLA HAS AN ALMOST METAPHYSICAL DIMENSION, TOO, AS THE CUBAN NOVELIST GUILLERMO CABRERA INFANTE MAKES CLEAR IN *HOLY SMOKE.* THE CHOICE OF VITOLA, REFERRING TO A CIGAR'S SHAPE, SIZE, AND COLOR, REFLECTS THE SMOKER WHO HAS SELECTED IT; IN THIS SENSE IT IS AN EXPRESSION OF HIS OR HER OWN PERSONAL, EVEN SPIRITUAL, VITOLA. BY WAY OF ILLUSTRATION, CABRERA INFANTE INVITES US TO IMAGINE CHURCHILL BLISSFULLY DRAWING ON A CHURCHILL. WHICH VITOLA DO YOU PREFER?

OPPOSITE

Fashioning the cigar head requires great dexterity.

and smell, and the quality of their work in the past, enter the room where they are to test the cigars in detail. This delicate operation is generally based on five criteria:

- Draw: very excessive, excessive, slightly excessive, correct, slightly insufficient, insufficient, very insufficient
- Strength: very strong, strong, slightly strong, average, slightly light, light, slightly weak, light, very light
- Aroma, combustibility, and savor: excellent, very good, good, acceptable, average, bad, very bad

From the sum of these criteria a cigar is defined as excellent, very good, good, acceptable, average, bad, or very bad. When these specialists have finished one tasting, they fill out an evaluation sheet and move on to the next cigar.

When all of the cigars have been tested, the head of the tasting committee takes note of each member's overall evaluation. The individual cigars are designated by a letter; only the committee head knows the identity of the torcedor who rolled this or that lot. A blind tasting is used to maintain objectivity among the participants, even though every torcedor can recognize at a glance the cigars he has rolled.

When a cigar receives a poor overall rating, the head of the committee asks the taster or tasters to justify their assessment. If the appraisal of a cigar differs radically from one taster to the next, another cigar from the same lot is evaluated by the taster who gave the lowest rating. If his opinion remains unchanged, the cigar is opened and its composition analyzed. Likewise, when all the tasters agree on the poor quality of a cigar, it too is opened and analyzed. The results of the analysis are conveyed to the galley production head in order to improve the work of the torcedor in question.

Following the tasting, a physical inspection of the cigars is carried out in a room next to the galley. With great care the inspector picks up a *media rueda* of fifty cigars, turns it over to make sure the heads are full, then flips it over once again to verify the regularity and finish of the tucks. Laying down the *media rueda,* he draws out ten cigars which he now examines closely one by one, checking such things as the uniformity of their color, the regularity of their shape, and the quality of their wrapper leaf. Next he presses the cigar with his fingers to make certain that its composition meets the manufacturer's standards. It must be firm without being too hard and rigid, a nuance that means all the difference in the world. If a cigar is too hard, that is, overfilled

A supple and shiny wrapper, an even body of uniform density: a Havana is born.
PAGES 104–05
On this arm rest five hundred brown ingots on their way to the quality control department.

102

with tobacco, it will draw poorly, diminishing the smoker's pleasure. If, on the other hand, the cigar is too soft and loose, it will burn too rapidly, heating up excessively, which again detracts from the smoker's pleasure.

Merely by feeling the cigar the expert can also tell whether it has been rolled correctly, whether the filler leaves, for example, have been twisted, which would harden the cigar and adversely affect how it burns. If a doubt persists, the inspectors will open the cigar by cutting the wrapper and binder lengthwise, take both ends of the filler in hand and squeeze lightly. In a cigar that has been properly rolled, this will cause the center of the filler to bulge. That does not occur when the leaves have been twisted.

Cigars may also be rejected because the wrapper reveals some flaw, a poor-quality leaf, a tear, or uneven coloring (in the case of a discolored *capa*, the cigar is called a *bandera*—literally, a flag). Such cigars are returned to the torcedores, who replace their wrapper leaves with new ones.

Twenty out of one hundred cigars produced by the same torcedor are thus inspected; of the twenty, two cigars with only minor flaws are allowed. Beyond that number, the entire lot of one hundred is examined one cigar at a time by a second inspector. A torcedor is granted a 4 percent margin of error. If he exceeds that percentage, his pay is docked accordingly. Rejected cigars, called *rezagos,* can be consumed by workers on the premises.

Inspected cigars are now put in wooden drawers, treated with smoke to eliminate any possible parasites, and stored in the manufacturer's cigar cellar, a veritable treasure trove in which tens of thousands of cigars of all sizes are sheltered.

The *escaparate* is an air-conditioned room with a dehumidifier. Its wooden cabinets contain a multitude of precious cigars arranged by *vitola,* the date when they were rolled, and the date when they were treated with smoke. Depending upon their size, they are either laid out or set upright on the cellar's shelves, where they are left to rest and dry from four days to a whole year, the time it takes to

OPPOSITE
*Neither too fat nor too thin, the Havana
maintains a refined profile.*
PAGES 108–09
*Pencils and checklists (and the senses) are
still the only tools used in controlling quality.*

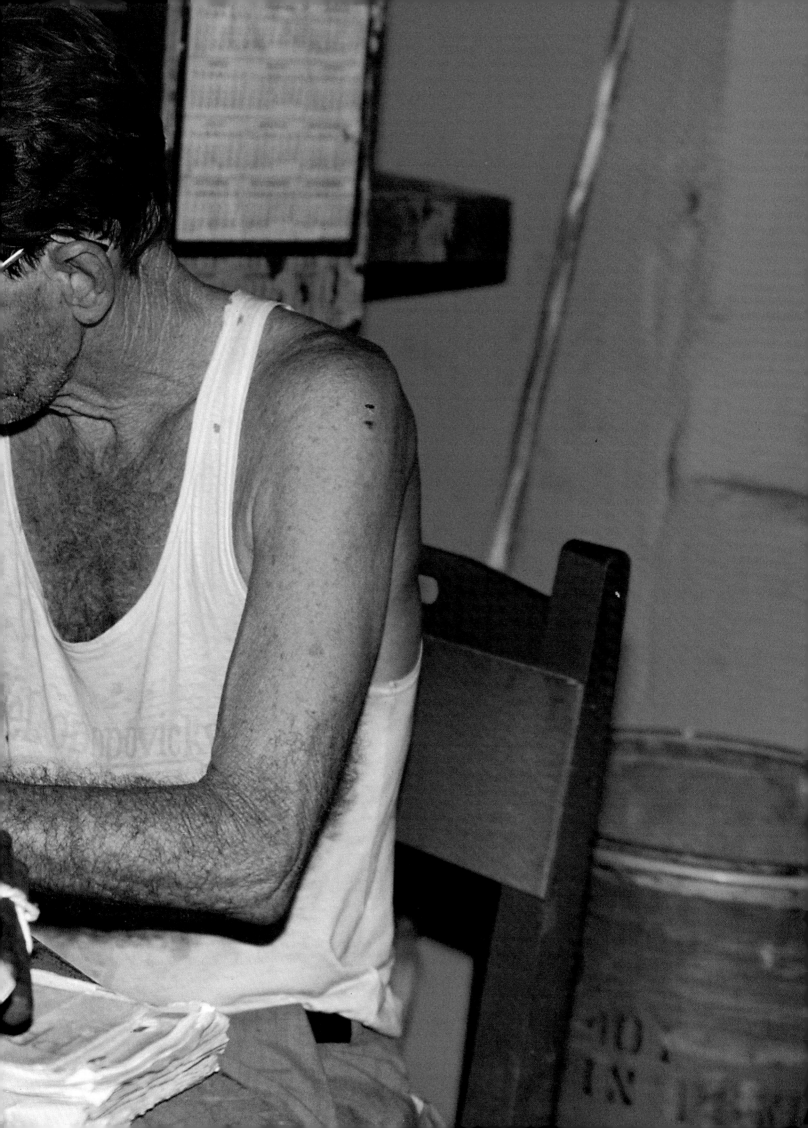

At 8 A.M. the manufacturer's tasters begin their task.

reduce their moisture by 12 to 16 percent. The tobacco has indeed suffered some in the normal course of being handled. During this period, wrapper leaves will take on an even shade of brown, losing their foxed or mottled appearance acquired over the course of their long journey here.

Aristocrat of the tobacco world, noble scion of the "queen's herb" that has produced innumerable coronas, the Havana cigar could hardly be content to enter the *beau monde* dressed in mundane attire. No, such a refined smoke needs to cut a fine figure, must sport a cigar band along with a few other ornaments. In its packaging, as in its production, the Havana is equally demanding.

First, the cigar has to be classified by color, a task performed in a department called the *escogida*. Standing before a great wooden table, the *escogedor* sorts the individual cigars of a single lot according to their shades *(matices)*. The standard palette of color categories offers between five and six shades of brown: *claro* (light brown), *colorado claro* (brown), *colorado* (dark brown) *colorado maduro* (very dark brown), and *maduro* (chestnut); or, as practiced by some manufacturers, *carmelita* (brown), *carmelita oscuro* (dark brown),

carmelita claro (light brown), *carmelita pajize* (straw-colored), *carmelita verdoso* (brownish green), and *verde* (green). Each of these shades can be further broken down into ten to fifteen different hues, sometimes even more.

The *escogedor* lays the cigars horizontally on the table, forming a mosaic of shades and nuances. From left to right and bottom to top, the cigars are arranged from the deepest hues to the lightest, the escogedor's sharp eye making out the barest distinctions of color. Looking over the possibilities before him, he determines at a glance to which pile a cigar corresponds and deposits it there. When all the cigars have been classified, as many small stacks as there are shades of Havanas have sprung up—some seventy different nuances in all. These pyramidal stacks are checked one after the other to make sure the various shades are perfectly uniform, then are broken down into batches of ten, twenty-five, or fifty cigars, depending on the volume of the cigar box used. They are now transferred to another worktable, the domain of the *envasador,* responsible for packaging the finished cigars.

In *boîtes natures* or *boîtes semi-natures* (that is, fine wooden boxes that are either bare or given a simple coat of

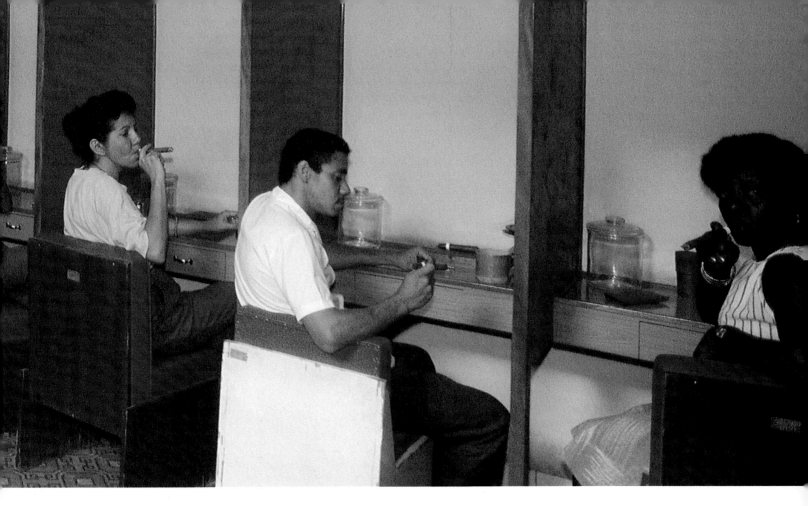

PAGES 112 AND 113
Natural cedar wood remains the Havana's surest refuge.
After so many tiring manipulations, the Havanas are allowed to rest in these
large wooden cabinets before continuing their journey through the cigar factory.

varnish), in individual containers of five, ten, twenty-five, or fifty cigars stacked layer upon layer, in bundles bound with a satin ribbon, or in aluminum tubes—these are some of the ways the Havana is presented to the buyer. The common denominator here remains their uncommon elegance. Either aligned in neat rows or tied in octagonal bundles *(mazos),* the cigars are carefully arranged to maintain their color harmony.

On his table the *envasador* separates the cigars into two groups that will form the upper and lower layers of the cigar box. Arrayed darkest to lightest from left to right, the Havanas are laid out in their box, the envasador taking care to place them with their best side facing up.

If, on the other hand, they are to be presented in mazos, the cigars are bound so that those displaying the shade of brown most alike are placed on the outside of the bundle. They may also be given a band before being assembled, depending on the brand. The *anillador,* the worker responsible for banding the cigar, must also scrupulously respect the color arrangement of the cigar boxes and the exact position given to each Havana.

In use for more than a century now, the lithographed paper cigar band or ring (*anillo*) is the token by which smokers immediately recognize a brand. This last refined touch is designed, printed, and slipped on the cigar according to the highest artistic standards. Producers of the bands employ a technique that was developed at the end of the nineteenth century. While still fresh, the newly printed sheets of cigar

FUMIGATION

TOBACCO IS FUMIGATED TO ELIMINATE INSECTS AND OTHER HARMFUL PESTS. BEFORE BEING PACKED IN THEIR BOXES, CASES OF CIGARS COVERED WITH A PIECE OF CLOTH ARE PLACED IN SPECIAL CHAMBERS AT THE MANU-FACTURER. THE AIR IS THEN EMPTIED OUT AT A PRESSURE OF -0.965 KG/CM^2 AND SPECIAL GAS USED TO TREAT THE CIGARS IS PUMPED IN UNDER PRESSURE (110 G/M^2) AT A TEMPERATURE THAT VARIES BETWEEN 79.9 AND 99.9°F (26.6–37.7°C). THE CIGARS WILL REMAIN IN THESE CHAMBERS BETWEEN SIX AND TWENTY-FOUR HOURS. ONCE THIS OPERATION IS COMPLETE, THE GAS IS EVACUATED THROUGH AN EXHAUST VENT AND THE DOORS OF THE CHAMBER ARE OPENED.

THE FOLLOWING FACTORS ARE RECORDED IN THE COURSE OF THIS OPERATION: THE TYPE AND QUANTITY OF SUBSTANCE USED TO FUMIGATE THE TOBACCO; THE PRESSURE WITHIN THE CHAMBER AT THE BEGINNING AND END OF THE OPERATION; THE TOTAL TIME THE TOBACCO WAS EXPOSED TO THE GAS. THIS INFORMATION ALLOWS EXPERTS TO ANALYZE ANY PROBLEM THAT MIGHT ARISE LATER.

bands, each of which contains seventy-two bands, are sprinkled with powdered gold leaf. After drying, each sheet is covered with a thin layer of clear varnish to lend it a shiny finish; certain bands may also be embossed here with various motifs. The printed bands are checked and then sent in groups of five hundred to the manufacturers.

Meticulously scrutinized throughout their production, Havanas are inspected yet again in their box. Workers make sure that the packaging is flawless; that the cigars show no signs of discoloring, tearing, or mold, and are correctly positioned and arranged by color; that their diameter and length are uniform; that their *boquillas* are full, their wrapper leaves are taut and without wrinkles, their bands reveal no defects nor unsightly excess paste, are placed at the same height and are not stuck together—and the list of details that have to be checked hardly stops there. Yet it is only by strictly adhering to these standards that manufacturers can guarantee a cigar of the highest quality. Overlook this or that element as a way of increasing sales and the Havana's position as the king of cigars begins to totter.

Sealed with a green ribbon indicating the official guarantee of the cigars' origin and labeled for tax purposes or stamped with health warnings, the cigar boxes are put in cardboard cartons and stocked in refrigerated rooms.

The Havana is now ready to set out for shops and private humidors the world over to offer smokers the unique taste and aroma of a cigar that is truly without equal. From earth to ash, some five centuries of tradition, three hundred individual operations and manipulations of the tobacco, months of hard work, and the collective experience of thousands of highly skilled *tabacaleros* have gone into making a few minutes of smoking pleasure available to genuine aficionados, a pleasure shared by the Taino Indians so many hundreds of years ago.

Cedar is the only wood used in making cigar boxes because of its great bitterness, which repels even the most voracious insects.

Although the Havana cigar has come to be a luxury item, for many years it traveled in mediocre packaging—bales tied together with *yagua* (leaves of the royal palm), or pig bladders containing a bit of vanilla whose aroma would permeate the cigars. As mentioned in an earlier chapter, the first wooden crates, which were easily counterfeited, only appeared in the early nineteenth century.

Manufacturers eventually understood that it was absolutely necessary for the Havana to travel in a case worthy of the cigar's origins. In 1845 Ramón Allones, for La Eminencia brand, invented the luxury cigar box. These handsome wooden containers were generously decorated with lithographed scenes. His competitors followed suit and by 1848 there were 232 different cigar labels. Over the years these lithographs, called *cromos,* were to flourish, so much so that they now number in the thousands. Featuring landscapes of fields growing tobacco, views of important edifices, or portraits of well-known people, the cromos show real

ENJOYING THE HAVANA

artistic talent. Each manufacturer would adopt an emblem for its cigar boxes—what came to be called after 1880 the *habilitación,* the packaging of the Havana.

The *fileteador* needs only a few minutes to decorate each box that passes through his hands. There are in fact several labels that he pastes on each container: the *cubierta* on the outside cover; the *vista* on the inside; the *bofetón* around the cigars; the *papeleta* along the smaller sides; the *larguero* on the longer front and back sides; the *contaseña* or *tapaclavo* hiding the small nail used to close the box; the *filetes* along the edges; and finally, since 1912, the national seal guaranteeing the origin of the cigars, a green ribbon pasted on the left side of the box.

Painstaking care is taken to conserve the Havana. Cuba's natural climate with its relative humidity of 70 percent must be reproduced by every means available, usually a humidifier, hygrometer, and thermostat (the temperature can

PAGES 118–19
This relatively newfangled calculator only recently replaced the shelved Russian adding machines.
OPPOSITE
To smoke a Havana remains a rare privilege for Cubans, which only makes the cigar taste that much better.

vary only between 64 and 68°F (18–20°C). It is generally thought that under the right conditions a cigar will keep from ten to twenty years.

Excessive humidity, like an overly dry environment, is harmful to a cigar's aroma. There exist a number of very effective ways for restoring dried-out cigars, although these demand infinite care and attention. A dry cigar is brittle and could develop mold if it absorbs too much moisture too quickly. And it must be remembered that the Havana cigar should never be enjoyed until after the summer following its production, since it continues to ferment slightly between June and August.

And so, from among exquisite, meticulously composed presentations, from among a range of very different categories of cigar and a wealth of unique aromas that have been patiently developed by generations of specialists, the Havana aficionado must now make his or her choice. Knowing how to savor a Havana, however, requires real training. It is an art that must satisfy all the senses. Impeccably arranged according to color, with a perfectly even, unblemished surface, the cigars reveal not the slightest flaw. Picking up a cigar, pressing it between thumb and index finger and releasing does not alter its shape. Rather the cigar emits a soft crackling that is easily heard and which attests to the Havana's perfect construction. At the same time, the tips of the smoker's fingers appreciate the touch of the absolutely smooth wrapper leaf. Finally, the cigar lover's sense of smell comes into play, for tobacco that is ready to be smoked gives off aromas that are full of promise. Naturally the enthusiast puts the finishing strokes on this process by striking a match, completely satisfying his or her sense of taste.

While the above traits are common to all Havanas, the same cannot be said about their size and strength. Thus one must pay attention to a few obvious criteria in moving from one *vitola* to the next. The inexperienced cigar smoker should begin with the smallest and lightest cigars, the coronitas, petits, and demitasses, for example, before tackling the

larger makes like the Julieta 2, the prominentes or the gran corona. These latter cigars' aromas are subtler and demand a connoisseur's palate.

Likewise each time of day corresponds to a certain size of cigar. A true aficionado will take a light cigar after breakfast, a demitasse, say, or crema or conchita. The coronas, superiores, and perlas are an excellent way to top off any light lunch, whereas the Cervantes, dalias, or ninfas are recommended after heavy midday meals or even a light supper. A large cigar with a complex aroma, Julieta 2, prominentes, or gran corona, makes a perfect end to the day. But the pleasure of a cigar is really best enjoyed after a meal for it should prolong the experience of good food, not work against or neutralize its effects. On the other hand, many smokers admit that they prefer cigars in the morning when their palate is still receptive enough to the aroma of tobacco.

First one chooses a cigar in its box according to its appearance and color. Because no two cigars are identical, each gives off tobacco aromas that are unique and must be appreciated—naturally an important part of the ceremony.

There are at least two competing methods for cutting off the *perilla,* the head of the cigar, namely, the straight cut and the V-cut. It is better to make a small clean cut and avoid the problems of a cigar that draws excessively or insufficiently—drawbacks in every sense of the word. In Cuba, many tobacco professionals choose to bite the perilla off, and generously wet the end of the cigar with their tongue while smoking. Now comes the question of removing the band. This can be a tricky operation since some *anillos* are lightly pasted to the wrapper leaf itself and removal could damage the *capa.* A few puffs will contract the body of the cigar somewhat, making it easier to slip the band off.

Before kindling the tuck, drawing a few times on the unlighted Havana is recommended in order to enjoy a foretaste of the aroma. Next, when lighting, a short, intense, odorless flame is used. It is no longer helpful to heat the cigar beforehand as in the days when the glue used in cigars

PAGE 122
*At every street corner, under every arcade,
the past refuses to disappear.*
PAGE 123
*While the Havana cigar continues to be an
emblem of masculinity . . .*
OPPOSITE
. . . the finest palates are often feminine.

124

from Seville had an unpleasant taste. The gum employed in Havana cigars nowadays is totally inodorous.

One must roll the Havana between one's fingers to make sure the cigar burns evenly, sometimes even shake it slightly in the air to fan the flame. The cigar is not immediately brought to one's lips; rather the smoker waits until a little crown of ash has formed at the tuck. The larger the cigar, the more time is needed to light it.

As with all cigars, smokers draw the Havana's smoke into the mouth where they hold it, then blow the bluish curls without trying to inhale. The whole of a cigar's quality lies in the flavors that then caress the palate and nose. A cigar smoker's lungs are in no danger of severe injury since the Havanas have the lowest amounts of nicotine of all known cigars. A cigar may go out if it is forgotten for a while, but the smoker only needs to relight the outer edge to rekindle the entire cigar right down to the very middle of the *bonche.*

Finally the smoker should refrain from tapping the cigar to remove the ash, which will drop off naturally when the end touches the ashtray. It is a good idea to keep an eighth of an inch (3 mm) or so of ash on the end since it tempers the flame and helps avoid overheating.

A Havana can be smoked down to three-quarters of its length or just over that, no more. And cigar lovers wouldn't think of stubbing or snubbing or snuffing out their Havana like a mere cigarette. Set on the edge of the ashtray the *cabo,* the cigar butt, will go out by itself in a short while.

Even though there exist strict criteria for evaluating a cigar, as I have laid out above when describing work at the manufacturers, in the end consumers should trust their own taste. It is personal taste, and that alone, once it has been trained, developed, and sharpened, that will lead the aficionado to prefer this or that brand and *vitola,* not a cigar's renown, not its overall appearance, not its popularity.

PAGE 126
For the visitor time does indeed come to a halt once in a while.
PAGE 127
Havana is a museum of old American cars.
OPPOSITE
For Cubans time has often passed too quickly.

LOS REYES DE ESPAÑA.

REGIAS

Catalogue Raisonné

Introduction to the Catalogue

The following catalogue raisonné shows Havana cigars in life-size view.

It comprises all of the brands officially sold by Cuba today, although some may prove difficult to find from one year to the next because of the ups and downs of tobacco growing.

Distribution in the countries that import Havanas is handled by Habano S.A., an independent commercial branch of Cubatabaco, following a thorough market study for each brand. As such, some brands of Havana cigars are only sold in certain countries and nowhere else—and of course all are, at least officially, unavailable in the United States.

The evaluation of each cigar is obviously subjective, conditioned by the quality of the harvest, the commercial availability of the product, and the smoker's personal taste. The evaluation provided for certain very rare makes was obtained from seasoned smokers inside Cuba and out, and draws on memories much more than any methodical appreciation.

The table on the bottom of each page of the catalogue lists, for each cigar shown, both the commercial name (first column) and production classification, or *vitola* (second column); length and diameter, in inches and millimeters; weight, in grams only; *cepo* (ring gauge); and taster's comments.

Belinda

Coronas   Panetelas   Petit   Petit Coronas   Preciosas   Princess   Superfinos

Name		Length	Diameter	Weight	Cepo	Comments
Coronas	Cremas	5⁹/₁₆ in. 140 mm	⁵/₈ in. 15.87 mm	7.64 g	40	This brand is produced in small quantities. The aromas found in the Coronas lack complexity.
Panetelas	Sports	4 ⁵/₈ in. 117 mm	⁹/₁₆ in. 13.89 mm	4.88 g	35	A simple, unsophisticated make that is earthy and a bit harsh.
Petit	Petit	4⁵/₁₆ in. 108 mm	¹/₂ in. 12.30 mm	3.57 g	31	A small, straightforward cigar that is fairly mild.
Petit Coronas	Petit Coronas	5¹/₈ in. 129 mm	¹¹/₁₆ in. 16.67 mm	7.77 g	42	Not especially flavorful, the Petit Coronas develops hints of fresh grass and green plants toward the middle.
Preciosas	Demi Tasse	4 in. 100 mm	¹/₂ in. 12.70 mm	3.50 g	32	A cigar with little character, suitable for a morning smoke.
Princess	Epicures	4³/₈ in. 110 mm	⁹/₁₆ in. 13.89 mm	4.60 g	35	Offers very weak, wispy flavors. Not especially interesting.
Superfinos	Coronitas	4⁵/₈ in. 117 mm	⁵/₈ in. 15.87 mm	6.35 g	40	Reveals no great refinement. Does not give a precise idea of the Havana.

Bolívar

Belicosos Finos   Belvederes   Bonitas   Coronas Extra

Name		Length	Diameter	Weight	Cepo	Comments
Belicosos Finos	Campanas	5½ in. 140 mm	⅞ in. 20.64 mm	12.37 g	52	A full-bodied, somewhat harsh cigar whose aromas build gradually after lighting. For the experienced smoker.
Belvederes	Belvederes	4¹⁵/₁₆ in. 125 mm	⅝ in. 15.48 mm	6.21 g	39	With its even combustion this make, turned out in small numbers, builds its aromas rather quickly.
Bonitas	Londres	5 in. 126 mm	⅝ in. 15.87 mm	7.29 g	40	Although comparable to the Belvederes, this cigar does prove harsher.
Coronas Extra	Franciscos	5¹¹/₁₆ in. 143 mm	¹¹/₁₆ in. 17.46 mm	9.94 g	44	A cigar with a big, full taste and complex aroma, able to assert its flavors after a heavy meal or strong spirits. For the connoisseur.

Bolívar

Coronas Gigantes   Coronas Junior   Coronas   Champions   Chicos

Name		Length	Diameter	Weight	Cepo	Comments
Coronas Gigantes	Julieta 2	7 in. 178 mm	¾ in. 18.65 mm	14.08 g	47	A relatively strong, slightly aromatic cigar with a long finish. For the aficionado.
Coronas Junior	Minutos	4³⁄₈ in. 110 mm	11.16 in. 16.67 mm	6.97 g	42	A relatively small cigar with complex aromas. Quite similar to the Coronas.
Coronas	Coronas	5⁵⁄₈ in. 142 mm	¹¹⁄₁₆ in. 16.67 mm	8.97 g	42	A powerful cigar that smacks of the earth. For experienced enthusiasts.
Champions	Cremas	5⁹⁄₁₆ in. 140 mm	⁵⁄₈ in. 15.87 mm	7.64 g	40	A cigar that is a bit too aggressive toward the end.
Chicos	Chicos	4³⁄₁₆ in. 106 mm	⁷⁄₁₆ in. 10.32 mm	3.00 g	29	A small, vigorous make whose aroma does not stand out especially.

Bolívar

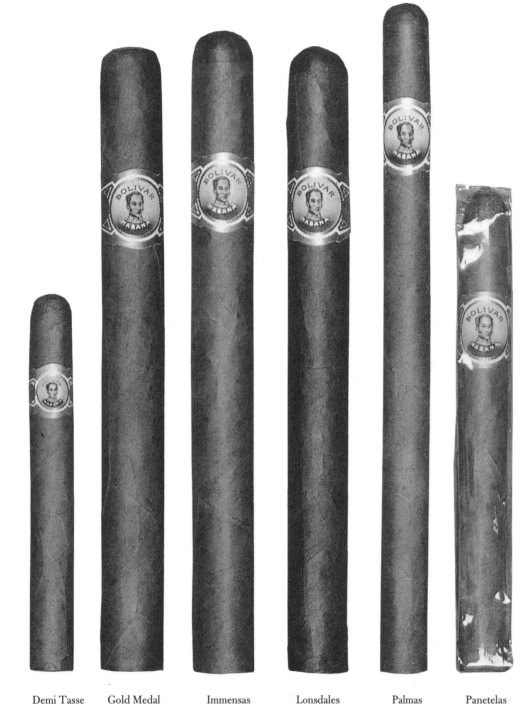

| Demi Tasse | Gold Medal | Immensas | Lonsdales | Palmas | Panetelas |

Name		Length	Diameter	Weight	Cepo	Comments
Demi Tasse	Entreactos	4 in. 100 mm	½ in. 11.91 mm	3.27 g	30	Don't be taken in by this cigar's small size: its pronounced taste may come as a surprise.
Gold Medal	Cervantes	6½ in. 165 mm	11/16 in. 16.67 mm	10.47 g	42	Full-bodied with a pronounced bouquet. Difficult to obtain nowadays, this cigar will please only a few connoisseurs in search of a powerful smoke.
Immensas	Dalias	6¾ in. 170 mm	11/16 in. 17.07 mm	11.32 g	43	Powerful and at times overly rough, a rather straightforward cigar that will delight those who prize the Havanas of old.
Lonsdales	Cervantes	6½ in. 165 mm	11/16 in. 16.67 mm	10.47 g	42	A light cigar in terms of its aromas and taste. Body lacks definition. For the beginner's palate.
Palmas	Ninfas	7 1/16 in. 178 mm	9/16 in. 13.10 mm	6.97 g	33	This long, thin cigar surprises smokers with the aggressive, rather blunt side of its character. Hard to smoke.
Panetelas	Conchitas	5 1/16 in. 127 mm	9/16 in. 13.89 mm	5.29 g	35	Slightly wanting in refinement, although it does develop spicy accents.

Bolívar

Petit Coronas   Petit Coronas   Regentes   Royal Coronas   Supremas Churchills
Especiales

Name		Length	Diameter	Weight	Cepo	Comments
Petit Coronas	Marevas	5⅛ in. 129 mm	¹¹/₁₆ in. 16.67 mm	8.14 g	42	A cigar that boasts a complex taste and aroma despite its medium size. Rather straightforward, it does not lose its force as it burns down.
Petit Coronas Especiales	Eminentes	5¼ in. 132 mm	¹¹/₁₆ in. 17.46 mm	8.74 g	44	Builds its flavors during its first third, although it remains somewhat harsh for its size.
Regentes	Placeras	4¹⁵/₁₆ in. 125 mm	⁹/₁₆ in. 13.49 mm	5.22 g	34	This cigar's earthy flavors might remain a handicap for some enthusiasts.
Royal Coronas	Robustos	4¹⁵/₁₆ in. 124 mm	¹³/₁₆ in. 19.84 mm	11.18 g	50	A balanced taste thanks in particular to its fine combustion. Generous in its aromas, this smooth cigar is the perfect end to a light meal.
Supremas Churchills	Julieta 2	7 in. 178 mm	¾ in. 18.65 mm	14.08 g	47	A powerful, aromatic cigar for lovers of traditional Havanas.

Cifuentes

Cubanitos   Cristal Tubo   Emboquillados   Habanitos   Petits Bouquets   Vegueritos   Super Estupendos

Name		Length	Diameter	Weight	Cepo	Comments
Cubanitos	Chicos	4³/₁₆ in. 106 mm	⁷/₁₆ in. 10.32 mm	3.00 g	29	A small, aromatic make. Like all the *vitolas* of this venerable brand, it is only rarely produced.
Cristal Tubo	Conservas	5³/₄ in. 145 mm	¹¹/₁₆ in. 17.46 mm	9.57 g	44	A rarity. To be held on to for its historic value.
Emboquillados	Demi Tip	5 in. 126 mm	¹/₂ in. 11.51 mm	3.68 g	29	A light, refined, unpretentious cigar.
Habanitos	Chicos	4³/₁₆ in. 106 mm	⁷/₁₆ in. 10.32 mm	3.00 g	29	A small make that is closer to a cigarillo than a cigar.
Petits Bouquets	Infantes	3¹⁵/₁₆ in. 98 mm	⁵/₈ in. 14.68 mm	4.03 g	37	A relatively full-bodied cigar devoid of any great complexity in its aromas.
Vegueritos	Vegueritos	5¹/₁₆ in. 127 mm	⁵/₈ in. 15.87 mm	6.10 g	37	Somewhat rough, the Vegueritos gives off the unsophisticated harshness of the smaller brands.
Super Estupendos	Gran Corona	9¹/₄ in. 235 mm	³/₄ in. 18.65 mm	18.63 g	47	This powerful cigar is unobtainable. The Super Estupendo's flavors smack of its native soil.

Cohiba

| Coronas Especiales | Panetelas | Esplendidos | Exquisitos | Coronas | Robusto | Lanceros |

Name		Length	Diameter	Weight	Cepo	Comments
Coronas Especiales	No. 2	5^{15}/$_{16}$ in. 152 mm	^{3}/$_8$ in. 9.50 mm	7.87 g	38	This cigar possesses a woody, though gentle bouquet and a pleasant, smooth taste. For smokers who wish to develop their palate.
Panetelas	No. 3	4^9/$_{16}$ in. 115 mm	^{7}/$_{16}$ in. 10.32 mm	2.81 g	26	Its small size detracts not a whit or whiff from its aggressive taste and solid aroma. For connoisseurs following coffee after dinner.
Esplendidos	Julieta 2	7 in. 178 mm	^{3}/$_4$ in. 18.65 mm	14.08 g	47	Rich, balanced flavor, and muscular aroma that is nonetheless rather mild. A cigar to be savored in peace and quiet. For enthusiasts.
Exquisitos	Seoanes	5 in. 126 mm	^{9}/$_{16}$ in. 13.10 mm	5.01 g	33	Light bouquet. Its woody taste when lighted makes itself felt on the palate despite its relative lack of complexity. To be smoked quickly.
Coronas	Coronas	5^5/$_8$ in. 142 mm	^{11}/$_{16}$ in. 16.67 mm	8.97 g	42	A rather mild, well-balanced cigar that is pleasant to smoke during the day. Very hard to obtain.
Robusto	Robustos	4^{15}/$_{16}$ in. 124 mm	^{13}/$_{16}$ in. 19.84 mm	11.18 g	50	An oily cigar that reveals great complexity in its flavors. As it burns, its taste lingers on the palate. For the aficionado.
Lanceros	No. 1	7^5/$_8$ in. 192 mm	^{5}/$_8$ in. 15.08 mm	10.03 g	38	Fidel Castro's favorite cigar, the Lancero is highly flavorful, perhaps too much so for certain aficionados. Its spicy taste remains quite consistent. For the seasoned enthusiast.

Cohiba

Siglo I   Siglo II   Siglo III   Siglo IV   Siglo V

Name		Length	Diameter	Weight	Cepo	Comments
Siglo I	Perlas	4$^{1}/_{16}$ in. 102 mm	$^{5}/_{8}$ in. 15.87 mm	5.91 g	40	A small cigar, quite pleasant and smooth. Its size and diameter make it burn quickly and evenly. Pleasing to women.
Siglo II	Marevas	5$^{1}/_{8}$ in. 129 mm	$^{11}/_{16}$ in. 16.67 mm	8.14 g	42	A cigar with character. The Siglo II is a small model among the bigger types of cigar that proves very easy to carry about.
Siglo III	Coronas Grandes	6$^{1}/_{8}$ in. 155 mm	$^{11}/_{16}$ in. 16.67 mm	9.89 g	42	A very pleasant cigar that is perfect after lunch.
Siglo IV	Coronas Gordas	5$^{11}/_{16}$ in. 143 mm	$^{11}/_{16}$ in. 16.67 mm	10.90 g	46	Its diameter gives the Siglo IV excellent combustibility. A full-bodied cigar that provides a well-rounded taste.
Siglo V	Dalias	6$^{3}/_{4}$ in. 170 mm	$^{11}/_{16}$ in. 17.07 mm	11.32 g	43	One of the best Havanas in this size. Possesses an aroma that smacks of its native soil. A smoke for special occasions.

Diplomaticos

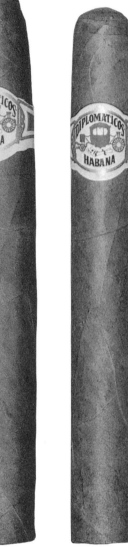

| Diplomaticos No. 1 | Diplomaticos No. 2 | Diplomaticos No. 3 | Diplomaticos No. 4 | Diplomaticos No. 5 | Diplomaticos No. 6 | Diplomaticos No. 7 |

Name		Length	Diameter	Weight	Cepo	Comments
Diplomaticos No. 1	Cervantes	6½ in. 165 mm	$^{11}/_{16}$ in. 16.07 mm	10.47 g	42	A cigar with a pleasant, though not especially pronounced, taste.
Diplomaticos No. 2	Piramides	6³/₁₆ in. 156 mm	⅞ in. 20.64 mm	12.19 g	52	A cigar that boasts a rather full and powerful taste. Mainly for experienced enthusiasts.
Diplomaticos No. 3	Coronas	5⅝ in. 142 mm	$^{11}/_{16}$ in. 16.67 mm	8.97 g	42	A cigar that fits in everywhere and can be enjoyed any time of day.
Diplomaticos No. 4	Marevas	5⅛ in. 129 mm	$^{11}/_{16}$ in. 16.67 mm	8.14 g	42	Doesn't obtrusively fill the air. A cigar for the morning.
Diplomaticos No. 5	Perlas	4¹/₁₆ in. 102 mm	⅝ in. 15.87 mm	5.91 g	40	May prove harsh without being especially flavorful.
Diplomaticos No. 6	No. 1	7⅝ in. 192 mm	⅝ in. 15.08 mm	10.03 g	38	An elegant cigar, though without the refinement of the Montecristo Especial.
Diplomaticos No. 7	No. 2	5¹⁵/₁₆ in. 152 mm	⅝ in. 15.08 mm	7.87 g	38	Similar to the No. 6, this *vitola* is somewhat wanting in staying power on the palate.

Flor de Cano

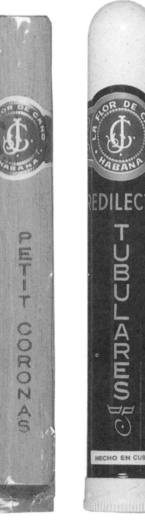

Coronas   Gran Coronas   Petit Coronas   Predilectos Tubulares   Preferidos   Selectos   Short Churchills   Diademas

Name		Length	Diameter	Weight	Cepo	Comments
Coronas	Marevas	5¹/₈ in. 129 mm	¹¹/₁₆ in. 16.67 mm	8.14 g	42	A light, smooth cigar with restrained aromas that will please inexperienced smokers all the same.
Gran Coronas	Coronas Gordas	5¹¹/₁₆ in. 143 mm	¹¹/₁₆ in. 16.67 mm	10.90 g	46	Supple, smooth. Burns evenly if it is not too tightly rolled. Very nice smoke for mid-morning or mid-afternoon.
Petit Coronas	Standard	4¹⁵/₁₆ in. 123 mm	⁵/₈ in. 15.87 mm	6.90 g	40	A light cigar, recommended for mornings.
Predilectos Tubulares	Standard	4¹⁵/₁₆ in. 123 mm	⁵/₈ in. 15.87 mm	6.90 g	40	A fresh, pleasant smoke that is also easy to carry about.
Preferidos	Vegueritos	5¹/₁₆ in. 127 mm	⁵/₈ in. 14.68 mm	6.10 g	37	A mild cigar that is sure to please beginners.
Selectos	Cristales	5¹⁵/₁₆ in. 150 mm	¹¹/₁₆ in. 16.27 mm	8.97 g	41	This mild cigar makes a perfect end to a light midday meal.
Short Churchills	Robustos	4¹⁵/₁₆ in. 124 mm	¹³/₁₆ in. 19.84 mm	11.18 g	50	This is a rather mild cigar whose taste appears from the very first whiffs to the very last whorls. Subtle though subdued aromas. A Havana for smokers of every stripe.
Diademas	Julieta 2	7 in. 178 mm	³/₄ in. 18.65 mm	14.08 g	47	A fresh, smooth cigar, one that will especially satisfy smokers eager to try the Julieta 2 or Churchill vitolas.

Flor de Juan Lopez

Coronas   Patricias   Petit Coronas   Panetela Superba

Name		Length	Diameter	Weight	Cepo	Comments
Coronas	Coronas	5⅝ in. 142 mm	11/16 in. 16.67 mm	8.97 g	42	This cigar is easy to smoke. Light and smooth, it can be enjoyed at any time of day. Recommended for the novice.
Patricias	Francis-canos	4⅝ in. 116 mm	⅝ in. 15.87 mm	6.72 g	40	The Patricias' fresh, light character makes it easy to smoke. With a flavor that is not especially striking, it remains a daytime cigar.
Petit Coronas	Marevas	5⅛ in. 129 mm	11/16 in. 16.67 mm	8.14 g	42	A cigar that boasts a discreet, very pleasant aroma. Never fails to delight smokers who are eager to try Havana cigars.
Panetela Superba	Placeras	4¹⁵/₁₆ in. 125 mm	9/16 in. 13.49 mm	5.22 g	34	An smooth, easy-to-smoke cigar that burns evenly, making it simple to control.

Flor del Caney

| Bouquet Finos | Canapé | Delgados | Especiales | Predilectos | Selectos | Vegueros |

Name		Length	Diameter	Weight	Cepo	Comments
Bouquet Finos	Vegueritos	5¹/₁₆ in. 127 mm	⁵/₈ in. 14.68 mm	6.10 g	37	Flor del Caney is a brand whose output largely depends on the tobacco harvest. Difficult to obtain.
Canapé	Chicos	4³/₁₆ in. 106 mm	⁷/₁₆ in. 10.32 mm	3.00 g	29	A small cigar that has kept its earthy fragrance.
Delgados	Vegueritos	5¹/₁₆ in. 127 mm	⁵/₈ in. 14.68 mm	6.10 g	37	Its aromas lack a certain refinement. Straightforward, blunt flavor.
Especiales	Culebras	5¹³/₁₆ in. 146 mm	⁵/₈ in. 15.48 mm	6.67 g	39	The Especiales' rough aromas recall the Havanas' taste of old.
Predilectos	Standard	4¹⁵/₁₆ in. 123 mm	⁵/₈ in. 15.87 mm	6.90 g	40	Not especially generous, this make proves a disappointment to enthusiasts who enjoy distinct aromas.
Selectos	Nacionales	5⁹/₁₆ in. 140 mm	⁵/₈ in. 15.87 mm	8.28 g	40	The Selectos' straight-out initial taste can surprise some smokers. Its flavors are not particularly complex.
Vegueros	Preferidos	5¹/₁₆ in. 127 mm	⁵/₈ in. 15.08 mm	7.02 g	38	Like all the Flor del Caney *vitolas*, the Vegueros remains a notch below the major brands of Havanas.

Fonseca

Cosacos   Delicias   Fonseca No. 1   Invictos   K.D.T. Cadetes

Name		Length	Diameter	Weight	Cepo	Comments
Cosacos	Cosacos	5³/₈ in. 135 mm	¹¹/₁₆ in. 16.67 mm	8.56 g	42	A very light, straightforward cigar with no particular complexity. For smokers eager to move up to the Havanas.
Delicias	Standard	4¹⁵/₁₆ in. 123 mm	⁵/₈ in. 15.87 mm	6.90 g	40	Leaves little impression on the palate, although the Delicias is not without flavor.
Fonseca No. 1	Cazadores	6⁷/₈ in. 162 mm	¹¹/₁₆ in. 17.46 mm	11.27 g	44	A gentle, generous make. Not especially aggressive, this is a fine cigar for enthusiasts looking to try the large sizes.
Invictos	Especiales	5⁵/₁₆ in. 158 mm	⁵/₈ in. 15.08 mm	10.03 g	45	The particular form of this make keeps its true character under wraps for the first third of its length, after which its flavors build to reveal a pleasant, light cigar.
K.D.T. Cadetes	Cadetes	4⁹/₁₆ in. 115 mm	⁵/₈ in. 14.29 mm	5.34 g	36	An unrefined, aggressive cigar that is disagreeable to the taste. Gives a poor idea of the Havanas.

Gispert

Coronas   Habaneras   Petit Coronas
No. 2   De Luxe

Name		Length	Diameter	Weight	Cepo	Comments
Coronas	Coronas	5⅝ in. 142 mm	11/16 in. 16.67 mm	8.97 g	42	A light, mild cigar that verges on being simply bland. For beginners.
Habaneras No. 2	Standard	4¹⁵/₁₆ in. 123 mm	⅝ in. 15.87 mm	6.90 g	40	A cigar that is somewhat lacking in individuality but will satisfy beginners.
Petit Coronas De Luxe	Marevas	5⅛ in. 129 mm	11/16 in. 16.67 mm	8.14 g	42	A light cigar, not especially harsh. Will please inexperienced cigar smokers.

Gloria Cubana

Cetros	Tapados	Minutos	Sabrosos	Médaille d'Or No. 1	Tainos	Médaille d'Or No. 4	Médaille d'Or No. 3	Médaille d'Or No. 2

Name		Length	Diameter	Weight	Cepo	Comments
Cetros	Cervantes	6½ in. 165 mm	11/16 in. 16.67 mm	10.47 g	42	Aromatic, though slightly harsh. This cigar's light character makes it pleasant, though not particularly memorable.
Tapados	Cosacos	5⅜ in. 135 mm	11/16 in. 16.67 mm	8.56 g	42	The Tapados' light taste develops throughout its even burn. Enjoyable any time of day.
Minutos	Franciscanos	4⅝ in. 116 mm	⅝ in. 15.87 mm	6.72 g	40	This light, evenly burning cigar leaves a pleasant sensation on the palate.
Sabrosos	Coronas Grandes	6⅛ in. 155 mm	11/16 in. 16.67 mm	9.89 g	42	A powerful, though only slightly aromatic, cigar. Round, full flavor.
Médaille d'Or No. 1	Delicados Extra	7 5/16 in. 235 mm	¾ in. 18.65 mm	18.63 g	36	Good combustibility allows aromas to develop fully. The taste becomes more aggressive in the last third of the cigar.
Tainos	Julieta 2	7 in. 178 mm	¾ in. 18.65 mm	14.08 g	47	Oily and fairly mild, the Tainos reveals a range of subtle flavors throughout its even burn.
Médaille d'Or No. 4	Palmitas	6 in. 152 mm	½ in. 12.70 mm	5.52 g	32	A smooth, mild cigar, can be enjoyed in the morning or the afternoon.
Médaille d'Or No. 3	Panetelas Largas	6 15/16 in. 175 mm	7/16 in. 11.11 mm	4.95 g	28	Burns evenly, making it easy to smoke. A light taste at first draw, this cigar becomes slightly aggressive in its last third.
Médaille d'Or No. 2	Dalias	6¾ in. 170 mm	11/16 in. 17.07 mm	11.32 g	43	The smooth, round taste of this cigar continues to build right up to the final puff. This is a mild make for seasoned cigar smokers.

Hoyo de Monterrey

Concorde   Coronation   Churchills   Epicure No. 1   Double Coronas   Particulares

Name		Length	Diameter	Weight	Cepo	Comments
Concorde	Julieta 2	7 in. 178 mm	¾ in. 18.65 mm	5.52 g	47	Harder to find than the Churchill, the Concorde offers light, complex flavors. For one and all.
Coronation	Marevas	5⅛ in. 129 mm	¹¹/₁₆ in. 16.67 mm	8.14 g	42	A light make of cigar that is perfectly suitable for mornings.
Churchills	Julieta 2	7 in. 178 mm	¾ in. 18.65 mm	5.52 g	47	A smooth restrained make whose flavors build towards the end of the cigar. Easy to smoke, this is a Havana to everyone's taste.
Epicure No. 1	Coronas Gordas	5¹¹/₁₆ in. 143 mm	¹¹/₁₆ in. 16.67 mm	10.90 g	46	A smooth cigar with a discreet, though pleasant taste. Easy to smoke. A long finish.
Double Coronas	Prominentes	7¹¹/₁₆ in. 194 mm	¹³/₁₆ in. 19.45 mm	16.70 g	49	A fragrant, smooth cigar, not particularly aggressive. Offers an oily, even taste to the very end.
Particulares	Gran Corona	9¼ in. 235 mm	¾ in. 18.65 mm	18.63 g	47	Despite its size, this cigar remains discreet in terms of its taste and aromas. Does not require an experienced palate, just a number of long leisurely hours.

Hoyo de Monterrey

Epicure No. 2   Exquisitos   Hoyo Coronas   Humidor No. 1   Jeanne d'Arc

Name		Length	Diameter	Weight	Cepo	Comments
Epicure No. 2	Robustos	4^{15}/$_{16}$ in. 124 mm	^{13}/$_{16}$ in. 19.84 mm	11.18 g	50	This cigar's light flavor charms the palate, although its lack of character may disappoint experienced smokers. For those who wish to discover the Robusto *vitola*.
Exquisitos	Petit Cetros	5^{1}/$_{8}$ in. 129 mm	^{5}/$_{8}$ in. 15.87 mm	7.04 g	40	With its light aromas, this make is easy to smoke. For enthusiasts of every stripe.
Hoyo Coronas	Coronas	5^{5}/$_{8}$ in. 142 mm	^{11}/$_{16}$ in. 16.67 mm	8.97 g	42	The Hoyo Coronas is a well-balanced cigar although it is produced in small quantities. Burns evenly throughout.
Humidor No. 1	Conservas	5^{3}/$_{4}$ in. 145 mm	^{11}/$_{16}$ in. 17.46 mm	9.57 g	44	Mild and slightly aromatic, this cigar has gradually disappeared from the market.
Jeanne d'Arc	Carlotas	5^{11}/$_{16}$ in. 143 mm	^{9}/$_{16}$ in. 13.89 mm	6.26 g	35	Elegant, though hard to find, the Jeanne d'Arc is especially worth savoring after a light midday meal.

Hoyo de Monterrey

Le Hoyo des Dieux	Le Hoyo du Dauphin	Le Hoyo du Gourmet	Le Hoyo du Député	Le Hoyo du Député	Le Hoyo du Prince

Name		Length	Diameter	Weight	Cepo	Comments
Le Hoyo des Dieux	Coronas Grandes	6¹/₈ in. 155 mm	¹¹/₁₆ in. 16.67 mm	9.89 g	42	A cigar that boasts great complexity and harmony, with well-balanced flavors easy to distinguish to the very end.
Le Hoyo du Dauphin	No. 2	5¹⁵/₁₆ in. 152 mm	⁵/₈ in. 15.08 mm	7.87 g	38	Difficult to smoke. Aggressive and not especially subtle.
Le Hoyo du Gourmet	Palmas	6³/₄ in. 170 mm	⁹/₁₆ in. 13.10 mm	6.65 g	33	Overheating renders this cigar harsh to the taste. Fails to develop its flavors. To be smoked slowly.
Le Hoyo du Député	Trabucos	4³/₈ in. 110 mm	⁵/₈ in. 15.08 mm	5.66 g	38	A vigorous cigar with rather indistinct aromas. For experienced aficionados.
Le Hoyo du Maire	Entreactos	4 in. 100 mm	¹/₂ in. 11.91 mm	3.27 g	30	Too small to be able to develop the qualities of a Havana. For smoking only occasionally.
Le Hoyo du Prince	Almuerzos	5¹/₈ in. 130 mm	⁵/₈ in. 15.87 mm	7.52 g	40	Quick to burn without overheating. An oily cigar rich in aroma, it remains relatively aggressive nonetheless.

Hoyo de Monterrey

Le Hoyo du Roi   Longos   Margaritas   Odéon   Opéra

Name		Length	Diameter	Weight	Cepo	Comments
Le Hoyo du Roi	Coronas	5⅝ in. 142 mm	11/16 in. 16.67 mm	8.97 g	42	A well-balanced, slightly acid taste. Redolent of its native soil.
Longos	Ninfas	7 1/16 in. 178 mm	9/16 in. 13.10 mm	6.97 g	33	Thin, elegant cigar that is not particularly harsh. Offers smokers a delicate, feminine sweetness.
Margaritas	Carolinas	4 13/16 in. 121 mm	7/16 in. 10.32 mm	2.94 g	26	A mild make, the Margaritas' restrained aromas make it a cigar for every palate.
Odéon	No. 2	5 15/16 in. 152 mm	5/8 in. 15.08 mm	7.87 g	38	The mildness of this cigar, with its light aromas, may eventually tire certain experienced palates.
Opéra	Coronas	5⅝ in. 142 mm	11/16 in. 16.67 mm	8.97 g	42	The subtlety of this light cigar makes it a pleasant smoke indeed.

Hoyo de Monterrey

Palmas Extras Petit Coronations Royal Coronations Short Hoyo Coronas Souvenirs De Luxe Versailles

Name		Length	Diameter	Weight	Cepo	Comments
Palmas Extras	Cremas	5⁹/₁₆ in. 140 mm	⁵/₈ in. 15.87 mm	7.64 g	40	A light, flavorful make of cigar for smokers of all stripes.
Petit Coronations	Franciscanos	4⁵/₈ in. 116 mm	⁵/₈ in. 15.87 mm	6.72 g	40	Not an especially distinctive cigar. Can be enjoyed any time of day.
Royal Coronations	Coronas	5⁵/₈ in. 142 mm	¹¹/₁₆ in. 16.67 mm	8.97 g	42	Subtle in its mildness, light in its aromas.
Short Hoyo Coronas	Marevas	5¹/₈ in. 129 mm	¹¹/₁₆ in. 16.67 mm	8.14 g	42	A pleasant cigar that offers a fine balance between its aromas and its taste. For any time of day.
Souvenirs De Luxe	Petit Coronas	5¹/₈ in. 129 mm	¹¹/₁₆ in. 16.67 mm	7.77 g	42	A hard-to-find cigar, the Souvenirs De Luxe is a mild smoke, more appropriate for the afternoon.
Versailles	Palmas	6³/₄ in. 170 mm	⁹/₁₆ in. 13.10 mm	6.65 g	33	A light cigar in terms of its taste and aromas. Rare.

José Gener   José L. Piedra

| Belvederes | Cazadores | Excepcionales | Longos | Perfectos | Superfinos | | Superiores |

Name		Length	Diameter	Weight	Cepo	Comments
Belvederes	Belvederes	4¹⁵/₁₆ in. 125 mm	⁵/₈ in. 15.48 mm	6.21 g	39	Fairly straightforward, this cigar is very hard to find on the market.
Cazadores	Cazadores	6⁷/₁₆ in. 162 mm	¹¹/₁₆ in. 17.46 mm	11.27 g	44	A powerful make possessing very spicy flavors. For enthusiasts.
Excepcionales	Standard	4¹⁵/₁₆ in. 123 mm	⁵/₈ in. 15.87 mm	6.90 g	40	A cigar that boasts quite strong, pronounced flavors. Rare.
Longos	Ninfas	7¹/₁₆ in. 178 mm	⁹/₁₆ in. 13.10 mm	6.97 g	33	The Longos' robust taste and heavy flavors make it a cigar for aficionados who appreciate an aggressive smoke.
Perfectos	Perfectos	5¹/₁₆ in. 127 mm	¹¹/₁₆ in. 17.46 mm	7.36 g	44	Slow combustion occasionally makes the Perfectos difficult to handle for the inexperienced smoker. Has practically disappeared from the market.
Superfinos	Coronitas	4⁵/₈ in. 117 mm	⁵/₈ in. 15.87 mm	6.35g	40	Full-bodied and rare make of cigar that will please enthusiasts only.
Superiores	Superiores	5¹³/₁₆ in. 146 mm	⁵/₈ in. 15.87 mm	8.46 g	40	This brand still figures in Cuban catalogs but is now only produced on rare occasions.

Montecristo

| Joyitas | Montecristo B | Montecristo Especial No. 2 | Montecristo Tubos | Montecristo No. 1 | Montecristo Especial |

Name		Length	Diameter	Weight	Cepo	Comments
Joyitas	No. 3	4⁹/₁₆ in. 115 mm	⁷/₁₆ in. 10.32 mm	2.81 g	26	This small cigar has only a slight bouquet and lacks flavor. Reveals little of the qualities that make a Havana.
Montecristo B	Cosacos	5³/₈ in. 135 mm	¹¹/₁₆ in. 16.67 mm	8.56 g	42	A light, mild make of cigar that has a smooth aromatic taste. First rate.
Montecristo Especial No. 2	No. 2	5¹⁵/₁₆ in. 152 mm	⁵/₈ in. 15.08 mm	7.87 g	38	A smooth, even cigar. Its low-key aroma makes it enjoyable to smoke.
Montecristo Tubos	Coronas Grandes	6¹/₈ in. 155 mm	¹¹/₁₆ in. 16.67 mm	9.89 g	42	Little taste, lean aroma. A cigar that is easier to carry about than it is enjoyable to smoke.
Montecristo No. 1	Cervantes	6¹/₂ in. 165 mm	¹¹/₁₆ in. 16.67 mm	10.47 g	42	A cigar that is turned out in great numbers. No special aroma or taste to set it apart. A smoke with broad appeal.
Montecristo Especial	No. 1	7⁵/₈ in. 192 mm	⁵/₈ in. 15.08 mm	10.03 g	38	Prized and praised for its elegance, this cigar can prove difficult to smoke. Its aggressive, powerful aroma rapidly fills the atmosphere.

Montecristo

Montecristo No. 2   Montecristo No. 3   Montecristo No. 4   Montecristo No. 5   Montecristo No. 6   Montecristo No. 7   Montecristo A

Name		Length	Diameter	Weight	Cepo	Comments
Montecristo No. 2	Piramides	6³/₁₆ in. 156 mm	⁷/₈ in. 20.64 mm	12.19 g	52	Can be exceptional or disappointing depending on the production year. A full-bodied cigar whose complex aromas are for the aficionado only.
Montecristo No. 3	Coronas	5⁵/₈ in. 142 mm	¹¹/₁₆ in. 16.67 mm	8.97 g	42	A dull cigar devoid of any particular qualities, probably because it suffers from overproduction.
Montecristo No. 4	Marevas	5¹/₈ in. 129 mm	¹¹/₁₆ in. 16.67 mm	8.14 g	42	Like the No. 3 above, this product is turned out in such massive quantities that what qualities it has make no mark in the world of the Havana cigar.
Montecristo No. 5	Perlas	4¹/₁₆ in. 102 mm	⁵/₈ in. 15.87 mm	5.91 g	40	Too high-strung to reveal any specific personality. Clearly the brand's poorest make.
Montecristo No. 6	Seoanes	5 in. 126 mm	⁹/₁₆ in. 13.10 mm	5.01 g	33	Produced in small quantities, the No. 6 has little character to recommend it.
Montecristo No. 7	Panetelas Largas	6¹⁵/₁₆ in. 175 mm	⁷/₁₆ in. 11.11 mm	4.95 g	28	Just like the No. 6, this make is only turned out in small numbers. Yet the No. 7 proves to be pleasant enough for neophytes.
Montecristo A	Gran Corona	9¹/₄ in. 235 mm	³/₄ in. 18.65 mm	18.63 g	47	A big cigar for connoisseurs, hard to obtain because of its great size, which demands large, high-quality leaves. This make of Montecristo offers an immense taste.

Partagás

Petit Bouquet   Petit Coronas   Petit Coronas   Petit Coronas Tubos   Petit Partagás   Presidentes
                                  Especiales

Name		Length	Diameter	Weight	Cepo	Comments
Petit Bouquet	Infantes	3¹⁵/₁₆ in. 98 mm	⅝ in. 14.68 mm	4.03 g	37	Quickly becomes a rather harsh smoke. Will largely please lovers of full-bodied cigars.
Petit Coronas	Marevas	5⅛ in. 129 mm	¹¹/₁₆ in. 16.67 mm	8.14 g	42	Enjoyable at first, this cigar can prove aggressive and so is recommended for aficionados of full-bodied cigars.
Petit Coronas Especiales	Eminentes	5¼ in. 132 mm	¹¹/₁₆ in. 17.46 mm	8.74 g	44	A full-bodied, full-flavored cigar. For enthusiasts.
Petit Coronas Tubos	Eminentes	5¼ in. 132 mm	¹¹/₁₆ in. 17.46 mm	8.74 g	44	A harsh, not especially subtle cigar. For experienced palates.
Petit Partagás	Petit Cetros	5⅛ in. 129 mm	⅝ in. 15.87 mm	7.04 g	40	Distinctive flavors leave a strong impression on the palate. May appear somewhat rough.
Presidentes	Tacos	6¼ in. 158 mm	¾ in. 18.65 mm	10.79 g	47	A powerful high-quality cigar. For experienced enthusiasts.

Partagás

| Serie D No. 4 | Selección privada No. 1 | Royales | Regalias de la Reina Bueno | Ramonitas | Princess |

Name		Length	Diameter	Weight	Cepo	Comments
Serie D No. 4	Robustos	4^{15}/$_{16}$ in. 124 mm	^{13}/$_{16}$ in. 19.84 mm	11.18 g	50	This make gives off very rich aromas from the first few puffs. Worth savoring in peace and quiet.
Selección privada No. 1	Dalias	6^{3}/$_{4}$ in. 170 mm	^{11}/$_{16}$ in. 17.07 mm	11.32 g	43	Powerful and full-bodied, very distinctive aromas. This make is best enjoyed alone because it can prove unpleasant to others.
Royales	Londres	5 in. 126 mm	^{5}/$_{8}$ in. 15.87 mm	7.29 g	40	Akin to the Partagás of old, the Royales is a full-bodied cigar with strong, though rather straightforward flavors.
Regalias de la Reina Bueno	Coronitas	4^{5}/$_{8}$ in. 117 mm	^{5}/$_{8}$ in. 15.87 mm	6.35 g	40	A mild cigar, though not especially refined.
Ramonitas	Carolinas	4^{13}/$_{16}$ in. 121 mm	^{7}/$_{16}$ in. 10.32 mm	2.94 g	26	A small cigar with real character, but one that may surprise beginners.
Princess	Conchitas	5^{1}/$_{16}$ in. 10.32 mm	^{9}/$_{16}$ in. 13.89 mm	5.29 g	35	A make whose aromas are fairly subdued, although rather mild.

Partagás

Très Petit Coronas   Toppers   Super Partagás   Shorts

Name		Length	Diameter	Weight	Cepo	Comments
Très Petit Coronas	Francis-canos	4⅝ in. 116 mm	⅝ in. 15.87 mm	6.72 g	40	A rough cigar that will certainly not go unremarked by smokers, and by those around them.
Toppers	Toppers	6⁵/₁₆ in. 160 mm	⅝ in. 15.48 mm	8.33 g	39	Its character, which is certainly affected by the Toppers being produced in large numbers, deserves to be more developed.
Super Partagás	Cremas	5⁹/₁₆ in. 140 mm	⅝ in. 15.87 mm	7.64 g	40	An occasionally harsh taste early on eventually gives way to distinctive flavors. For enthusiasts.
Shorts	Minutos	4³⁄₈ in. 110 mm	¹¹/₁₆ in. 16.67 mm	6.97 g	42	Refreshing and light. This cigar's bracing aromas cannot fail to please beginner cigar smokers.

Partagás

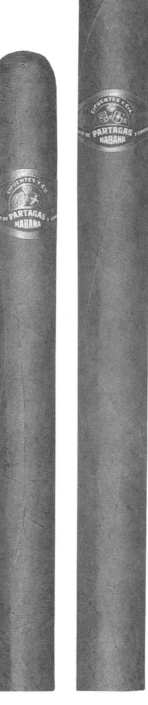

Lonsdales   Mille Fleurs   8-9-8 Cabinet   8-9-8 Varnished   Lusitanias

Name		Length	Diameter	Weight	Cepo	Comments
Lonsdales	Cervantes	6½ in. 165 mm	11/16 in. 16.67 mm	10.47 g	42	A rich variety of aromas and a distinct taste make this a high-quality cigar. For experienced enthusiasts.
Mille Fleurs	Petit Coronas	5⅛ in. 129 mm	11/16 in. 16.67 mm	7.77 g	42	A light make of cigar that is only slightly aromatic, though pleasant nonetheless.
8-9-8 Cabinet	Coronas Grandes	6⅛ in. 155 mm	11/16 in. 16.67 mm	9.89 g	42	A mild cigar whose taste and aromas are not especially pronounced. Could do with a little more body. A good choice for the novice smoker.
8-9-8 Varnished	Dalias	6¾ in. 170 mm	11/16 in. 17.07 mm	11.32 g	43	Its heavy aroma and complex flavors are suitable for enthusiasts who are capable of mastering the giddiness that comes with such smoke.
Lusitanias	Promi-nentes	7 11/16 in. 194 mm	13/16 in. 19.45 mm	16.70 g	49	A great cigar among the Havanas, the Lusitanias offers rich, spicy aromas whose savors build unflaggingly right to the end. Made for connoisseurs.

Partagás

Coronas Grandes   Coronas Junior   Coronas Senior   Culebras   Charlottes   Chicos   Churchill De Luxe

Name		Length	Diameter	Weight	Cepo	Comments
Coronas Grandes	Coronas Grandes	6⅛ in. 155 mm	¹¹/₁₆ in. 16.67 mm	9.89 g	42	This make may disappoint some because of its lack of individuality.
Coronas Junior	Coronitas	4⅝ in. 117 mm	⅝ in. 15.87 mm	6.35 g	40	Fairly mild, the Coronas Junior's packaging in a tube makes it easy to carry about.
Coronas Senior	Eminentes	5¼ in. 132 mm	¹¹/₁₆ in. 17.46 mm	8.74 g	44	A cigar that borders on being overly harsh. Distinctive thanks to its strong flavors.
Culebras	Culebras	5¹³/₁₆ in. 146 mm	⅝ in. 15.48 mm	6.67 g	39	Prized more for its original shape, this make maintains a light touch in its aromas despite uneven burning.
Charlottes	Carlotas	5¹¹/₁₆ in. 143 mm	⁹/₁₆ in. 13.89 mm	6.26 g	35	A full-flavored cigar, a bit harsh at times. For enthusiasts.
Chicos	Chicos	4³/₁₆ in. 106 mm	⁷/₁₆ in. 10.32 mm	3.00 g	29	A small cigar that has a general appeal despite its full distinctive flavor.
Churchill De Luxe	Julieta 2	7 in. 178 mm	¾ in. 18.65 mm	14.08 g	47	A very powerful cigar, rich in flavor but not very subtle. For connoisseurs who enjoy full-bodied smoke.

Partagás

| Palmas Grandes | Panetelas | Parisianos | Partagás De Luxe | Partagás de Partagás No. 1 | Perfectos | Personales |

Name		Length	Diameter	Weight	Cepo	Comments
Palmas Grandes	Ninfas	7¹/₁₆ in. 178 mm	⁹/₁₆ in. 13.10 mm	6.97 g	33	Burns well, is rather mild, but offers aromas that are not especially distinctive.
Panetelas	Conchitas	5¹/₁₆ in. 127 mm	⁹/₁₆ in. 13.89 mm	5.29 g	35	Just slightly full-bodied, the Panetelas has kept the taste of the traditional Havana.
Parisianos	Petit Cetros	5¹/₈ in. 129 mm	⁵/₈ in. 15.87 mm	7.04 g	40	The Parisianos' aromas lack a certain subtlety. Occasionally biting.
Partagás De Luxe	Cremas	5⁹/₁₆ in. 140 mm	⁵/₈ in. 15.87 mm	7.64 g	40	Rather full-bodied, the Partagás De Luxe makes its mark on the palate thanks to its pronounced flavors.
Partagás de Partagás No. 1	Dalias	6³/₄ in. 170 mm	¹¹/₁₆ in. 17.07 mm	11.32 g	43	Full-bodied without great subtlety. Will satisfy enthusiasts of the Havanas of old.
Perfectos	Perfectos	5¹/₁₆ in. 127 mm	¹¹/₁₆ in. 17.46 mm	7.36 g	44	Aromas could do with more nuance. This full-bodied cigar is for aficionados.
Personales	Petit Cetros	5¹/₈ in. 129 mm	⁵/₈ in. 15.87 mm	7.64 g	40	A pleasant make, though its taste is hardly as nuanced as that of the cigars of old.

Partagás

| Demi Tip | Eminentes | Filipos | Habaneros | Londres en Cedro | Londres Extra | Londres Finos |

Name		Length	Diameter	Weight	Cepo	Comments
Demi Tip	Demi Tip	5 in. 126 mm	1/2 in. 11.51 mm	3.68 g	29	A thin cigar that barely develops its aromas as it burns.
Eminentes	Eminentes	5 1/4 in. 132 mm	11/16 in. 17.46 mm	8.74 g	44	Its rough aromas leave their mark on both the palate and the atmosphere.
Filipos	Placeras	4 15/16 in. 125 mm	9/16 in. 13.49 mm	5.22 g	34	Relatively mild, the Filipos is enjoyable to smoke despite its unsophisticated flavors.
Habaneros	Belvederes	4 15/16 in. 125 mm	5/8 in. 15.48 mm	6.21 g	39	Inconsistent in terms of its flavors, this make can prove hard to smoke.
Londres en Cedro	Petit Cetros	5 1/8 in. 129 mm	5/8 in. 15.87 mm	7.04 g	40	More flavorful than the Londres Extra, the Londres en Cedro develops aromatic accents.
Londres Extra	Petit Cetros	5 1/8 in. 129 mm	5/8 in. 15.87 mm	7.04 g	40	A cigar whose aromas lack nuance, although they are quite distinct during its first third.
Londres Finos	Petit Cetros	5 1/8 in. 129 mm	5/8 in. 15.87 mm	7.04 g	40	The mildest of the three Londres, the Finos, like the two preceding *vitolas*, is rarely found on the market.

Partagás

Aristocrats   Astoria   Belvederes   Bonito
Extra Mild   Coronas   Coronas
A. Mejorado

Name		Length	Diameter	Weight	Cepo	Comments
Aristocrats	Petit Cetros	5¹/₈ in. 129 mm	⁵/₈ in. 15.87 mm	7.04 g	40	An occasionally rough cigar that boasts very pronounced aromas. For enthusiasts.
Astoria	Cosacos	5³/₈ in. 135 mm	¹¹/₁₆ in. 16.67 mm	8.56 g	42	A fairly harsh cigar. The Astoria, like the Aristocrats, has gradually disappeared from the market.
Belvederes	Belvederes	4¹⁵/₁₆ in. 125 mm	⁵/₈ in. 15.48 mm	6.21 g	39	Its aromas lack a certain subtlety. For enthusiasts.
Bonito Extra Mild	Chicos	4³/₁₆ in. 106 mm	⁷/₁₆ in. 10.32 mm	3.00 g	29	A mild cigar that goes well with an aperitif.
Coronas	Coronas	5⁵/₈ in. 142 mm	¹¹/₁₆ in. 16.67 mm	8.97 g	42	Rich in flavor and very aromatic, this cigar is quite pleasing to smoke. Will completely satisfy lovers of coronas.
Coronas A. Mejorado	Coronas	5⁵/₈ in. 142 mm	¹¹/₁₆ in. 16.67 mm	8.97 g	42	A rarely seen, flavorful *vitola* whose forceful taste makes it a cigar for true enthusiasts.

Por Larrañaga

| Belvederes | Corona | Coronitas | Curritos | Juanito | Largos de Larrañaga | Lolas en Cedro | Lonsdales |

Name		Length	Diameter	Weight	Cepo	Comments
Belvederes	Belvederes	4¹⁵/₁₆ in. 125 mm	⁵/₈ in. 15.48 mm	6.21 g	39	Mild and flavorful, this make is hard to obtain, like the majority of cigars put out by this brand.
Corona	Coronas	5⁵/₈ in. 142 mm	¹¹/₁₆ in. 16.67 mm	8.97 g	42	Cigar with a rich taste and discreet aromas. Requires an experienced palate.
Coronitas	Panetelas	4⁵/₈ in. 117 mm	⁹/₁₆ in. 13.49 mm	4.85 g	34	A mild cigar that is perfectly suitable for mornings.
Curritos	Chicos	4³/₁₆ in. 106 mm	⁷/₁₆ in. 10.32 mm	3.00 g	29	Rather mild, this cigar builds its oily flavors despite its limited size.
Juanito	Chicos	4³/₁₆ in. 106 mm	⁷/₁₆ in. 10.32 mm	3.00 g	29	Comparable to the Curritos, this cigar is also just as hard to find on the market.
Largos de Larrañaga	Deliciosos	6⁵/₁₆ in. 159 mm	⁹/₁₆ in. 13.89 mm	6.67 g	35	A flavorful *vitola* with good burning qualities, suitable for after a light midday meal.
Lolas en Cedro	Petit Coronas	5¹/₈ in. 129 mm	¹¹/₁₆ in. 16.67 mm	7.77 g	42	Powerful yet not especially aggressive, the Lolas builds its pleasant aromas in its middle third.
Lonsdales	Cervantes	6¹/₂ in. 165 mm	¹¹/₁₆ in. 16.67 mm	10.47 g	42	Mild yet powerful, this aromatic Lonsdales is hard to come by.

Por Larrañaga

Montecarlos   Panetelas   Petit Coronas   Small Coronas   Super Cedros

Name		Length	Diameter	Weight	Cepo	Comments
Montecarlos	Deliciosos	6⁵/₁₆ in. 159 mm	⁹/₁₆ in. 13.89 mm	6.67 g	35	A mild, flavorful cigar with an even burn.
Panetelas	Vegueritos	5¹/₁₆ in. 127 mm	⁵/₈ in. 14.68 mm	6.10 g	37	A light, mild make whose aromas come to the fore in the first third of the cigar.
Petit Coronas	Marevas	5⅛ in. 129 mm	¹¹/₁₆ in. 16.67 mm	8.14 g	42	Rich in flavor, the Petit Coronas builds subtle aromas that prove quite sweet.
Small Coronas	Franciscanos	4⅝ in. 116 mm	⁵/₈ in. 15.87 mm	6.72 g	40	Despite its compact, stubby shape, this cigar is fairly mild. To be enjoyed in the morning or early afternoon.
Super Cedros	Standard	4¹⁵/₁₆ in. 123 mm	⁵/₈ in. 15.87 mm	6.90 g	40	This fragrant cigar is rich in taste. Burns well.

Punch

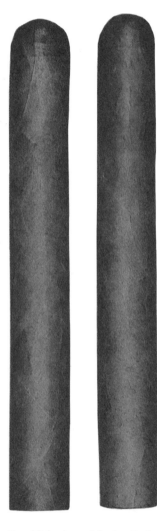

Royal
Coronation

Royal Selection
No. 11

Royal Selection
No. 12

Selection De Luxe
No. 2

Name		Length	Diameter	Weight	Cepo	Comments
Royal Coronation	Coronas	5⅝ in. 142 mm	11/16 in. 16.67 mm	8.97 g	42	An aroma-rich, very well balanced, mild cigar. Perfectly blended. For enthusiasts.
Royal Selection No. 11	Coronas Gordas	5 11/16 in. 143 mm	11/16 in. 16.67 mm	10.90 g	46	Rich taste and aromas. This enjoyable cigar develops its flavors toward the middle. For experienced aficionados.
Royal Selection No. 12	Marevas	5⅛ in. 129 mm	11/16 in. 16.67 mm	8.14 g	42	A cigar that tends to be aggressive, with discreet aromas. Can be disappointing.
Selection De Luxe No. 2	Marevas	5⅛ in. 129 mm	11/16 in. 16.67 mm	8.14 g	42	Less harsh than the Royal Selection No. 12, this cigar's aromas remain fairly discreet.

Punch

Souvenir De Luxe   Souvenir De Luxe   Super Selection No. 1   Super Selection No. 2   Très Petit Coronas   Gran Coronas

Name		Length	Diameter	Weight	Cepo	Comments
Souvenir De Luxe	Petit Coronas	5¹/₈ in. 129 mm	¹¹/₁₆ in. 16.67 mm	7.77 g	42	Builds interesting aromas as it burns down. Enjoyable.
Souvenir De Luxe	Londres	5 in. 126 mm	⁵/₈ in. 15.87 mm	7.29 g	40	A mild cigar whose aromas smack of its native soil.
Super Selection No. 1	Coronas Grandes	6¹/₈ in. 155 mm	¹¹/₁₆ in. 16.67 mm	9.89 g	42	Develops a rich, though somewhat rough taste, one that makes itself felt nonetheless. Its aromas clearly assert themselves as it burns down. For aficionados.
Super Selection No. 2	Coronas Gordas	5¹¹/₁₆ in. 143 mm	¹¹/₁₆ in. 16.67 mm	10.90 g	46	This make burns evenly, allowing its aromas and rich flavor to build nicely. A full-bodied cigar mainly for enthusiasts.
Très Petit Coronas	Minutos	4³/₈ in. 110 mm	¹¹/₁₆ in. 16.67 mm	6.97 g	42	A powerful, full-bodied cigar with very discreet aromas. For the aficionado.
Gran Coronas	Superiores	5¹³/₁₆ in. 146 mm	⁵/₈ in. 15.87 mm	8.46 g	40	The Gran Coronas offers woody accents. To be savored in the afternoon.

Punch

Ninfas   Palmas Reales   Panetelas   Panetelas   Petit Coronas   Diademas Extra
                                         Grandes   del Punch

Name		Length	Diameter	Weight	Cepo	Comments
Ninfas	Ninfas	7^1/$_{16}$ in. 178 mm	^{9}/$_{16}$ in. 13.10 mm	6.97 g	33	Mild with good burning qualities, this cigar is retiring yet rewarding. Especially enjoyable during the day.
Palmas Reales	Cremas	5^9/$_{16}$ in. 140 mm	^{5}/$_8$ in. 15.87 mm	7.64 g	40	Not especially rough, this cigar yields a number of pleasant flavors as it burns down.
Panetelas	Panetelas	4^5/$_8$ in. 117 mm	^{9}/$_{16}$ in. 13.49 mm	4.85 g	34	A mild cigar, not particularly nuanced. Suitable for mornings.
Panetelas Grandes	Ninfas	7^1/$_{16}$ in. 13.49 mm	^{9}/$_{16}$ in. 13.10 mm	6.97 g	33	Poor combustion makes it difficult to smoke. For aficionados who favor full-bodied cigars.
Petit Coronas del Punch	Marevas	5^1/$_8$ in. 129 mm	^{11}/$_{16}$ in. 16.67 mm	8.14 g	42	Cigar with a slightly spicy taste and weak aromas, although a reasonably good quality make.
Diademas Extra	Gran Corona	9^1/$_4$ in. 235 mm	^{3}/$_4$ in. 18.65 mm	18.63 g	47	Despite its size, relatively mild and aromatic. Like all cigars in this *vitola*, needs plenty of time to be enjoyed.

Punch

Petit Coronations   Petit Punch   Petit Punch De Luxe   Presidentes   Punchinellos   Punch Punch

Name		Length	Diameter	Weight	Cepo	Comments
Petit Coronations	Francis-canos	4⅝ in. 116 mm	⅝ in. 15.87 mm	6.72 g	40	Restrained, this cigar offers woody flavors in its first third.
Petit Punch	Perlas	4¹/₁₆ in. 102 mm	⅝ in. 15.87 mm	5.91 g	40	Well-balanced cigar with a rich taste and mild aromas that are not overpowering. A good choice for beginners.
Petit Punch De Luxe	Perlas	4¹/₁₆ in. 102 mm	⅝ in. 15.87 mm	5.91 g	40	Enjoyable because it doesn't overpower the palate yet gives off light aromas.
Presidentes	Marevas	5⅛ in. 129 mm	¹¹/₁₆ in. 16.67 mm	8.14 g	42	A light cigar whose aromas lack nuance. For the neophyte.
Punchinellos	Panetelas	4⅝ in. 117 mm	⁹/₁₆ in. 13.49 mm	4.85 g	34	Mild and enjoyable. To be savored in the morning or afternoon.
Punch Punch	Coronas Gordas	5¹¹/₁₆ in. 143 mm	¹¹/₁₆ in. 16.67 mm	10.90 g	46	Well-balanced flavorful cigar, mild, harmonious. For enthusiasts.

Punch

Belvederes   Black Prince   Cigarillos   Coronas   Coronations

Name		Length	Diameter	Weight	Cepo	Comments
Belvederes	Belvederes	4 15/16 in. 125 mm	5/8 in. 15.48 mm	6.21 g	39	A light cigar, pretty straightforward in its flavors. For one and all.
Black Prince	Coronas Gordas	5 11/16 in. 143 mm	11/16 in. 16.67 mm	10.90 g	46	Mild and discreet, this is a light cigar for smokers of every stripe.
Cigarillos	Chicos	4 3/16 in. 106 mm	7/16 in. 10.32 mm	3.00 g	29	A small *vitola* that makes for an enjoyable smoke. A cigar that anyone can handle.
Coronas	Coronas	5 5/8 in. 142 mm	11/16 in. 16.67 mm	8.97 g	42	Light aromas that leave little impression. Lacks subtlety. To be enjoyed during the day.
Coronations	Marevas	5 1/8 in. 129 mm	11/16 in. 16.67 mm	8.14 g	42	A light cigar whose great plus is that it can be carried about very easily.

Punch

Churchills   Exquisitos   Margaritas   Monarcas   Double Coronas   Nacionales

Name		Length	Diameter	Weight	Cepo	Comments
Churchills	Julieta 2	7 in. 178 mm	³/₄ in. 18.65 mm	14.08 g	47	Builds its aromas with moderation. Easy and pleasant to smoke, this Churchill is a well-balanced cigar.
Exquisitos	Petit Cetros	5¹/₈ in. 129 mm	⁵/₈ in. 15.87 mm	7.04 g	40	A not especially rough, rather restrained cigar whose aromas remain discreet.
Margaritas	Carolinas	4¹³/₁₆ in. 121 mm	⁷/₁₆ in. 10.32 mm	2.94 g	26	Aroma and body pleasantly balance one another right to the end. For smoking in the morning, after breakfast, or over an aperitif.
Monarcas	Julieta 2	7 in. 178 mm	³/₄ in. 18.65 mm	14.08 g	47	The Monarcas offer rich savors and light aromas. Although it lacks subtlety, this cigar is nonetheless an enjoyable smoke.
Double Coronas	Promi-nentes	7¹¹/₁₆ in. 194 mm	¹³/₁₆ in. 19.45 mm	16.70 g	49	A high-quality cigar, powerful without being aggressive, whose taste develops to the very last draw. For the experienced enthusiast.
Nacionales	Cosacos	5³/₈ in. 135 mm	¹¹/₁₆ in. 16.67 mm	8.56 g	42	A well-balanced, flavorful cigar that makes an enjoyable afternoon smoke.

Quai d'Orsay

Coronas Claro   Coronas Claro Claro   Gran Coronas   Imperiales   Panetelas

Name		Length	Diameter	Weight	Cepo	Comments
Coronas Claro	Coronas	5⅝ in. 142 mm	11/16 in. 16.67 mm	8.97 g	42	An oily cigar dominated by its earthy flavors. Its good qualities build as it burns.
Coronas Claro Claro	Coronas	5⅝ in. 142 mm	11/16 in. 16.67 mm	8.97 g	42	Comparable to the Coronas Claro, though this cigar's wrapper is a lighter shade.
Gran Coronas	Coronas Grandes	6⅛ in. 155 mm	11/16 in. 16.67 mm	9.89 g	42	A rather straightforward aroma and a taste that develops woody notes make this cigar easy to smoke. For after the midday meal.
Imperiales	Julieta 2	7 in. 178 mm	¾ in. 18.65 mm	14.08 g	47	Offers a fine range of aromas. This cigar's mildness makes it easy to smoke. Thoroughly accessible to inexperienced cigar smokers.
Panetelas	Ninfas	7 1/16 in. 178 mm	9/16 in. 13.10 mm	6.97 g	33	A mild, aromatic cigar that all smokers will enjoy.

Quintero

| Brevas | Coronas Selectas | Coronas | Churchills | Londres |

Name		Length	Diameter	Weight	Cepo	Comments
Brevas	Nacionales	5⁹/₁₆ in. 140 mm	⁵/₈ in. 15.87 mm	8.28 g	40	A full-bodied cigar, rich in flavor, with distinctive aromas. For the connoisseur.
Coronas Selectas	Coronas	5⁵/₈ in. 142 mm	¹¹/₁₆ in. 16.67 mm	8.97 g	42	A strong, earthy cigar. For enthusiasts.
Coronas	Coronas	5⁵/₈ in. 142 mm	¹¹/₁₆ in. 16.67 mm	8.97 g	42	Revealing no great subtlety, this *vitola* remains well within the Quinteros line of cigars.
Churchills	Cervantes	6½ in. 165 mm	¹¹/₁₆ in. 16.67 mm	10.47 g	42	With aromas smacking of its native soil, this Cervantes might appear somewhat rough when smoked. For aficionados who favor full-bodied cigars.
Londres	Standard	4¹⁵/₁₆ in. 123 mm	⁵/₈ in. 15.87 mm	6.90 g	40	A full-bodied cigar, though rather stinting in its aromas.

Quintero

| Londres Extra | Medias Coronas | Medias Coronas Selectas | Nacionales | Panetelas | Puritos |

Name		Length	Diameter	Weight	Cepo	Comments
Londres Extra	Standard	4^{15}/16 in. 123 mm	^{5}/8 in. 15.87 mm	6.90 g	40	Although it boasts greater aroma than the Londres, this make proves less aggressive to the palate.
Medias Coronas	Londres	5 in. 126 mm	^{5}/8 in. 15.87 mm	7.29 g	40	A full-bodied cigar with earthy aromas.
Medias Coronas Selectas	Londres	5 in. 126 mm	^{5}/8 in. 15.87 mm	7.29 g	40	Builds rather straightforward aromas while maintaining its full-bodied character.
Nacionales	Nacionales	5^9/16 in. 140 mm	^{5}/8 in. 15.87 mm	8.28 g	40	The first puffs of this make are fairly harsh. Its earthy aromas remain constant throughout.
Panetelas	Vegueritos	5^1/16 in. 127 mm	^{5}/8 in. 14.68 mm	6.10 g	37	Like all the *vitolas* of this brand, the Panetelas is both full-bodied and rare.
Puritos	Chicos	4^3/16 in. 106 mm	^{7}/16 in. 10.32 mm	3.00 g	29	Don't be taken in by the Puritos' small size: it can be surprisingly rough.

Rafaël Gonzales

Cigarritos   Coronas Extra   Demi Tasse   Lonsdales   Panetelas

Name		Length	Diameter	Weight	Cepo	Comments
Cigarritos	No. 3	4⁹⁄₁₆ in. 115 mm	⁷⁄₁₆ in. 10.32 mm	2.81 g	26	A very enjoyable cigarrito, aromatic and well-balanced. An excellent choice for women and beginner smokers.
Coronas Extra	Coronas Gordas	5¹¹⁄₁₆ in. 143 mm	¹¹⁄₁₆ in. 16.67 mm	10.90 g	46	A cigar that has a pleasant range of aromas, powerful without being overpowering. Burns evenly.
Demi Tasse	Entreactos	4 in. 100 mm	½ in. 11.91 mm	3.27 g	30	With its even burn, the Demi Tasse remains enjoyable to the very last puff.
Lonsdales	Cervantes	6½ in. 165 mm	¹¹⁄₁₆ in. 16.67 mm	10.47 g	42	Revealing subtle aromas, this make pleases most smokers because it is rather oily and not overpowering.
Panetelas	Panetelas	4⁵⁄₈ in. 117 mm	⁹⁄₁₆ in. 13.49 mm	4.85 g	34	A light cigar that barely marks the palate. Easy to smoke despite being somewhat short on flavor. For neophytes.

Rafaël Gonzales

Petit Coronas   Petit Lonsdales   Slenderellas   Très Petit   Panetelas
                                                     Lonsdales   Extra

Name		Length	Diameter	Weight	Cepo	Comments
Petit Coronas	Marevas	5¹/₈ in. 129 mm	¹¹/₁₆ in. 16.67 mm	8.14 g	42	A light, fresh, discreetly aromatic cigar that lacks a distinctive character. Good for savoring during the day.
Petit Lonsdales	Marevas	5¹/₈ in. 129 mm	¹¹/₁₆ in. 16.67 mm	8.14 g	42	Mild, although it boasts a full-bodied flavor, this rather aggressive cigar is largely for enthusiasts.
Slenderellas	Panetelas Largas	6¹⁵/₁₆ in. 175 mm	⁷/₁₆ in. 11.11 mm	4.95 g	28	Rich in flavor. Its mildness and fresh flavors win smokers over. For inexperienced enthusiasts, men or women.
Très Petit Lonsdales	Franciscanos	4⁵/₈ in. 116 mm	⁵/₈ in. 15.87 mm	6.72 g	40	A powerful cigar despite its small size. Its flavors are brought out nicely after a solid midday meal.
Panetelas Extra	Vegueritos	5¹/₁₆ in. 127 mm	⁵/₈ in. 14.68 mm	6.10 g	37	Delightfully flavorful. The range of its aromas is quite pleasing for a cigar of this caliber.

Ramón Allones

| Mille Fleurs | Panetelas | Petit Coronas | 8-9-8 Varnished | 8-9-8 Cabinet | Gigantes | Delgados |

Name		Length	Diameter	Weight	Cepo	Comments
Mille Fleurs	Petit Coronas	5⅛ in. 129 mm	¹¹/₁₆ in. 16.67 mm	7.77 g	42	Somewhat wanting in aroma, the Mille Fleurs offers a taste that evokes its native soil.
Panetelas	Conchitas	5¹/₁₆ in. 127 mm	⁹/₁₆ in. 13.89 mm	5.29 g	35	Relatively mild, this make has a fine range of restrained aromas.
Petit Coronas	Marevas	5⅛ in. 129 mm	¹¹/₁₆ in. 16.67 mm	8.14 g	42	Burns rapidly making it overpowering. Its aromas are not particularly striking. For the enthusiast fond of cigars that smack of the earth.
8-9-8 Varnished	Dalias	6¾ in. 170 mm	¹¹/₁₆ in. 17.07 mm	11.32 g	43	Mild, with an even burn, this cigar does not overpower. For the experienced enthusiast.
8-9-8 Cabinet	Coronas	5⅝ in. 142 mm	¹¹/₁₆ in. 16.67 mm	8.97 g	42	Not especially flavorful, this lightly aromatic cigar is still quite pleasant to smoke during the day.
Gigantes	Prominentes	7¹¹/₁₆ in. 194 mm	¹³/₁₆ in. 19.45 mm	16.70 g	49	Excellent aroma, with a pronounced taste and complex flavors. For experienced enthusiasts.
Delgados	Toppers	6⁵/₁₆ in. 160 mm	⅝ in. 15.48 mm	8.33 g	39	Rich in taste and aromas, the Delgados has no trouble holding its own after a good meal.

Ramón Allones

| Ramondos | Allones Specially Selected | Ramonitas | Small Club Coronas | Toppers | Belvederes | Bits of Havana | Coronas |

Name		Length	Diameter	Weight	Cepo	Comments
Ramondos	Cremas	5⁹/₁₆ in. 140 mm	⁵/₈ in. 15.87 mm	7.64 g	40	Rather restrained cigar, enjoyable after lunch.
Allones Specially Selected	Robustos	4¹⁵/₁₆ in. 124 mm	¹³/₁₆ in. 19.84 mm	11.18 g	50	A generous, aromatic cigar with a pronounced taste. For experienced enthusiasts.
Ramonitas	Carolinas	4¹³/₁₆ in. 121 mm	⁷/₁₆ in. 10.32 mm	2.94 g	26	A small rough cigar that hardly reflects the Havanas.
Small Club Coronas	Minutos	4³/₈ in. 110 mm	¹¹/₁₆ in. 16.67 mm	6.97 g	42	A pleasing cigar with good burning qualities, quite enjoyable during the day.
Toppers	Toppers	6⁵/₁₆ in. 160 mm	⁵/₈ in. 15.48 mm	8.33 g	39	Rich in taste, this cigar builds its flavors after the first third. For experienced smokers.
Belvederes	Belvederes	4¹⁵/₁₆ in. 125 mm	⁵/₈ in. 15.48 mm	6.21 g	39	This straightforward cigar occasionally lacks nuance in its aromas.
Bits of Havana	Chicos	4³/₁₆ in. 106 mm	⁷/₁₆ in. 10.32 mm	3.00 g	29	Relatively harsh for its small size. Not a good cigar for the inexperienced smoker.
Coronas	Coronas	5⁵/₈ in. 142 mm	¹¹/₁₆ in. 16.67 mm	8.97 g	42	An enjoyable cigar with a traditional flavor, easy to savor. For one and all.

El Rey Del Mundo

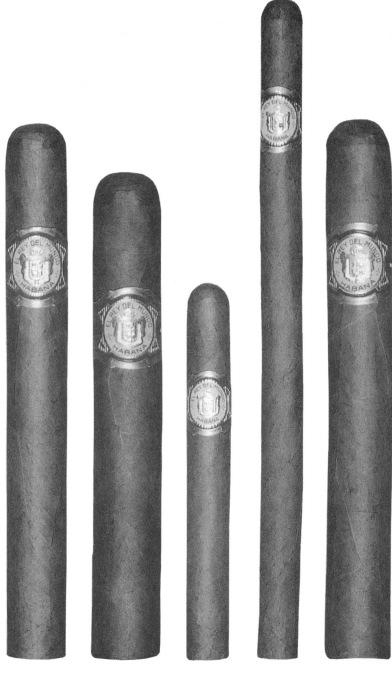

Coronas De Luxe   Choix Suprême   Demi Tasse   Elegantes   Gran Corona

Name		Length	Diameter	Weight	Cepo	Comments
Coronas De Luxe	Coronas	5⅝ in. 142 mm	¹¹⁄₁₆ in. 16.67 mm	8.97 g	42	A cigar with rather flat aromas, mild yet lacking subtlety. Especially good in the morning. Recommended for beginner smokers.
Choix Suprême	Hermosos No. 4	5⅙ in. 127 mm	¾ in. 19.05 mm	10.47 g	48	An aromatic cigar that wants a little refinement. Its mildness makes it accessible to smokers of every stripe.
Demi Tasse	Entreactos	4 in. 100 mm	½ in. 11.91 mm	3.27 g	30	A small, light cigar that burns evenly. Well balanced. Can be smoked like a cigarillo.
Elegantes	Panetelas Largas	6¹⁵⁄₁₆ in. 175 mm	⁷⁄₁₆ in. 11.11 mm	4.95 g	28	An overly strong character detracts from the aroma and taste. Balanced only when it is perfectly rolled.
Gran Corona	Coronas Gordas	5¹¹⁄₁₆ in. 143 mm	¹¹⁄₁₆ in. 16.67 mm	10.90 g	46	A mild, light cigar whose aromas are a bit too discreet. Not especially representative of the Coronas Gordas in general.

El Rey Del Mundo

Petit Coronas   Petit Lonsdales   Señoritas   Tainos   Variedales

Name		Length	Diameter	Weight	Cepo	Comments
Petit Coronas	Marevas	5⅛ in. 129 mm	¹¹/₁₆ in. 16.67 mm	8.14 g	42	A mild cigar wanting in taste when lighted. Builds only a precious few of its range of aromas.
Petit Lonsdales	Marevas	5⅛ in. 129 mm	¹¹/₁₆ in. 16.67 mm	8.14 g	42	Too light for some, this cigar may eventually weary those aficionados in search of strong cigars rich in aromas.
Señoritas	No. 3	4⁹/₁₆ in. 115 mm	⁷/₁₆ in. 10.32 mm	2.81 g	26	Perfectly suitable for beginner cigar smokers.
Tainos	Julieta 2	7 in. 178 mm	¾ in. 18.65 mm	14.08 g	47	The Taino's lack of body makes it a fresh, light cigar that is quite enjoyable to smoke. For those who wish to try this size.
Variedales	Chicos	4³/₁₆ in. 106 mm	⁷/₁₆ in. 10.32 mm	3.00 g	29	Would be ideal for smokers of every stripe if only it were easy to find.

El Rey Del Mundo

| Isabel | Lonsdales | Lunch Club | Panetelas Largas | Grandes de España |

Name		Length	Diameter	Weight	Cepo	Comments
Isabel	Carlotas	5¹¹/₁₆ in. 143 mm	⁹/₁₆ in. 13.89 mm	6.26 g	35	This fresh, winning cigar cannot fail to please beginners.
Lonsdales	Cervantes	6½ in. 165 mm	¹¹/₁₆ in. 16.67 mm	10.47 g	42	A lack of body makes this a light cigar. Somewhat flat, needs a rounder flavor. Accessible to all smokers.
Lunch Club	Franciscanos	4⁵/₈ in. 116 mm	⁵/₈ in. 15.87 mm	6.72 g	40	Small cigar that is not overly rough. A fine introduction to the Havanas.
Panetelas Largas	Panetelas Largas	6¹⁵/₁₆ in. 175 mm	⁷/₁₆ in. 11.11 mm	4.95 g	28	An elegant, mild cigar, enjoyable any time of day.
Grandes de España	Delicados	7⁹/₁₆ in. 192 mm	⁵/₈ in. 15.08 mm	10.03 g	38	Mild, with little in the way of aroma, yet an enjoyable cigar to smoke. Good burning qualities.

Romeo y Julieta

Belvederes	Cazadores	Culebras	Cedros De Luxe No. 1	Cedros De Luxe No. 2	Cedros De Luxe No. 3	Celestiales Finos

Name		Length	Diameter	Weight	Cepo	Comments
Belvederes	Belvederes	4^{15}/$_{16}$ in. 125 mm	^{5}/$_8$ in. 15.48 mm	6.21 g	39	Hard to find, this cigar is a full-bodied smoke rich in aromas.
Cazadores	Cazadores	6^7/$_{16}$ in. 162 mm	^{11}/$_{16}$ in. 17.46 mm	11.27 g	44	A very powerful cigar that boasts a range of quite distinctive aromas. Aggressive, for those who love strong tastes.
Culebras	Culebras	5^{13}/$_{16}$ in. 146 mm	^{5}/$_8$ in. 15.48 mm	6.67 g	39	A rarity. And easier to hail than inhale.
Cedros De Luxe No. 1	Cervantes	6^1/$_2$ in. 165 mm	^{11}/$_{16}$ in. 16.67 mm	10.47 g	42	A cigar with little character. A weak aroma coupled with a fresh taste will please beginner cigar smokers.
Cedros De Luxe No. 2	Coronas	5^5/$_8$ in. 142 mm	^{11}/$_{16}$ in. 16.67 mm	8.97 g	42	A fresh, easy-to-smoke cigar perfectly suited to the neophyte.
Cedros De Luxe No. 3	Marevas	5^1/$_8$ in. 129 mm	^{11}/$_{16}$ in. 16.67 mm	8.14 g	42	A light and not especially interesting cigar. Easy to smoke.
Celestiales Finos	Britanicas	5^7/$_{16}$ in. 137 mm	^{3}/$_4$ in. 18.26 mm	9.34 g	46	A powerful cigar with a full, round taste and a range of aromas that clearly stand out. This cigar's well-balanced flavors are sure to please experienced enthusiasts.

Romeo y Julieta

| Clarines | Clemenceau | Club Kings | Coronas | Coronas Grandes |

Name		Length	Diameter	Weight	Cepo	Comments
Clarines	Coronitas	4⅝ in. 117 mm	⅝ in. 15.87 mm	6.35 g	40	A rare cigar, easy to smoke.
Clemenceau	Julieta 2	7 in. 178 mm	¾ in. 18.65 mm	14.08 g	47	A milder and less full-bodied cigar than the Churchill, but with subtler aromas. For the enthusiast.
Club Kings	Marevas	5⅛ in. 129 mm	¹¹⁄₁₆ in. 16.67 mm	8.14 g	42	Mild, with an even burn, the Club Kings' aromas are subdued.
Coronas	Coronas	5⅝ in. 142 mm	¹¹⁄₁₆ in. 16.67 mm	8.97 g	42	This discreetly aromatic cigar is easy to smoke. Even, mild, it is one of the best examples of the coronas.
Coronas Grandes	Coronas Grandes	6⅛ in. 155 mm	¹¹⁄₁₆ in. 16.67 mm	9.89 g	42	A mild, pleasing make of cigar, lightly aromatic.

Romeo y Julieta

Coronitas   Coronitas en Cedro   Exceptionales   Exhibición No. 3   Exhibición No. 4   Churchills

Name		Length	Diameter	Weight	Cepo	Comments
Coronitas	Petit Cetros	5⅛ in. 129 mm	⅝ in. 15.87 mm	7.04 g	40	Not especially strong, the Coronitas is somewhat lacking in individuality.
Coronitas en Cedro	Petit Cetros	5⅛ in. 129 mm	⅝ in. 15.87 mm	7.04 g	40	Lightly aromatic and fairly mild. Enjoyable.
Exceptionales	Petit Coronas	5⅛ in. 129 mm	¹¹⁄₁₆ in. 16.67 mm	7.77 g	42	This mild cigar's aromas begin to assert themselves midway through its length.
Exhibición No. 3	Coronas Gordas	5¹¹⁄₁₆ in. 143 mm	¹¹⁄₁₆ in. 16.67 mm	10.90 g	46	Though a powerful cigar with distinctive aromas, this one lacks complexity. For the aficionado.
Exhibición No. 4	Hermosos No. 4	5¹⁄₁₆ in. 127 mm	¾ in. 19.05 mm	10.47 g	48	A full-flavored, subtle cigar that offers a very round taste, with very pronounced aromas. One of the brand's best cigars.
Churchills	Julieta 2	7 in. 178 mm	¾ in. 18.65 mm	14.08 g	47	A powerful full-bodied taste, together with a range of distinctive aromas, makes this cigar a true benchmark. For experienced aficionados.

Romeo y Julieta

Exquisitos   Favoritas   Julietas   Mille Fleurs   Montagues   Nacionales

Name		Length	Diameter	Weight	Cepo	Comments
Exquisitos	Petit Cetros	5¹⁄₈ in. 129 mm	⁵⁄₈ in. 15.87 mm	7.04 g	40	A light, straightforward cigar that anybody can enjoy.
Favoritas	Belvederes	4¹⁵⁄₁₆ in. 125 mm	⁵⁄₈ in. 15.48 mm	6.21 g	39	An even cigar, discreet in terms of its aromas. Suitable after a light midday meal.
Julietas	Franciscanos	4⁵⁄₈ in. 116 mm	⁵⁄₈ in. 15.87 mm	6.72 g	40	The aroma-rich Julieta makes for a mild, even smoke.
Mille Fleurs	Petit Coronas	5¹⁄₈ in. 129 mm	¹¹⁄₁₆ in. 16.67 mm	7.77 g	42	Turned out in very small numbers, this subtly aromatic cigar truly lives up to the "thousand flowers" of its name.
Montagues	Toppers	6⁵⁄₁₆ in. 160 mm	⁵⁄₈ in. 15.48 mm	8.33 g	39	This make's aromas are restrained. At times lacks individuality.
Nacionales	Cosacos	5³⁄₈ in. 135 mm	¹¹⁄₁₆ in. 16.67 mm	8.56 g	42	Builds its powerful aromas as it burns down. Fairly restrained.

Romeo y Julieta

Palmas Reales   Panetelas   Perfectos   Petit Coronas   Petit Julietas   Chicos

Name		Length	Diameter	Weight	Cepo	Comments
Palmas Reales	Ninfas	7¹/₁₆ in. 178 mm	⁹/₁₆ in. 13.10 mm	6.97 g	33	This thin, elegant cigar offers a number of light aromas.
Panetelas	Panetelas	4⁵/₈ in. 117 mm	⁹/₁₆ in. 13.49 mm	4.85 g	34	Although mild, this Panetelas occasionally seems to cry out for greater subtlety.
Perfectos	Perfectos	5¹/₁₆ in. 127 mm	¹¹/₁₆ in. 17.46 mm	7.36 g	44	This make sometimes lacks nuance although it remains relatively strong and flavorful.
Petit Coronas	Marevas	5¹/₈ in. 129 mm	¹¹/₁₆ in. 16.67 mm	8.14 g	42	Although rather powerful, this cigar offers little aroma. Wants nuance. Suitable for afternoons.
Petit Julietas	Entreactos	4 in. 100 mm	¹/₂ in. 11.91 mm	3.27 g	30	Mild, almost innocuous. For beginners.
Chicos	Chicos	4³/₁₆ in. 106 mm	⁷/₁₆ in. 10.32 mm	3.00 g	29	Fresh and light, the Chicos is suitable for mornings or over an aperitif.

Romeo y Julieta

| Romeo No. 1 De Luxe | Romeo No. 1 | Romeo No. 2 De Luxe | Romeo No. 2 | Romeo No. 3 De Luxe | RomeoNo. 3 | Shakespeare | Sport Largos |

Name		Length	Diameter	Weight	Cepo	Comments
Romeo No. 1 De Luxe	Coronas	5⁵/₈ in. 142 mm	11/₁₆ in. 16.67 mm	8.97 g	42	This light, mild cigar is perfectly suited to beginners.
Romeo No. 1	Cremas	5⁹/₁₆ in. 140 mm	⁵/₈ in. 15.87 mm	7.64 g	40	Lacks a distinctive character of its own. A cigar of general appeal.
Romeo No. 2 De Luxe	Marevas	5¹/₈ in. 129 mm	11/₁₆ in. 16.67 mm	8.14 g	42	A lack of aroma makes this cigar too light. For inexperienced smokers.
Romeo No. 2	Petit Coronas	5¹/₈ in. 129 mm	11/₁₆ in. 16.67 mm	7.77 g	42	A cigar that makes no demands on the smoker. For beginners.
Romeo No. 3 De Luxe	Franciscanos	4⁵/₈ in. 116 mm	⁵/₈ in. 15.87 mm	6.72 g	40	A morning cigar, light and not particularly subtle.
Romeo No. 3	Coronitas	4⁵/₈ in. 117 mm	⁵/₈ in. 15.87 mm	6.35 g	40	Needs to develop its individuality. Can be enjoyed any time of day.
Shakespeare	Panetelas Largas	6¹⁵/₁₆ in. 175 mm	⁷/₁₆ in. 11.11 mm	4.95 g	28	Light and rich in aromas, this is an easy-going, enjoyable cigar.
Sport Largos	Sports	4⁵/₈ in. 117 mm	⁹/₁₆ in. 13.89 mm	4.88 g	35	A light, pleasing cigar worth savoring over an aperitif.

Romeo y Julieta

| Petit Princess | Plateados de Romeo | Plateados de Romeo | Prince of Wales | Regalias de Londres | Regalias de la Habana | Très Petit Coronas |

Name		Length	Diameter	Weight	Cepo	Comments
Petit Princess	Perlas	4¹/₁₆ in. 102 mm	⅝ in. 15.87 mm	5.91 g	40	Light and refreshing, the Petit Princess can be smoked any time of day.
Plateados de Romeo	Marevas	5⅛ in. 129 mm	¹¹/₁₆ in. 16.67 mm	8.14 g	42	The Plateados de Romeo's rich taste makes it more of a cigar for experienced enthusiasts.
Plateados de Romeo	Petit Cetros	5⅛ in. 129 mm	⅝ in. 15.87 mm	7.04 g	40	More straightforward than the Mareva *vitola* above, this is still a cigar for experienced palates.
Prince of Wales	Julieta 2	7 in. 178 mm	¾ in. 18.65 mm	14.08 g	47	Milder than the Clemenceau and rather restrained. Accessible to beginner cigar smokers.
Regalias de Londres	Coronitas	4⅝ in. 117 mm	⅝ in. 15.87 mm	6.35 g	40	Well balanced. This cigar's aromas continue to please even as it burns.
Regalias de la Habana	Belvederes	4¹⁵/₁₆ in. 125 mm	⅝ in. 15.48 mm	6.21 g	39	This is a full-bodied make, although its aromas remain fairly discreet.
Très Petit Coronas	Francis-canos	4⅝ in. 116 mm	⅝ in. 15.87 mm	6.72 g	40	A small aromatic cigar with a pleasing taste. Perfect for the morning.

Sancho Panza

Bachilleres   Belicosos   Coronas

Name		Length	Diameter	Weight	Cepo	Comments
Bachilleres	Francis-canos	4⅝ in. 116 mm	⅝ in. 15.87 mm	6.72 g	40	A small, light cigar, not very original but enjoyable just the same. For beginners.
Belicosos	Campanas	5½ in. 140 mm	⅞ in. 20.64 mm	12.37 g	52	A mild, full-flavored cigar with a well-rounded taste and good burning qualities. Enjoyable thanks to its fine aroma.
Coronas	Coronas	5⅝ in. 142 mm	11/16 in. 16.67 mm	8.97 g	42	A refined cigar, mild and aromatic. Very representative of this range of cigars.

Sancho Panza

Non Plus   Tronquitos   Molinos   Dorados   Coronas Gigantes   Sanchos

Name		Length	Diameter	Weight	Cepo	Comments
Non Plus	Marevas	5⅛ in. 129 mm	11/16 in. 16.67 mm	8.14 g	42	A rather powerful cigar, but pleasant on the palate. Burns well. Can be smoked any time of day.
Tronquitos	Coronas	5⅝ in. 142 mm	11/16 in. 16.67 mm	8.97 g	42	A mild, refined cigar, the Tronquitos can be enjoyed at any time of day.
Molinos	Cervantes	6½ in. 165 mm	11/16 in. 16.67 mm	10.47 g	42	An especially well-balanced, smooth taste. Delightful, refined aromas. Will please experienced aficionados and beginning smokers alike.
Dorados	Cervantes	6½ in. 165 mm	11/16 in. 16.67 mm	10.47 g	42	A full-flavored cigar with delightfully refined aromas. The Dorados' even burn adds to the pleasure of smoking it.
Coronas Gigantes	Julieta 2	7 in. 178 mm	¾ in. 18.65 mm	14.08 g	47	A choice, sophisticated, and relatively mild cigar. Good combustion allows its pleasant aromas to develop. A cigar best enjoyed after meals.
Sanchos	Gran Corona	9¼ in. 235 mm	¾ in. 18.65 mm	18.63 g	47	Despite its large size, this is a mild and relatively light cigar. Intended for a wide range of smokers with a few hours to spare.

San Luis Rey

| Coronas | Regios | Série A | Coronas | Churchills | Lonsdales | Petit Coronas | Double Coronas |

Name		Length	Diameter	Weight	Cepo	Comments
Coronas	Coronas	5⅝ in. 142 mm	¹¹/₁₆ in. 16.67 mm	8.97 g	42	Boasting a full, round taste, this cigar may become overbearing, although that does not alter its qualities. For aficionados.
Regios	Hermosos No. 4	5¹/₁₆ in. 127 mm	¾ in. 19.05 mm	10.47 g	48	Mild, with unremarkable, albeit pleasant, aromas, this cigar can be enjoyed in the company of others, though not particularly suitable after meals.
Série A	Coronas Gordas	5¹¹/₁₆ in. 143 mm	¹¹/₁₆ in. 16.67 mm	10.90 g	46	Mild, aromatic, and well balanced. Pleasing after a midday meal.
Coronas	Coronas	5⅝ in. 142 mm	¹¹/₁₆ in. 16.67 mm	8.97 g	42	Less aggressive than the Coronas above, this *vitola* maintains its rich taste. For experienced aficionados.
Churchills	Julieta 2	7 in. 178 mm	¾ in. 18.65 mm	14.08 g	47	Rich in flavor and smooth. For connoisseurs of not overly strong cigars.
Lonsdales	Cervantes	6½ in. 165 mm	¹¹/₁₆ in. 16.67 mm	10.47 g	42	Aromatic and smooth, becomes rough toward the end. For enthusiasts, after dinner.
Petit Coronas	Marevas	5⅛ in. 129 mm	¹¹/₁₆ in. 16.67 mm	8.14 g	42	A small, powerful, oily cigar that fits in well after a fine meal.
Double Coronas	Promi-nentes	7¹¹/₁₆ in. 194 mm	¹³/₁₆ in. 19.45 mm	16.70 g	49	The strong taste of the very first whorls of smoke becomes more full-bodied as the cigar burns down. Develops its subtle, quite distinctive aromas nicely. For experienced aficionados.

Statos De Luxe

Troya

Brevas Cremas Delirios Dobles Selectos Universales Coronas Club Tubulares

Name		Length	Diameter	Weight	Cepo	Comments
Brevas	Nacionales	5⁹/₁₆ in. 140 mm	⁵/₈ in. 15.87 mm	8.28 g	40	Like all of this brand's *vitolas*, the Brevas is produced in small numbers. Develops its aromas in the course of its first third.
Cremas	Nacionales	5⁹/₁₆ in. 140 mm	⁵/₈ in. 15.87 mm	8.28 g	40	With less pronounced aromas than the Brevas, this cigar is still very pleasing.
Delirios	Standard	4¹⁵/₁₆ in. 123 mm	⁵/₈ in. 15.87 mm	6.90 g	40	Not an especially distinctive cigar. A good smoke for all occasions.
Dobles	Standard	4¹⁵/₁₆ in. 123 mm	⁵/₈ in. 15.87 mm	6.90 g	40	Not particularly subtle in terms of its aromas. A daytime cigar.
Selectos	Nacionales	5⁹/₁₆ in. 140 mm	⁵/₈ in. 15.87 mm	8.28 g	40	Although it doesn't especially assert itself, the Selectos remains an enjoyable cigar.
Universales	Universales	5⁵/₁₆ in. 134 mm	⁵/₈ in. 15.08 mm	7.13 g	38	As rare as the Coronas below, the Universales belongs more to the Havanas of old.
Coronas Club Tubulares	Standard	4¹⁵/₁₆ in. 123 mm	⁵/₈ in. 15.87 mm	6.90 g	38	Extremely rare, this cigar has had a hard time surmounting various bad years for Cuban tobacco.

H. Upmann

| Amatistas | Aromaticos | Aromaticos | Belvederes | Cinco Bocas | Connaisseur No. 1 | Coronas |

Name		Length	Diameter	Weight	Cepo	Comments
Amatistas	Superiores	5¹³/₁₆ in. 146 mm	⅝ in. 15.87 mm	8.46 g	40	A very-hard-to-find cigar that will surely please those who go in for the traditional taste of the Havanas.
Aromaticos	Petit Coronas	5⅛ in. 129 mm	¹¹/₁₆ in. 16.67 mm	7.77 g	42	Quite straightforward, the Aromaticos easily asserts its flavors after a good midday meal. Rare.
Aromaticos	Coronitas	4⅝ in. 117 mm	⅝ in. 15.87 mm	6.35 g	40	Full-bodied, fairly blunt make that roughly asserts itself.
Belvederes	Belvederes	4¹⁵/₁₆ in. 125 mm	⅝ in. 15.48 mm	6.21 g	39	Uncomplicated cigar whose flavors are too light at times and leave little impression on the palate.
Cinco Bocas	Cervantes	6½ in. 165 mm	¹¹/₁₆ in. 16.67 mm	10.47 g	42	Produced in small numbers. Enjoyable enough to smoke, but hardly asserts its flavors.
Connaisseur No. 1	Hermosos No. 4	5¹/₁₆ in. 127 mm	¾ in. 19.05 mm	10.47 g	48	This fresh, light cigar leaves only a slight impression on the palate. Good burning qualities. Accessible to experienced aficionados and beginning smokers alike.
Coronas	Coronas	5⅝ in. 142 mm	¹¹/₁₆ in. 16.67 mm	8.97 g	42	A full-bodied, direct cigar in the purest tradition of the H. Upmanns.

H. Upmann

Coronas Major	Coronas Minor	Cristales	Culebras	El Prado	Epicures	Especiales

Name		Length	Diameter	Weight	Cepo	Comments
Coronas Major	Eminentes	5¼ in. 132 mm	¹¹/₁₆ in. 17.46 mm	8.74 g	44	A full-bodied make that lacks a certain refinement. For aficionados.
Coronas Minor	Coronitas	4⅝ in. 117 mm	⅝ in. 15.87 mm	6.35 g	40	Relatively light and smooth, the Coronas Minor is enjoyable throughout the day.
Cristales	Cosacos	5⅜ in. 135 mm	¹¹/₁₆ in. 16.67 mm	8.56 g	42	This is the only cigar to be sold in a glass container. A smooth, light Havana with a discreet woody aroma. Hard to find.
Culebras	Culebras	5¹³/₁₆ in. 146 mm	⅝ in. 15.48 mm	6.67 g	39	Rare. Worth collecting rather than smoking.
El Prado	Deliciosos	6⁵/₁₆ in. 159 mm	⁹/₁₆ in. 13.89 mm	6.67 g	35	A mild cigar with light aromas. Burns evenly.
Epicures	Epicures	4³/₈ in. 110 mm	⁹/₁₆ in. 13.89 mm	4.60 g	35	Occasionally harsh, this make of cigar lacks nuance.
Especiales	Cremas	5⁹/₁₆ in. 140 mm	⅝ in. 15.87 mm	7.64 g	40	The Especiales is rich in taste. Not a cigar to hide its earthy origins.

H. Upmann

Petit Upmann   Preciosas   Regalias   Royal Coronas   Short Coronas   Singulares

Name		Length	Diameter	Weight	Cepo	Comments
Petit Upmann	Petit	4⁵/₁₆ in. 108 mm	¹/₂ in. 12.70 mm	3.57 g	31	A light cigar, but one without much refinement.
Preciosas	Demi Tasse	4 in. 100 mm	¹/₂ in. 12.70 mm	3.50 g	32	Not too full-bodied, the Preciosas goes well with an aperitif.
Regalias	Petit Coronas	5¹/₈ in. 129 mm	¹¹/₁₆ in. 16.67 mm	7.77 g	42	Like all of the cigars of this selection, this make is hard to find. The petit coronas *vitola* is forthright and direct on the palate.
Royal Coronas	Conservas	5³/₄ in. 145 mm	¹¹/₁₆ in. 17.46 mm	9.57 g	44	A strong cigar that asserts itself from the first puffs. Builds its earthy aromas especially towards the middle.
Short Coronas	Cosacos	5³/₈ in. 135 mm	¹¹/₁₆ in. 16.67 mm	8.56 g	42	A squat cigar that is not particularly refined, although squarely in the Upmann tradition.
Singulares	Coronitas	4⁵/₈ in. 117 mm	⁵/₈ in. 15.87 mm	6.35 g	40	Although less powerful than the preceding *vitolas*, the Coronitas retains its characteristic lingering taste.

H. Upmann

| | Magnum 46 | Naturals | Noellas | Petit Coronas | Petits Palatinos | Monarchs |

Name		Length	Diameter	Weight	Cepo	Comments
Magnum 46	Coronas Gordas	5^{11}/$_{16}$ in. 143 mm	^{11}/$_{16}$ in. 16.67 mm	10.90 g	46	Rare. The Magnum's flavors come out fully toward the middle.
Naturals	Naturales	6^{1}/$_{8}$ in. 155 mm	^{5}/$_{8}$ in. 14.68 mm	3.57 g	37	Produced in very small numbers, this light cigar is pleasing to the palate even if it never builds any particularly subtle aromas.
Noellas	Cosacos	5^{3}/$_{8}$ in. 135 mm	^{11}/$_{16}$ in. 16.67 mm	8.56 g	42	As difficult to find as the Naturales, the Cosacos is a more full-bodied smoke.
Petit Coronas	Marevas	5^{1}/$_{8}$ in. 129 mm	^{11}/$_{16}$ in. 16.67 mm	8.14 g	42	Fairly full-bodied, this cigar lacks a certain refinement, especially toward the middle.
Petits Palatinos	Cadetes	4^{9}/$_{16}$ in. 115 mm	^{5}/$_{8}$ in. 14.29 mm	5.34 g	36	Aromas are a bit underdeveloped in terms of their nuance. Not overly strong.
Monarchs	Julieta 2	7 in. 178 mm	^{3}/$_{4}$ in. 18.65 mm	14.08 g	47	Full-bodied Havana whose aromas, though lacking complexity, are particularly striking. A cigar rich in flavor. For connoisseurs.

H. Upmann

| Sir Winston | Super Coronas | Upmann No. 1 | Upmann No. 2 | Upmann No. 3 | Upmann No. 4 |

Name		Length	Diameter	Weight	Cepo	Comments
Sir Winston	Julieta 2	7 in. 178 mm	$^3/_4$ in. 18.65 mm	14.08 g	47	A powerful cigar with rough, unrefined aromas and long-lasting flavor. This Havana's qualities hold up throughout its regular combustion. For experienced enthusiasts.
Super Coronas	Coronas Gordas	$5^{11}/_{16}$ in. 143 mm	$^{11}/_{16}$ in. 16.67 mm	10.90 g	46	A mild cigar that burns evenly. Very aromatic but unfortunately rare.
Upmann No. 1	Cervantes	$6^1/_2$ in. 165 mm	$^{11}/_{16}$ in. 16.67 mm	10.47 g	42	Not particularly harsh, the Upmann No. 1 is too straightforward.
Upmann No. 2	Piramides	$6^3/_{16}$ in. 156 mm	$^7/_8$ in. 20.64 mm	12.19 g	52	Robust, though wanting in subtlety, the Upmann No. 2 boasts very distinctive aromas that smack of its native earth. Its strength makes it a cigar for aficionados only.
Upmann No. 3	Coronas	$5^5/_8$ in. 142 mm	$^{11}/_{16}$ in. 16.67 mm	8.97 g	42	This make's aromas need refining. May prove rough.
Upmann No. 4	Marevas	$5^1/_8$ in. 129 mm	$^{11}/_{16}$ in. 16.67 mm	8.14 g	42	The lightest of the series, the Upmann No. 4 is still intended for smokers who appreciate full-bodied cigars.

H. Upmann

Exquisitos	Kings	Lonsdales	Majestic	Medias Coronas	Medias Coronas	Monarcas

Name		Length	Diameter	Weight	Cepo	Comments
Exquisitos	Petit Coronas	5⅛ in. 129 mm	¹¹⁄₁₆ in. 16.67 mm	7.77 g	42	Full-bodied, this Petit Coronas can prove uneven.
Kings	Petit Coronas	5⅛ in. 129 mm	¹¹⁄₁₆ in. 16.67 mm	7.77 g	42	Builds a taste that smacks of the soil during its first third. Full-bodied.
Lonsdales	Cervantes	6½ in. 165 mm	¹¹⁄₁₆ in. 16.67 mm	10.47 g	42	A lightly aromatic cigar lacking depth. Not especially aggressive.
Majestic	Cremas	5⁹⁄₁₆ in. 140 mm	⅝ in. 15.87 mm	7.64 g	40	A mild cigar with weak aromas. For one and all.
Medias Coronas	Eminentes	5¼ in. 132 mm	¹¹⁄₁₆ in. 17.46 mm	8.74 g	44	A powerful, though not especially subtle cigar. For enthusiasts.
Medias Coronas	Marevas	5⅛ in. 129 mm	¹¹⁄₁₆ in. 16.67 mm	8.14 g	42	Lighter than the Eminentes, the Marevas is produced mainly for aficionados who prize a traditional taste.
Monarcas	Julieta 2	7 in. 178 mm	¾ in. 18.65 mm	14.08 g	47	A powerful cigar, this Julieta 2 is even stronger than the Monarchs produced for the British market.

Vitolas

Brand Names and Sizes

Three hundred nine brands made up the prerevolutionary hierarchy of the Havana cigar; today only thirty-six remain, some of which have practically disappeared from the market because of shortages of raw material. Together the thirty-six brands produce over five hundred different types of individual Havanas, available in any of seventy-two formats, or *vitolas.*

The *vitola* corresponds to a set size and shape. The manufacturers in Havana actually have two families of vitolas. In the rolling departments, the names given to the different calibers of cigars are the *vitolas de galera,* production vitolas. They define the length, diameter, and weight of each type of Havana, and are common to all makers of Havana cigars. The names of each size of cigar produced by any one brand are called the *vitolas de salida,* commercial vitolas. These are the names that confront the cigar buyer and differ from one brand to the next.

The two tables found in the following pages indicate the connection between the different brands of Havanas and the various vitolas, both production and commercial, and cover the current production of Cuban cigar manufacturers in its entirety. They show which brands put out the same vitolas and under what names each brand markets them.

The first table lists the Havanas by brand. Beneath each brand name are the commercial vitolas (on the left) and the corresponding production vitolas (on the right). The code number before each production vitola relates to how the cigar is produced.

The second table lists the production vitolas alphabetically. Diameter, *cepo* (or ring gauge), length, and weight are given for each vitola. The left-hand column lists the brands producing the cigars of these given dimensions and, to the right, the "public" name they themselves bestow on these cigars (their commercial vitola).

While most of the vitolas in the second table are made exclusively by hand, some are made both by hand *(hecho a mano)* and by machine. These vitolas thus have two code numbers: machine-made cigars have a code number that begins with 2, handmades with 7. (The dual classifications largely concern small cigars.) For example, in the first table under the brand name "Bolívar" the commercial vitola "Champions" corresponds to the production vitola "Cremas"; the code here is 708 when the cigar is rolled by hand, and 208 when it is produced by machine. In the second table under "Cremas" we read that the cigars with this vitola have a diameter of $^5/_8$ in. (15.87 mm), are $5^9/_{16}$ in. (140 mm) long, and weigh 7.64 g. Among the brands marketing the same type of cigar we find Romeo y Julieta with its Romeo No. 1 and Punch with its Palmas Reales.

Commercial Vitolas

COMMERCIAL VITOLA	PRODUCTION VITOLA
BELINDA	
Belvederes	Belvederes Mano (290, 790)
Coronas	Cremas (208)
Demi-Tasse	Demitasse (213)
Panetelas	Sports Mano (224, 724)
Petit	Petit (218)
Petit Coronas	Petit Coronas Mano (220, 720)
Petit Princess	Epicures (215)
Preciosas	Demi Tasse (213)
Princess	Epicures Mano (215, 715)
Superfinos	Coronitas (207)
BOLÍVAR	
Amado Selección C	Franciscos (508)
Amado Selección E	Robusto (435)
Amado Selección G	Minutos (423)
Belicosos Finos	Campanas (581)
Belvederes	Belvederes Mano (290, 790)
Bolívar Tubos no. 1	Coronas (504)
Bolívar Tubos no. 2	Mareva (421)
Bolívar Tubos no. 3	Placeras (433)
Bonitas	Londres (420)
Champions	Cremas Mano (208, 708)
Chicos	Chicos Mano (261, 761)
Churchills	Julieta 2 (609)
Coronas	Coronas (504)
Coronas Extra	Franciscos (508)
Coronas Gigantes	Julieta 2 (609)
Coronas Junior	Minutos (423)
Demi-Tasse	Entreactos (412)
Especiales	Delicados (604)
Gold Medal	Cervantes (503)
Inmensas	Dalias (507)
Lonsdales	Cervantes (503)

COMMERCIAL VITOLA	PRODUCTION VITOLA
Palmas	Ninfas (512)
Panatelas	Conchitas Mano (205, 705)
Petit Coronas	Mareva (421)
Petit Coronas Especiales	Eminentes Mano (214, 714)
Regentes	Placeras (433)
Royal Coronas	Robusto (435)
Supremas Churchills	Julieta 2 (609)
CABAÑAS	
Belvederes	Belvederes Mano (290, 790)
Chiquitos	Infantes Mano (291, 791)
Coronitas	Chicos (261)
Perfectos	Perfectos Mano (292, 792)
Suaves	Sports Mano (224, 724)
Superfinos	Coronitas Mano (207, 707)
FLOR DEL CANEY	
Bouquets Finos	Vegueritos Mano (274, 774)
Canapé	Chicos Mano (261, 761)
Delgados	Vegueritos Mano (274, 774)
Especiales	Culebras (210)
Predilectos	Standard Mano (273, 773)
Selectos	Nacionales Mano (272, 772)
Vegueros	Preferidos Mano (264, 764)
CIFUENTES	
Cristal tubo	Conservas Mano (206, 706)
Cubanitos	Chicos Mano (261, 761)
Emboquillados no. 5	Demi Tip Mano (262, 762)
Habanitos	Chicos Mano (261, 761)
Petit Bouquets	Infantes Mano (291, 791)
Super Estupendos	Gran Corona (607)
Vegueritos	Vegueritos Mano (274, 774)

COHIBA

Coronas . . . . Coronas (504)
Coronas Especiales . . . . Numero 2 (513)
Esplendidos . . . . Julieta 2 (609)
Exquisitos . . . . Seoane (517)
Lanceros . . . . Numero 1 (611)
Panetelas . . . . Numero 3 (428)
Robusto . . . . Robusto (435)
Siglo I . . . . Perlas (432)
Siglo II . . . . Mareva (421)
Siglo III . . . . Coronas Grandes (506)
Siglo IV . . . . Coronas Gordas (505)
Siglo V . . . . Dalias (507)

DIPLOMATICOS

Diplomaticos no. 1 . . . . Cervantes (503)
Diplomaticos no. 2 . . . . Piramides (681)
Diplomaticos no. 3 . . . . Coronas (504)
Diplomaticos no. 4 . . . . Mareva (421)
Diplomaticos no. 5 . . . . Perlas (432)
Diplomaticos no. 6 . . . . Numero 1 (611)
Diplomaticos no. 7 . . . . Numero 2 (513)

DUNHILL

Abajo . . . . Piramides (681)
Atados . . . . Panetelas Largas (515)
Cabinetta . . . . Robusto (435)
Chico Minor . . . . Chicos Mano (761)
Chicola Minor . . . . Chicos Mano (761)
Chicos . . . . Chicos Mano (761)
Demi-Tasse . . . . Entreactos (412)
Estupendos . . . . Julieta 2 (609)
Havana Club . . . . Gran Corona (607)
Malecón . . . . Cervantes (503)
Mojito . . . . Coronas (504)
Princess . . . . Placeras (433)
Supremas . . . . Franciscanos (416)
Tubos . . . . Coronas Grandes (506)
Varadero . . . . Mareva (421)

FONSECA

Cosacos . . . . Cosacos (408)
Delicias . . . . Standard Mano (273, 773)
Fonseca no. 1 . . . . Cazadores (406)
Invictos . . . . Especiales (582)
Kdt Cadetes . . . . Cadetes (404)

GISPERT

Coronas . . . . Coronas (504)
Habaneras no. 2 . . . . Standard Mano (273, 773)
Petit Coronas de luxe . . . . Mareva (421)

HOYO DE MONTERREY

Churchills . . . . Julieta 2 (609)
Concorde . . . . Julieta 2 (609)
Coronations . . . . Mareva (421)
Coronations . . . . Petit Coronas Mano (220, 720)
Double Coronas . . . . Prominentes (612)
Epicure no. 1 . . . . Coronas Gordas (505)
Epicure no. 2 . . . . Robusto (435)

Exquisitos . . . . Petit Cetros Mano (219, 719)
Hoyo Coronas . . . . Coronas (504)
Humidor no. 1 . . . . Conservas Mano (206, 706)
Jeanne D'Arc . . . . Carlotas (501)
Le Hoyo des Dieux . . . . Coronas Grandes (506)
Le Hoyo du Dauphin . . . . Numero 2 (513)
Le Hoyo du Député . . . . Trabucos (439)
Le Hoyo du Gourmet . . . . Palmas (514)
Le Hoyo du Maire . . . . Entreactos (412)
Le Hoyo du Prince . . . . Almuerzos (401)
Le Hoyo du Roi . . . . Coronas (504)
Longos . . . . Ninfas (512)
Margaritas . . . . Carolinas (405)
Odéon . . . . Numero 2 (513)
Opéra . . . . Coronas (504)
Palmas Extra . . . . Cremas Mano (208, 708)
Particulares . . . . Gran Corona (607)
Petit Coronations . . . . Coronitas Mano (207, 707)
Petit Coronations . . . . Franciscanos (416)
Royal Coronations . . . . Conservas Mano (206, 706)
Royal Coronations . . . . Coronas (504)
Short Hoyo Coronas . . . . Mareva (421)
Souvenir De Luxe . . . . Petit Coronas Mano (220, 720)
Super Selection no. 1 . . . . Coronas Grandes (506)
Versailles . . . . Palmas (514)

JOSÉ L. PIEDRA

Superiores . . . . Superiores (438)

FLOR DE JUAN LOPEZ

Coronas . . . . Coronas (504)
Panetela Superba . . . . Placeras (433)
Patricias . . . . Franciscanos (416)
Petit Coronas . . . . Mareva (421)
Selección no. 1 . . . . Coronas Gordas (505)
Selección no. 2 . . . . Robusto (435)

LA CORONA

Belvederes . . . . Belvederes Mano (290, 790)
Coronas . . . . Cremas Mano (208, 708)
Coronitas . . . . Chicos Mano (261, 761)
Demi-Tasse . . . . Demi Tasse Mano (213, 713)
Panatelas . . . . Conchitas Mano (205, 705)
Perfectos . . . . Perfectos Mano (292, 792)
Petit . . . . Petit Mano (218, 718)
Petit Cetros . . . . Petit Cetros Mano (219, 719)
Petit Coronas . . . . Petit Coronas (220)

FLOR DE CANO

Coronas . . . . Mareva (421)
Diademas . . . . Julieta 2 (609)
Gran Corona . . . . Coronas Gordas (505)
Petit Coronas . . . . Standard Mano (273, 773)
Predilectos Tubulares . . . . Standard Mano (273, 773)
Preferidos . . . . Vegueritos Mano (274, 774)
Selectos . . . . Cristales Mano (271, 771)
Short Churchill . . . . Robusto (435)

GLORIA CUBANA

Cetros . . . . Cervantes (503)

Médaille d'Or no. 1 . . . . Delicados Extra (605)
Médaille d'Or no. 2 . . . . Dalias (507)
Médaille d'Or no. 3 . . . . Panetelas Largas (515)
Médaille d'Or no. 4 . . . . Palmitas (430)
Minutos . . . . Franciscanos (416)
Sabrosos . . . . Coronas Grandes (506)
Tainos . . . . Julieta 2 (609)
Tapados . . . . Cosacos (408)

JOSÉ GENER

Belvederes . . . . Belvederes Mano (290, 790)
Cazadores . . . . Cazadores (406)
Excepcionales . . . . Standard Mano (273, 773)
Longos . . . . Ninfas (512)
Perfectos . . . . Perfectos Mano (292, 792)
Superfinos . . . . Coronitas (207)

MARIA GUERRERO

Grandes de España . . . . Delicados (604)

MONTECRISTO

Dunhill Especial . . . . Numero 1 (611)
Dunhill Selección Suprema no. 1 . . . . Cervantes (503)
Dunhill Selección Suprema no. 2 . . . . Piramides (681)
Dunhill Selección Suprema no. 3 . . . . Coronas (504)
Dunhill Selección Suprema no. 4 . . . . Mareva (421)
Dunhill Selección Suprema no. 5 . . . . Perlas (432)
Dunhill Selección Suprema Tubos . . . . Coronas Grandes (506)
Joyitas . . . . Numero 3 (428)
Montecristo A . . . . Gran Corona (607)
Montecristo B . . . . Cosacos (408)
Montecristo Especial . . . . Numero 1 (611)
Montecristo Especial no. 2 . . . . Numero 2 (513)
Montecristo no. 1 . . . . Cervantes (503)
Montecristo no. 2 . . . . Piramides (681)
Montecristo no. 3 . . . . Coronas (504)
Montecristo no. 4 . . . . Mareva (421)
Montecristo no. 5 . . . . Perlas (432)
Montecristo no. 6 . . . . Seoane (517)
Montecristo no. 7 . . . . Panetelas Largas (515)
Montecristo Tubos . . . . Coronas Grandes (506)
Petit Tubos . . . . Mareva (421)

NUEVA MARCA

8-9-8 . . . . Dalias (507)
Especial no. 2 . . . . Numero 2 (513)
Especiales . . . . Numero 1 (611)
Joyitas . . . . Numero 3 (428)
no. 1 . . . . Cervantes (503)
no. 2 . . . . Piramides (681)
no. 3 . . . . Coronas (504)
no. 4 . . . . Mareva (421)
no. 5 . . . . Perlas (432)
Tubos . . . . Coronas Grandes (506)

PARTAGÁS

8-9-8 . . . . Coronas Grandes (506)
8-9-8 . . . . Dalias (507)
Aristocrats . . . . Petit Cetros Mano (219, 719)
Astorias . . . . Cosacos (408)

Belvederes . . . . Belvederes Mano (290, 790)
Bonitos Extra Mild . . . . Chicos Mano (261, 761)
Capitols . . . . Petit Cetros Mano (219, 719)
Charlottes . . . . Carlotas (501)
Chicos . . . . Chicos Mano (261, 761)
Churchills De Luxe . . . . Julieta 2 (609)
Coronas . . . . Coronas (504)
Coronas A. Mejorado . . . . Coronas (504)
Coronas Grandes . . . . Coronas Grandes (506)
Coronas Junoir . . . . Coronitas Mano (207, 707)
Coronas Senior . . . . Eminentes Mano (214, 714)
Cubanos . . . . Placeras (433)
Culebras . . . . Culebras Mano (210, 710)
Demi-Tip . . . . Demi Tip Mano (262, 762)
Dunhill Selección Suprema no. 151 . . . . Placeras (433)
Eminentes . . . . Eminentes Mano (214, 714)
Filipos . . . . Placeras (433)
Habaneros . . . . Belvederes Mano (290, 790)
Half Coronas . . . . Minutos (423)
Londres en Cedro . . . . Petit Cetros Mano (219, 719)
Londres Extra . . . . Petit Cetros Mano (219, 719)
Londres Finos . . . . Petit Cetros Mano (219, 719)
Lonsdales . . . . Cervantes (503)
Lusitanias . . . . Prominentes (612)
Mille Fleurs . . . . Petit Coronas Mano (220, 720)
Palmas Grandes . . . . Ninfas (512)
Panatelas . . . . Conchitas Mano (205, 705)
Parisianos . . . . Petit Cetros Mano (219, 719)
Partagás De Luxe . . . . Cremas Mano (208, 708)
Partagás de Partagás no. 1 . . . . Dalias (507)
Partagás Pride . . . . Minutos (423)
Perfectos . . . . Perfectos Mano (292, 792)
Personales . . . . Petit Cetros Mano (219, 719)
Petit Bouquets . . . . Infantes Mano (291, 791)
Petit Coronas . . . . Mareva (421)
Petit Coronas Especiales . . . . Eminentes Mano (214, 714)
Petit Coronas Tubos . . . . Eminentes Mano (214, 714)
Petit Partagás . . . . Petit Cetros Mano (219, 719)
Petit Privados . . . . Mareva (421)
Presidentes . . . . Tacos (586)
Princess . . . . Conchitas Mano (205, 705)
Privados . . . . Coronas (504)
Ramonitas . . . . Carolinas (405)
Regalias de la Reina Bueno . . . . Coronitas Mano (207, 707)
Royales . . . . Londres (420)
Selección Fox no. 7 . . . . Minutos (423)
Selección Fox no. 11 . . . . Placeras (433)
Selección Privada no. 1 . . . . Dalias (507)
Serie D no. 4 . . . . Robusto (435)
Série du Connaisseur no. 1 . . . . Delicados (604)
Série du Connaisseur no. 2 . . . . Parejos (516)
Série du Connaisseur no. 3 . . . . Carlotas (501)
Shorts . . . . Minutos (423)
Super Partagás . . . . Cremas Mano (208, 708)
Toppers . . . . Toppers Mano (225, 725)
Très Petit Coronas . . . . Franciscanos (416)

Por Larrañaga

Belvederes	Belvederes (290)
Coronas	Coronas (504)
Coronitas	Panetelas (431)
Curritos	Chicos Mano (261, 761)
Dunhill Selección Suprema no. 32	Mareva (421)
Eduardos	Numero 3 (428)
Juanitos	Chicos Mano (261, 761)
Lanceros	Coronas (504)
Largos de Larrañaga	Deliciosos Mano (212, 712)
Lolas en Cedro	Petit Coronas Mano (220, 720)
Lonsdales	Cervantes (503)
Montecarlos	Deliciosos Mano (212, 712)
Panetelas	Veguerito Mano (274, 774)
Petit Coronas	Mareva (421)
Petit Lanceros	Mareva (421)
Small Coronas	Franciscanos (416)
Super Cedros	Standard Mano (773)

Punch

Belvederes	Belvederes Mano (290, 790)
Black Prince	Coronas Gordas (505)
Churchills	Julieta 2 (609)
Cigarillos	Chicos Mano (261, 761)
Coronas	Coronas (504)
Coronations	Mareva (421)
Coronations	Petit Coronas Mano (220, 720)
Coronets	Panetelas (431)
Diademas Extra	Gran Corona (607)
Double Coronas	Prominentes (612)
Exquisitos	Petit Cetros Mano (219, 719)
Gran Corona	Superiores (438)
Margaritas	Carolinas (405)
Monarcas	Julieta 2 (609)
Nacionales	Cosacos (408)
Nectares no. 2	Coronas Gordas (505)
Nectares no. 4	Franciscanos (416)
Nectares no. 5	Ninfas (512)
Ninfas	Ninfas (512)
Palmas Reales	Cremas Mano (208, 708)
Panatelas Grandes	Ninfas (512)
Panetelas	Panetelas (431)
Petit Coronas del Punch	Mareva (421)
Petit Coronas del Punch Ones	Mareva (421)
Petit Coronations	Franciscanos (416)
Petit Coronations	Coronitas Mano (207, 707)
Petit Punch	Perlas (432)
Petit Punch De Luxe	Perlas (432)
Presidentes	Mareva (421)
Punch Punch	Coronas Gordas (505)
Punchinellos	Panetelas (431)
Royal Coronations	Conservas Mano (206, 706)
Royal Coronations	Coronas (504)
Royal Selection no. 11	Coronas Gordas (505)
Royal Selection no. 12	Mareva (421)
S/N (Rayados)	Londres (420)
Selección de luxe no. 1	Coronas Gorda (505)
Selección de luxe no. 2	Mareva (421)
Souvenir de luxe	Londres (420)

Souvenir de luxe	Petit Coronas Mano (220, 720)
Super Selection no. 1	Coronas Grandes (506)
Super Selection no. 2	Coronas Gordas (505)
Très Petit Coronas	Minutos (423)

Quai d'Orsay

Coronas Claro	Coronas (504)
Coronas Claro Claro	Coronas (504)
Gran Corona	Coronas Grandes (506)
Imperiales	Julieta 2 (609)
Panetelas	Ninfas (512)

Quintero

Brevas	Nacionales Mano (272, 772)
Churchills	Cervantes (503)
Coronas	Coronas (504)
Coronas Selectas	Coronas (504)
Londres	Standard Mano (773)
Londres Extra	Standard Mano (773)
Medias Coronas	Londres (420)
Medias Coronas Selectas	Londres (420)
Nacionales	Nacionales Mano 272 (272, 772)
Panetelas	Vegueritos Mano 274 (274, 774)
Puritos	Chicos Mano (261, 761)

Rafaël Gonzalez

Cigarritos	Numero 3 (428)
Coronas Extra	Coronas Gorda (505)
Demi-Tasse	Entreactos (412)
Lonsdales	Cervantes (503)
Panetelas	Panetelas (431)
Panetelas Extra	Vegueritos Mano (274, 774)
Petit Coronas	Mareva (421)
Petit Lonsdales	Mareva (421)
Slenderellas	Panetelas Largas (515)
Très Petit Lonsdales	Franciscanos (416)

Ramón Allones

8-9-8	Coronas (504)
8-9-8	Dalias (507)
Allones Specially Selected	Robusto (435)
Belvederes	Belvederes Mano (290, 790)
Bits of Havana	Chicos Mano (261, 761)
Coronas	Coronas (504)
Delgados	Toppers Mano (225, 725)
Dunhill Selección Suprema no. 11	Petit Cetros Mano (219, 719)
Dunhill Selección Suprema no. 81	Toppers Mano (225, 725)
Dunhill Selección Suprema no. 82	Cremas Mano (208, 708)
Dunhill Selección Suprema no. 280	Cosacos (408)
Dunhill Selección Suprema no. 622	Conchitas (205)
Gigantes	Prominentes (612)
Mille Fleurs	Petit Coronas Mano (220, 720)
Palmitas	Palmitas (430)
Panatelas	Conchitas Mano (205, 705)
Petit Coronas	Mareva (421)
Ramondos	Cremas Mano (208, 708)
Ramonitas	Carolinas (405)
Small Club Coronas	Minutos (423)
Toppers	Toppers Mano (225, 725)

El Rey del Mundo

Commercial Vitola	Production Vitola
Choix Suprême	Hermosos no. 4 (417)
Coronas de luxe	Coronas (504)
Demi-Tasse	Entreactos (412)
Elegantes	Panetelas Largas (515)
Fox Selection no. 47	Hermosos no. 4 (417)
Gran Corona	Coronas Gordas (505)
Grandes de España	Delicados (604)
Isabel	Carlotas (501)
Lonsdales	Cervantes (503)
Lunch Club	Franciscanos (416)
Panetelas Largas	Panetelas Largas (515)
Petit Coronas	Mareva (421)
Petit Lonsdales	Mareva (421)
Señoritas	Numero 3 (428)
Tainos	Julieta 2 (609)
Tubo no. 1	Coronas (504)
Tubo no. 2	Mareva (421)
Tubo no. 3	Franciscanos (416)
Variedales	Chicos Mano (261, 761)

Romeo y Julieta

Commercial Vitola	Production Vitola
Belicosos	Campanas (581)
Belvederes	Belvederes Mano (290, 790)
Cazadores	Cazadores (406)
Cedros de luxe no. 1	Cervantes (503)
Cedros de luxe no. 2	Coronas (504)
Cedros de luxe no. 3	Mareva (421)
Celestiales Finos	Britanicas (481)
Chicos	Chicos (261)
Churchills	Julieta 2 (609)
Clarines	Coronitas Mano (207, 707)
Clemenceau	Julieta 2 (609)
Club Kings	Mareva (421)
Club Kings	Petit Coronas Mano (220, 720)
Coronas	Coronas (504)
Coronas Grandes	Coronas Grandes (506)
Coronitas	Petit Cetros Mano (219, 719)
Coronitas en Cedro	Petit Cetros Mano (219, 719)
Culebras	Culebras (210)
Dunhill Selección Suprema no. 1	Cervantes (503)
Dunhill Selección Suprema no. 2	Coronas (504)
Dunhill Selección Suprema no. 3	Mareva (421)
Dunhill Selección Suprema no. 11	Petit Cetros (219)
Dunhill Selección Suprema no. 620	Julieta 2 (609)
Excepcionales	Petit Coronas Mano (220, 720)
Exhibición no. 3	Coronas Gordas (505)
Exhibición no. 4	Hermosos no. 4 (17)
Exquisitos	Petit Cetros Mano (219, 179)
Favoritas	Belvederes Mano (290, 790)
Julietas	Franciscanos (416)
Mille Fleurs	Petit Coronas Mano (220, 720)
Montagues	Toppers Mano (225, 725)
Nacionales	Cosacos (408)
Palmas Reales	Ninfas (512)
Panetelas	Panetelas (431)
Panetelas	Sports Mano (224, 724)
Perfectos	Perfectos Mano (292, 792)
Petit Coronas	Mareva (421)

(Romeo y Julieta continued)

Commercial Vitola	Production Vitola
Petit Julietas	Entreactos (412)
Petit Princess	Perlas (432)
Plateados de Romeo	Mareva (421)
Plateados de Romeo	Petit Cetros Mano (219, 719)
Prince of Wales	Julieta 2 (609)
Regalias de la Habana	Belvederes Mano (290, 790)
Regalias de Londres	Coronitas Mano (207, 707)
Romeo no. 1	Cremas Mano (208, 708)
Romeo no. 1 de luxe	Coronas (504)
Romeo no. 2	Petit Coronas Mano (220, 720)
Romeo no. 2 de luxe	Mareva (421)
Romeo no. 3	Coronitas Mano (207, 707)
Romeo no. 3 de luxe	Franciscanos (416)
Sanchos	Gran Corona (607)
Shakespeare	Panetelas Largas (515)
Sport Largos	Sports Mano -224 (224, 724)
Très Petit Coronas	Franciscanos (416)

Sancho Panza

Commercial Vitola	Production Vitola
Bachilleres	Franciscanos (416)
Belicosos	Campanas (581)
Coronas	Coronas (504)
Coronas Gigantes	Julieta 2 (609)
Dorados	Cervantes (503)
Molinos	Cervantes (503)
Non Plus	Mareva (421)
Sanchos	Gran Corona (607)
Tronquitos	Coronas (504)

San Luis Rey

Commercial Vitola	Production Vitola
Churchills	Julieta 2 (609)
Coronas	Cervantes (503)
Coronas	Coronas (504)
Double Coronas	Prominentes (612)
Lonsdales	Cervantes (503)
Mini-Habanos	Chicos Mano (761)
Petit Coronas	Mareva (421)
Regios	Hermosos no. 4 (417)
Série A	Coronas Gordas (505)

Siboney

Commercial Vitola	Production Vitola
Especiales	Numero 2 (513)

Statos de Luxe

Commercial Vitola	Production Vitola
Delirios	Standard Mano (773)
Dobles	Standard Mano (773)
Brevas	Nacionales Mano (272, 772)
Cremas	Nacionales Mano (272, 772)
Selectos	Nacionales Mano (272, 772)

Troya

Commercial Vitola	Production Vitola
Coronas Club Tubulares	Standard Mano (773)
Universales	Universales Mano (270, 770)

H. Upmann

Commercial Vitola	Production Vitola
Amatistas	Superiores (438)
Aromaticos	Coronitas Mano (207, 707)
Aromaticos	Petit Coronas Mano (220, 770)
Belvederes	Belvederes Mano (290, 790)
Cinco Bocas	Cervantes (503)

Connoissieur no. 1 . . . . Hermosos no. 4 (417)

Coronas. . . . . Coronas (504)

Coronas Junior . . . . Cadetes (404)

Coronas Major . . . . Eminentes Mano (214, 714)

Coronas Mayor . . . . Mareva (421)

Coronas Minor . . . . Coronitas Mano (207, 707)

Coronas Minor . . . . Franciscanos (416)

Cristales. . . . . Cosacos (408)

Culebras . . . . Culebras (210)

El Prado . . . . Deliciosos Mano (212, 712)

Epicures . . . . Epicures Mano (215, 715)

Especiales . . . . Cremas Mano (208, 708)

Excepcionales Rothschild . . . . Perfectos Mano (292, 792)

Exquisitos . . . . Petit Coronas Mano (220, 720)

Glorias . . . . Epicures Mano (215, 715)

Grand Coronas . . . . Superiores (438)

Kings . . . . Petit Coronas Mano (220, 720)

Lonsdales . . . . Cervantes (503)

Magnum 46 . . . . Coronas Gordas (505)

Majestic. . . . . Cremas Mano (208, 708)

Medias Coronas . . . . Eminentes (214)

Medias Coronas . . . . Mareva (421)

Monarcas. . . . . Julieta 2 (609)

Monarchs. . . . . Julieta 2 (609)

Naturals . . . . Naturales Mano (217, 717)

Noellas . . . . Cosacos (408)

Petit Coronas . . . . Mareva (421)

Petit Palatinos. . . . . Cadetes (404)

Petit Upmann. . . . . Cadetes (404)

Petit Upmann. . . . . Petit Mano (218, 718)

Preciosas. . . . . Demi Tasse Mano (213, 713)

Regalias . . . . Petit Coronas Mano (220, 720)

Royal Coronas. Conservas Mano (206, 706)

Royal Coronas. . . . . Coronas (504)

Selección 303 . . . . Coronas (504)

Selección Suprema no. 11. . . . . Petit Coronas Mano (220, 720)

Selección Suprema no. 13 . . . . Cremas Mano (208, 708)

Selección Suprema no. 23. . . . . Ninfas (512)

Selección Suprema no. 25 . . . . Mareva (421)

Selección Suprema no. 30 . . . . Cervantes (503)

Short Coronas . . . . Cosacos (408)

Singulares . . . . Coronitas Mano (207, 707)

Sir Winston . . . . Julieta 2 (609)

Super Coronas. . . . . Coronas Gordas (505)

Upmann no. 1 . . . . Cervantes (503)

Upmann no. 2 . . . . Piramides (681)

Upmann no. 3 . . . . Coronas (504)

Upmann no. 4 . . . . Mareva (421)

Upmann no. 5 . . . . Perlas (432)

Production Vitolas

(Machine-made cigars are in *italic;* all others are handmade.)

BRAND	COMMERCIAL VITOLA

ALMUERZOS (401)
Cepo: 40   Diameter: ⅝ in. (15.87 mm)
Length: 5⅛ in. (130 mm)   Weight: 7.52 g

Hoyo de Monterrey	Le Hoyo du Prince

BELVEDERES (*290, 790*)
Cepo: 39   Diameter: ⅝ in. (15.48 mm)
Length: 4¹⁵⁄₁₆ in. (125 mm)   Weight: 6.21 g

Belinda	Belvederes
Bolívar	Belvederes
Cabañas	Belvederes
La Corona	Belvederes
La Escepción	Belvederes
Partagás	Belvederes
Partagás	Habaneros
Por Larrañaga	*Belvederes*
Punch	Belvederes
Ramón Allones	Belvederes
Romeo y Julieta	Belvederes
Romeo y Julieta	Favoritas
Romeo y Julieta	Regalias de la Habana
H. Upman	Belvederes

BRITANICAS (481)
Cepo: 46   Diameter: ¾ in. (18.26 mm)
Length: 5⁷⁄₁₆ in. (137 mm)   Weight: 9.34 g

Romeo y Julieta	Celestiales Finos

CADETES (404)
Cepo: 36   Diameter: ⅝ in. (14.29 mm)
Length: 4⁹⁄₁₆ in. (115 mm)   Weight: 5.34 g

Fonseca	Kdt Cadetes
H. Upmann	Coronas Junior
H. Upmann	Petit Palatinos
H. Upmann	Petit Upmann

CAMPANAS (581)
Cepo: 52   Diameter: ⅞ in. (20.64 mm)
Length: 5½ in. (140 mm)   Weight: 12.37 g

Bolívar	Belicosos Finos
Romeo y Julieta	Belicosos
Sancho Panza	Belicosos

CARLOTAS (501)
Cepo: 35   Diameter: ⁹⁄₁₆ in. (13.89 mm)
Length: 5¹¹⁄₁₆ in. (143 mm)   Weight: 6.26 g

Hoyo de Monterrey	Jeanne D'Arc
Partagás	Charlottes
Partagás	Série du Connaisseur no. 3
Rey del Mundo	Isabel

CAROLINAS (405)
Cepo: 26   Diameter: ⁷⁄₁₆ in. (10.32 mm)
Length: 4¹³⁄₁₆ in. (121 mm)   Weight: 2.94 g

Hoyo de Monterrey	Margaritas
Partagás	Ramonitas
Punch	Margaritas
Ramón Allones	Ramonitas

CAZADORES (406)
Cepo: 44   Diameter: ¹¹⁄₁₆ in. (17.46 mm)
Length: 6⁷⁄₁₆ in. (162 mm)   Weight: 11.27 g

Fonseca	Fonseca no. 1
La Escepción	Cazadores
Romeo y Julieta	Cazadores

Cervantes (503)

Cepo: 42   Diameter: $^{11}/_{16}$ in. (16.67 mm)
Length: 6$^1/_2$ in. (165 mm)   Weight: 10.47 g

Bolívar . . . . Gold Medal
Bolívar . . . . Lonsdales
Diplomaticos . . . . Diplomaticos no. 1
Dunhill . . . . Malecón
La Gloria Cubana . . . . Cetros
Montecristo . . . . Dunhill Selección Suprema no. 1
Montecristo . . . . Montecristo no. 1
Nueva Marca . . . . no. 1
Partagás . . . . Lonsdales
Por Larrañaga . . . . Lonsdales
Quintero . . . . Churchills
Rafaël Gonzales . . . . Lonsdales
Rey del Mundo . . . . Lonsdales
Romeo y Julieta . . . . Cedros De Luxe no. 1
Romeo y Julieta . . . . Dunhill Selección Suprema no. 1
San Luis Rey . . . . Coronas
San Luis Rey . . . . Lonsdales
Sancho Panza . . . . Dorados
Sancho Panza . . . . Molinos
H. Upmann . . . . Cinco Bocas
H. Upmann . . . . Lonsdales
H. Upmann . . . . Selección Suprema no. 30
H. Upmann . . . . Upmann no. 1

Chicos (261, 761)

Cepo: 29   Diameter: $^1/_2$ in. (11.51 mm)
Length: 4$^3/_{16}$ in. (106 mm)   Weight: 3.00 g

Bolívar . . . . Chicos
Cabañas . . . . *Coronitas*
Caney . . . . Canape
Cifuentes . . . . Cubanitos
Cifuentes . . . . Habanitos
Dunhill . . . . *Chico Minor Mano*
Dunhill . . . . *Chicola Minor Mano*
Dunhill . . . . *Chicos Mano*
La Corona . . . . Coronitas
Partagás . . . . Bonitos Extra Mild
Partagás . . . . Chicos
Por Larrañaga . . . . Curritos
Por Larrañaga . . . . Juanitos
Punch . . . . Cigarillos
Quintero . . . . Puritos
Ramón Allones . . . . Bits of Havana
Rey del Mundo . . . . Variedades
Romeo y Julieta . . . . *Chicos*
San Luis Rey . . . . *Mini-Habanos Mano*

Conchitas (205, 705)

Cepo: 35   Diameter: $^9/_{16}$ in. (13.89 mm)
Length: 5$^1/_{16}$ in. (127 mm)   Weight: 5.29 g

Bolívar . . . . Panatelas
La Corona . . . . Panatelas
Partagás . . . . Panatelas
Partagás . . . . Princess
Ramón Allones . . . . *Dunhill Selección Suprema no. 622*
Ramón Allones . . . . Panatelas

Conservas (206, 706)

Cepo: 44   Diameter: $^{11}/_{16}$ in. (17.46 mm)
Length: 5$^3/_4$ in. (145 mm)   Weight: 9.57 g

Cifuentes . . . . Cristal Tubo
Hoyo de Monterrey . . . . *Humidor no. 1*
Hoyo de Monterrey . . . . Royal Coronations
Punch . . . . Royal Coronations
H. Upmann . . . . Royal Coronas

Coronas (504)

Cepo: 42   Diameter: $^{11}/_{16}$ in. (16.67 mm)
Length: 5$^5/_8$ in. (142 mm)   Weight: 8.97 g

Bolívar . . . . Bolívar Tubos no. 1
Bolívar . . . . Coronas
Cohiba . . . . Coronas
Diplomaticos . . . . Diplomaticos no. 3
Dunhill . . . . Mojito
Gispert . . . . Coronas
Hoyo de Monterrey . . . . Hoyo Coronas
Hoyo de Monterrey . . . . Le Hoyo du Roi
Hoyo de Monterrey . . . . Opéra
Hoyo de Monterrey . . . . Royal Coronations
Juan Lopez . . . . Coronas
Montecristo . . . . Dunhill Selección Suprema no. 3
Montecristo . . . . Montecristo no. 3
Nueva Marca . . . . no. 3
Partagás . . . . Coronas
Partagás . . . . Coronas "A" Mejorado
Partagás . . . . Privados
Por Larrañaga . . . . Coronas
Por Larrañaga . . . . Lanceros
Punch . . . . Coronas
Punch . . . . Royal Coronations
Quai d'Orsay . . . . Coronas Claro
Quai d'Orsay . . . . Coronas Claro Claro
Quintero . . . . Coronas
Quintero . . . . Coronas Selectas
Ramón Allones 8-9-8
Ramón Allones . . . . Coronas
Rey del Mundo . . . . Coronas De Luxe
Rey del Mundo . . . . Tubo no. 1
Romeo y Julieta . . . . Cedros de Luxe no. 2
Romeo y Julieta . . . . Coronas
Romeo y Julieta . . . . Dunhill Selección Suprema no. 2
Romeo y Julieta . . . . Romeo no. 1 De Luxe
San Luis Rey . . . . Coronas
Sancho Panza . . . . Coronas
Sancho Panza . . . . Tronquitos
H. Upmann . . . . Coronas
H. Upmann . . . . Royal Coronas
H. Upmann . . . . Selección 303
H. Upmann . . . . Upmann no. 3

CORONAS GORDAS (505)

Cepo: 42   Diameter: $^{11}/_{16}$ in. (16.67 mm)

Length: $5^{11}/_{16}$ in. (143 mm)   Weight: 10.90 g

Cohiba . . . . Siglo IV
Hoyo de Monterrey. . . . . Epicure no. 1
Juan Lopez. . . . . Selección no. 1
La Flor de Cano. . . . . Gran Corona
Punch. . . . . Black Prince
Punch . . . . Nectares no. 2
Punch. . . . . Punch Punch
Punch . . . . Royal Selection no. 11
Punch. . . . . Selección De Luxe no. 1
Punch . . . . Super Selection no. 2
Rafaël Gonzales . . . . Coronas Extra
Rey del Mundo . . . . Gran Corona
Romeo y Julieta . . . . Exhibición no. 3
San Luis Rey . . . . Serie A
H. Upmann. . . . . Magnum 46
H. Upmann . . . . Super Coronas

CORONAS GRANDES (506)

Cepo: 42   Diameter: $^{11}/_{16}$ in. (16.67 mm)

Length: $6^1/_8$ in. (155 mm)   Weight: 9.89 g

Cohiba . . . . Siglo III
Dunhill . . . . Tubos
Hoyo de Monterrey . . . . Le Hoyo des Dieux
Hoyo de Monterrey. Super Selection no. 1
La Gloria Cubana. . . . . Sabrosos
Montecristo. . . . . Dunhill Selección Suprema Tubos
Montecristo . . . . Montecristo Tubos
Nueva Marca . . . . Tubos
Partagás. 8-9-8
Partagás . . . . Coronas Grandes
Punch. . . . . Super Selection no. 1
Quai d'Orsay. . . . . Gran Corona
Romeo y Julieta. . . . . Coronas Grandes

CORONITAS (207, 707)

Cepo: 40   Diameter: $^5/_8$ in. (15.87 mm)

Length: $4^5/_8$ in. (117 mm)   Weight: 6.35 g

Belinda . . . . *Superfinos*
Cabañas. . . . . *Superfinos*
Hoyo de Monterrey. Petit Coronations
La Escepción . . . . *Superfinos*
Partagás . . . . Coronas Junoir
Partagás . . . . Regalias de la Reina Bueno
Punch. . . . . Petit Coronations
Romeo y Julieta. . . . . Clarines
Romeo y Julieta. . . . . Regalias de Londres
Romeo y Julieta . . . . Romeo no. 3
H. Upmann . . . . Aromaticos
H. Upmann . . . . Coronas Minor
H. Upmann . . . . Singulares

COSACOS (408)

Cepo: 42   Diameter: $^{11}/_{16}$ in. (16.67 mm)

Length: $5^3/_8$ in. (135 mm)   Weight: 8.56 g

Fonseca . . . . Cosacos
La Gloria Cubana. . . . . Tapados
Montecristo . . . . Montecristo B
Partagás . . . . Astorias
Punch. . . . . Nacionales
Ramón Allones . . . . Dunhill Selección Suprema no. 280
Romeo y Julieta. . . . . Nacionales
H. Upmann . . . . Cristales
H. Upmann . . . . Noellas
H. Upmann . . . . Short Coronas

CREMAS (*208, 708*)

Cepo: 40   Diameter: $^5/_8$ in. (15.87 mm)

Length: $5^9/_{16}$ in. (140 mm)   Weight: 7.64 g

Belinda . . . . *Coronas*
Bolívar. . . . . Champions
Hoyo de Monterrey . . . . Palmas Extra
La Corona . . . . Coronas
Partagás . . . . Partagás De Luxe
Partagás . . . . Super Partagás
Punch . . . . Palmas Reales
Ramón Allones . . . . Dunhill Selección Suprema no. 82
Ramón Allones . . . . Ramondos
Romeo y Julieta . . . . Romeo no. 1
H. Upmann . . . . Especiales
H. Upmann. . . . . Majestic
H. Upmann . . . . Selección Suprema no. 13

CRISTALES (*271, 771*)

Cepo: 41   Diameter: $^{11}/_{16}$ in. (16.27 mm)

Length: $5^{15}/_{16}$ in. (150 mm)   Weight: 8.97 g

La Flor de Cano . . . . Selectos

CULEBRAS (*210, 710*)

Cepo: 39   Diameter: $^5/_8$ in. (15.48 mm)

Length: $5^{13}/_{16}$ in. (146 mm)   Weight: 6.67 g

Caney. . . . . *Especiales*
Partagás. . . . . Culebras
Romeo y Julieta . . . . *Culebras*
H. Upmann . . . . *Culebras*

DALIAS (507)

Cepo: 43   Diameter: $^{11}/_{16}$ in. (17.07 mm)

Length: $6^3/_4$ in. (170 mm)   Weight: 11.32 g

Bolívar. . . . . Immensas
Cohiba. . . . . Siglo V
La Gloria Cubanav. Medaille d'Or no. 2
Nueva Marca. 8-9-8
Partagás. 8-9-8
Partagás . . . . Partagás de Partagás no. 1
Partagás . . . . Selección Privada no. 1
Ramón Allones 8-9-8

DELICADOS (604)

Cepo: 38   Diameter: 5/8 in. (15.08 mm)

Length: 7 9/16 in. (192 mm)   Weight: 10.03 g

Bolívar . . . . Especiales

Maria Guerrero . . . . Grandes de España

Partagás . . . . Série du Connaisseur no. 1

Rey del Mundo . . . . Grandes de España

DELICADOS EXTRA (605)

Cepo: 36   Diameter: 5/8 in. (14.29 mm)

Length: 7 5/16 in. (185 mm)   Weight: 8.56 g

La Gloria Cubana . . . . Médaille d'Or no. 1

DELICIOSOS (212, 712)

Cepo: 35   Diameter: 9/16 in. (13.89 mm)

Length: 6 5/16 in. (159 mm)   Weight: 6.67 g

Por Larrañaga . . . . Largos de Larrañaga

Por Larrañaga . . . . Montecarlos

H. Upmann . . . . El Prado

DEMI TASSE (213, 713)

Cepo: 32   Diameter: 1/2 in. (12.70 mm)

Length: 4 in. (100 mm)   Weight: 3.50 g

Belinda . . . . *Demitasse*

Belinda . . . . *Preciosas*

La Corona . . . . Demitasse

H. Upmann . . . . Preciosas

DEMI TIP (262, 762)

Cepo: 29   Diameter: 1/2 in. (11.51 mm)

Length: 5 in. (126 mm)   Weight: 3.68 g

Cifuentes . . . . Emboquillados no. 5

Partagás . . . . Demi Tip

EMINENTES (214, 714)

Cepo: 44   Diameter: 11/16 in. (17.46 mm)

Length: 5 1/4 in. (132 mm)   Weight: 8.74 g

Bolívar . . . . Petit Coronas Especiales

Partagás . . . . Coronas Senior

Partagás . . . . Eminentes

Partagás . . . . Petit Coronas Especiales

Partagás . . . . Petit Coronas Tubos

H. Upmann . . . . Coronas Major

H. Upmann . . . . *Medias Coronas*

ENTREACTOS (412)

Cepo: 30   Diameter: 1/2 in. (11.91 mm)

Length: 4 in. (100 mm)   Weight: 3.27 g

Bolívar . . . . Demi Tasse

Dunhill . . . . Demi Tasse

Hoyo de Monterrey . . . . Le Hoyo du Maire

Rafaël Gonzalez . . . . Demi Tasse

Rey del Mundo . . . . Demi Tasse

Romeo y Julieta . . . . Petit Julietas

EPICURES (215, 715)

Cepo: 35   Diameter: 9/16 in. (13.89 mm)

Length: 4 3/8 in. (110 mm)   Weight: 4.60 g

Belinda . . . . *Petit Princess*

Belinda . . . . Princess

H. Upmann . . . . Epicures

H. Upmann . . . . Glorias

ESPECIALES (582)

Cepo: 45   Diameter: 3/4 in. (17.86 mm)

Length: 5 15/16 in. (134 mm)   Weight: 8.63 g

Fonseca . . . . Invictos

FRANCISCANOS (416)

Cepo: 40   Diameter: 5/8 in. (15.87 mm)

Length: 4 5/8 in. (116 mm)   Weight: 6.72 g

Dunhill . . . . Supremas

Hoyo de Monterrey . . . . Petit Coronations

Juan Lopez . . . . Patricias

La Gloria Cubana . . . . Minutos

Partagás . . . . Très Petit Coronas

Por Larrañaga . . . . Small Coronas

Punch . . . . Nectares no. 4

Punch . . . . Petit Coronation

Rafaël Gonzales . . . . Très Petit Lonsdales

Rey del Mundo . . . . Lunch Club

Rey del Mundo . . . . Tubo no.3

Romeo y Julieta . . . . Julietas

Romeo y Julieta . . . . Romeo no. 3 De Luxe

Romeo y Julieta . . . . Très Petit Coronas

Sancho Panza . . . . Bachilleres

H. Upmann . . . . Coronas Minor

FRANCISCOS (508)

Cepo: 44   Diameter: 11/16 in. (17.46 mm)

Length: 5 11/16 in. (143 mm)   Weight: 9.94 g

Bolívar . . . . Amado Selección C

Bolívar . . . . Coronas Extra

GRAN CORONA (607)

Cepo: 47   Diameter: 3/4 in. (18.65 mm)

Length: 9 1/4 in. (235 mm)   Weight: 18.63 g

Cifuentes . . . . Super Estupendos

Dunhill . . . . Havana Club

Hoyo de Monterrey . . . . Particulares

Montecristo . . . . Montecristo A

Punch . . . . Diademas Extra

Romeo y Julieta . . . . Sanchos

Sancho Panza . . . . Sanchos

HERMOSOS NO. 4 (417)

Cepo: 48   Diameter: 3/4 in. (19.05 mm)

Length: 5 1/16 in. (127 mm)   Weight: 10.47 g

Rey del Mundo . . . . Choix Suprême

Rey del Mundo . . . . Fox Selection no. 47

Romeo y Julieta . . . . Exhibición no. 4

San Luis Rey . . . . Regios

H. Upmann . . . . Connaisseur no. 1

INFANTES (*291, 791*)

Cepo: 37   Diameter: ⅝ in. (14.68 mm)

Length: 3¹⁵⁄₁₆ in. (98 mm)   Weight: 4.03 g

Cabañas . . . . Chiquitos
Cifuentes . . . . Petit Bouquets
Partagás . . . . Petit Bouquets

JULIETA 2 (*609*)

Cepo: 47   Diameter: ¾ in. (18.65 mm)

Length: 7 in. (178 mm)   Weight: 14.08 g

Bolívar . . . . Churchills
Bolívar . . . . Coronas Gigantes
Bolívar . . . . Supremas Churchills
Cohiba . . . . Esplendidos
Dunhill . . . . Estupendos
Hoyo de Monterrey . . . . Churchills
Hoyo de Monterrey . . . . Concorde
La Flor de Cano . . . . Diademas
La Gloria Cubana . . . . Tainos
Partagás . . . . Churchills De Luxe
Punch . . . . Churchills
Punch . . . . Monarcas
Quai d'Orsay . . . . Imperiales
Rey del Mundo . . . . Tainos
Romeo y Julieta . . . . Churchills
Romeo y Julieta . . . . Clemenceau
Romeo y Julieta . . . . Dunhill Selección Suprema no. 620
Romeo y Julieta . . . . Prince of Wales
San Luis Rey . . . . Churchills
Sancho Panza . . . . Coronas Gigantes
H. Upmann . . . . Monarcas
H. Upmann . . . . Monarchs
H. Upmann . . . . Sir Winston

LONDRES (420)

Cepo: 40   Diameter: ⅝ in. (15.87 mm)

Length: 5 in. (126 mm)   Weight: 7.29 g

Bolívar . . . . Bonitas
Partagás . . . . Royales
Punch . . . . S/N (Rayados)
Punch . . . . Souvenir de Luxe
Quintero . . . . Medias Coronas
Quintero . . . . Medias Coronas Selectas

MAREVAS (421)

Cepo: 42   Diameter: ¹¹⁄₁₆ in. (16.67 mm)

Length: 5⅛ in. (129 mm)   Weight: 8.14 g

Bolívar . . . . Bolívar Tubos no. 2
Bolívar . . . . Petit Coronas
Cohiba . . . . Siglo II
Diplomaticos . . . . Diplomaticos no. 4
Dunhill . . . . Varadero
Gispert . . . . Petit Coronas De Luxe
Hoyo de Monterrey . . . . Coronations
Hoyo de Monterrey . . . . Short Hoyo Coronas
Juan Lopez . . . . Petit Coronas
La Flor de Cano . . . . Coronas
Montecristo . . . . Dunhill Selección Suprema no. 4
Montecristo . . . . Montecristo no. 4

Montecristo . . . . Petit Tubos
Nueva Marca . . . . no. 4
Partagás . . . . Petit Coronas
Partagás . . . . Petit Privados
Por Larrañaga . . . . Dunhill Selección Suprema no. 32
Por Larrañaga . . . . Petit Coronas
Por Larrañaga . . . . Petit Lanceros
Punch . . . . Coronations
Punch . . . . Petit Coronas del Punch
Punch . . . . Petit Coronas del Punch Ones
Punch . . . . Presidentes
Punch . . . . Royal Selection no. 12
Punch . . . . Selección De Luxe no. 2
Rafaël Gonzalez . . . . Petit Coronas
Rafaël Gonzalez . . . . Petit Lonsdales
Ramón Allones . . . . Petit Coronas
Rey del Mundo . . . . Petit Coronas
Rey del Mundo . . . . Petit Lonsdales
Rey del Mundo . . . . Tubo no. 2
Romeo y Julieta . . . . Cedros De Luxe no. 3
Romeo y Julieta . . . . Club Kings
Romeo y Julieta . . . . Dunhill Selección Suprema no. 3
Romeo y Julieta . . . . Petit Coronas
Romeo y Julieta . . . . Plateados de Romeo
Romeo y Julieta . . . . Romeo no. 2 De Luxe
San Luis Rey . . . . Petit Coronas
Sancho Panza . . . . Non Plus
H. Upmann . . . . Coronas Mayor
H. Upmann . . . . Medias Coronas
H. Upmann . . . . Petit Coronas
H. Upmann . . . . Selección Suprema no. 25
H. Upmann . . . . Upmann no. 4

MINUTOS (423)

Cepo: 42   Diameter: ¹¹⁄₁₆ in. (16.67 mm)

Length: 4⅜ in. (110 mm)   Weight: 6.97 g

Bolívar . . . . Amado Selección G
Bolívar . . . . Coronas Junior
Partagás . . . . Half Coronas
Partagás . . . . Partagás Pride
Partagás . . . . Selección Fox no. 7
Partagás . . . . Shorts
Punch . . . . Très Petit Coronas
Ramón Allones . . . . Small Club Coronas

NACIONALES (*272, 772*)

Cepo: 40   Diameter: ⅝ in. (15.87 mm)

Length: 5⁹⁄₁₆ in. (140 mm)   Weight: 8.28 g

Caney . . . . Selectos
Quintero . . . . Brevas
Quintero . . . . Nacionales
Statos de Luxe . . . . Brevas
Statos de Luxe . . . . Cremas
Statos de Luxe . . . . Selectos

NATURALES (217, 717)

Cepo: 37   Diameter: $5/8$ in. (14.68 mm)
Length: $6\,1/8$ in. (155 mm)   Weight: 7.25 g
H. Upmann . . . . Naturals

NINFAS (512)

Cepo: 33   Diameter: $9/16$ in. (13.10 mm)
Length: $7\,1/16$ in. (178 mm)   Weight: 6.97 g
Bolívar . . . . Palmas
Hoyo de Monterrey . . . . Longos
La Escepción . . . . Longos
Partagás . . . . Palmas Grandes
Punch . . . . Nectares no. 5
Punch . . . . Ninfas
Punch . . . . Panatelas Grandes
Quai d'Orsay . . . . Panatelas
Romeo y Julieta . . . . Palmas Reales
H. Upmann . . . . Selección Suprema no. 23

NUMERO 1 (611)

Cepo: 38   Diameter: $5/8$ in. (15.08 mm)
Length: $7\,5/8$ in. (192 mm)   Weight: 10.03 g
Cohiba . . . . Lanceros
Diplomaticos . . . . Diplomaticos no. 6
Montecristo . . . . Dunhill Especial
Montecristo . . . . Montecristo Especial
Nueva Marca . . . . Especiales

NUMERO 2 (513)

Cepo: 38   Diameter: $5/8$ in. (15.08 mm)
Length: 6 in. (152 mm)   Weight: 7.87 g
Cohiba . . . . Coronas Especiales
Diplomaticos . . . . Diplomaticos no. 7
Hoyo de Monterrey . . . . Le Hoyo du Dauphin
Hoyo de Monterrey . . . . Odéon
Montecristo . . . . Montecristo Especial no. 2
Nueva Marca . . . . Especial no. 2
Siboney . . . . Especiales

NUMERO 3 (428)

Cepo: 26   Diameter: $7/16$ in. (10.32 mm)
Length: $4\,9/16$ in. (115 mm)   Weight: 2.81 g
Cohiba . . . . Panetelas
Montecristo . . . . Joyitas
Nueva Marca . . . . Joyitas
Por Larrañaga . . . . Eduardos
Rafaël Gonzalez . . . . Cigarritos
Rey del Mundo . . . . Señoritas

PALMAS (514)

Cepo: 33   Diameter: $9/16$ in. (13.10 mm)
Length: $6\,3/4$ in. (170 mm)   Weight: 6.65 g
Hoyo de Monterrey . . . . Le Hoyo du Gourmet
Hoyo de Monterrey . . . . Versailles

PALMITAS (430)

Cepo: 32   Diameter: $1/2$ in. (12.70 mm)
Length: 6 in. (152 mm)   Weight: 5.52 g
La Gloria Cubana . . . . Médaille d'Or no. 4
Ramón Allones . . . . Palmitas

PANETELAS (431)

Cepo: 34   Diameter: $9/16$ in. (13.49 mm)
Length: $4\,5/8$ in. (117 mm)   Weight: 4.85 g
Por Larrañaga . . . . Coronitas
Punch . . . . Coronets
Punch . . . . Panetelas
Punch . . . . Punchinellos
Rafaël Gonzalez . . . . Panetelas
Romeo y Julieta . . . . Panetelas

PANETELAS LARGAS (515)

Cepo: 28   Diameter: $7/16$ in. (11.11 mm)
Length: $6\,15/16$ in. (175 mm)   Weight: 4.95 g
Dunhill . . . . Atados
La Gloria Cubana . . . . Medaille d'Or no. 3
Montecristo . . . . Montecristo no. 7
Rafaël Gonzalez . . . . Slenderellas
Rey del Mundo . . . . Elegantes
Rey del Mundo . . . . Panetelas Largas
Romeo y Julieta . . . . Shakespeare

PAREJOS (516)

Cepo: 38   Diameter: $5/8$ in. (15.08 mm)
Length: $6\,9/16$ in. (166 mm)   Weight: 8.60 g
Partagás . . . . Serie du Connaisseur no. 2

PERFECTOS (292, 792)

Cepo: 44   Diameter: $11/16$ in. (17.46 mm)
Length: $5\,1/16$ in. (127 mm)   Weight: 7.36 g
Cabañas . . . . Perfectos
H. Upmann . . . . Excepcionales Rothschild
La Corona . . . . Perfectos
La Escepción . . . . Perfectos
Partagás . . . . Perfectos
Romeo y Julieta . . . . Perfectos

PERLAS (432)

Cepo: 40   Diameter: $5/8$ in. (15.87 mm)
Length: $4\,1/16$ in. (102 mm)   Weight: 5.91 g
Cohiba . . . . Siglo I
Diplomaticos . . . . Diplomaticos no. 5
Montecristo . . . . Dunhill Selección Suprema no. 5
Montecristo . . . . Montecristo no. 5
Nueva Marca . . . . no. 5
Punch . . . . Petit Punch
Punch . . . . Petit Punch De Luxe
Romeo y Julieta . . . . Petit Princess
H. Upmann . . . . Upmann no. 5

PETIT (*218*, 718)

Cepo: 31   Diameter: $^{1}/_{2}$ in. (12.30 mm)

Length: $4^{5}/_{16}$ in. (108 mm)   Weight: 3.57 g

Belinda . . . . *Petit*

La Corona . . . . Petit

H. Upmann . . . . Petit Upmann

PETIT CETROS (*219*, 719)

Cepo: 40   Diameter: $^{5}/_{8}$ in. (15.87 mm)

Length: $5^{1}/_{8}$ in. (129 mm)   Weight: 7.04 g

Hoyo de Monterrey . . . . Exquisitos

La Corona . . . . Petit Cetros

Partagás . . . . Aristocrats

Partagás . . . . Capitols

Partagás . . . . Londres en Cedro

Partagás . . . . Londres Extra

Partagás . . . . Londres Finos

Partagás . . . . Parisianos

Partagás . . . . Personales

Partagás . . . . Petit Partagás

Punch . . . . Exquisitos

Ramón Allones . . . . Dunhill Selección Suprema no. 11

Romeo y Julieta . . . . Coronitas

Romeo y Julieta . . . . Coronitas en Cedro

Romeo y Julieta . . . . *Dunhill Selección Suprema no. 11*

Romeo y Julieta . . . . Exquisitos

Romeo y Julieta . . . . Plateados de Romeo

PETIT CORONAS (220, 720)

Cepo: 42   Diameter: $^{11}/_{16}$ in. (16.67 mm)

Length: $5^{1}/_{8}$ in. (129 mm)   Weight: 7.77 g

Belinda . . . . Petit Coronas

Hoyo de Monterrey . . . . Coronations

Hoyo de Monterrey . . . . Souvenir de Luxe

La Corona . . . . *Petit Coronas*

Partagás . . . . Mille Fleurs

Por Larrañaga . . . . Lolas en Cedro

Punch . . . . Coronations

Punch . . . . Souvenir de Luxe

Ramón Allones . . . . Mille Fleurs

Romeo y Julieta . . . . Club Kings

Romeo y Julieta . . . . Excepcionales

Romeo y Julieta . . . . Mille Fleurs

Romeo y Julieta . . . . Romeo no. 2

H. Upmann . . . . Aromaticos

H. Upmann . . . . Exquisitos

H. Upmann . . . . Kings

H. Upmann . . . . Regalias

H. Upmann . . . . Selección Suprema no. 11

PIRAMIDES (681)

Cepo: 52   Diameter: $^{7}/_{8}$ in. (20.64 mm)

Length: $6^{3}/_{16}$ in. (156 mm)   Weight: 12.19 g

Diplomaticos . . . . Diplomaticos no. 2

Dunhill . . . . Abajo

Montecristo . . . . Dunhill Selección Suprema no. 2

Montecristo . . . . Montecristo no. 2

Nueva Marca . . . . no. 2

H. Upmann . . . . Upmann no. 2

PLACERAS (433)

Cepo: 34   Diameter: $^{9}/_{16}$ in. (13.49 mm)

Length: $4^{15}/_{16}$ in. (125 mm)   Weight: 5.22 g

Bolívar . . . . Bolívar Tubos no. 3

Bolívar . . . . Regentes

Dunhill . . . . Princess

Juan Lopez . . . . Panetela Superba

Partagás . . . . Cubanos

Partagás . . . . Dunhill Selección Suprema no. 151

Partagás . . . . Filipos

Partagás . . . . Selección Fox no. 11

PREFERIDOS (*264*, 764)

Cepo: 38   Diameter: $^{5}/_{8}$ in. (15.08 mm)

Length: $5^{1}/_{16}$ in. (127 mm)   Weight: 7.02 g

Caney . . . . Vegueros

PROMINENTES (612)

Cepo: 49   Diameter: $^{13}/_{16}$ in. (19.45 mm)

Length: $7^{11}/_{16}$ in. (194 mm)   Weight: 16.70 g

Hoyo de Monterrey . . . . Double Coronas

Partagás . . . . Lusitanias

Punch . . . . Double Coronas

Ramón Allones . . . . Gigantes

San Luis Rey . . . . Double Coronas

ROBUSTOS (435)

Cepo: 50   Diameter: $^{13}/_{16}$ in. (19.84 mm)

Length: $4^{15}/_{16}$ in. (124 mm)   Weight: 11.18 g

Bolívar . . . . Amado Selección E

Bolívar . . . . Royal Coronas

Cohiba . . . . Robusto

Dunhill . . . . Cabinetta

Hoyo de Monterrey . . . . Epicure no. 2

Juan Lopez . . . . Selección no. 2

La Flor de Cano . . . . Short Churchill

Partagás . . . . Serie D no. 4

Ramón Allones . . . . Allones Specially Selected

SEOANES (517)

Cepo: 33   Diameter: $^{9}/_{16}$ in. (13.10 mm)

Length: 5 in. (126 mm)   Weight: 5.01 g

Cohiba . . . . Exquisitos

Montecristo . . . . Montecristo no. 6

SPORTS (224, 724)

Cepo: 35   Diameter: $^{9}/_{16}$ in. (13.89 mm)

Length: $4^{5}/_{8}$ in. (117 mm)   Weight: 4.88 g

Belinda . . . . Panetelas

Cabañas . . . . Suaves

Romeo y Julieta . . . . Panetelas

Romeo y Julieta . . . . Sport Largos

STANDARD (273, 773)
Cepo: 40   Diameter: ⅝ in. (15.87 mm)
Length: 4¹⁵/₁₆ in. (123 mm)   Weight: 6.90 g

Caney . . . . Predilectos
Fonseca . . . . Delicias
Gispert . . . . Habaneras no. 2
La Escepción . . . . Excepcionales
La Flor de Cano . . . . Petit Coronas
La Flor de Cano . . . . Predilectos Tubulares
Por Larrañaga . . . . Super Cedros
Quintero . . . . Londres
Quintero . . . . Londres Extra
Statos De Luxe . . . . Delirios
Statos De Luxe . . . . Dobles
Troya . . . . Coronas Club Tubulares

SUPERIORES (438)
Cepo: 40   Diameter: ⅝ in. (15.87 mm)
Length: 5¹³/₁₆ in. (146 mm)   Weight: 8.46 g

José L. Piedra . . . . Superiores
Punch . . . . Gran Corona
H. Upmann . . . . Amatistas
H. Upmann . . . . Grand Coronas

TACOS (586)
Cepo: 47   Diameter: ¾ in. (18.65 mm)
Length: 6¼ in. (158 mm)   Weight: 10.79 g

Partagás . . . . Presidentes

TOPPERS (225, 725)
Cepo: 39   Diameter: ⅝ in. (15.48 mm)
Length: 6⁵/₁₆ in. (160 mm)   Weight: 8.33 g

Partagás . . . . Toppers
Ramón Allones . . . . Delgados
Ramón Allones . . . . Dunhill Selección Suprema no. 81
Ramón Allones . . . . Toppers
Romeo y Julieta . . . . Montagues

TRABUCOS (439)
Cepo: 38   Diameter: ⅝ in. (15.08 mm)
Length: 4 3⁄8 in. (110 mm)   Weight: 5.66 g

Hoyo de Monterrey . . . . Le Hoyo du Député

UNIVERSALES (270, 770)
Cepo: 38   Diameter: ⅝ in. (15.08 mm)
Length: 5⁵/₁₆ in. (134 mm)   Weight: 7.13 g

Troya . . . . Universales

VEGUERITOS (274, 774)
Cepo: 37   Diameter: ⅝ in. (14.68 mm)
Length: 5¹/₁₆ in. (127 mm)   Weight: 6.10 g

Caney . . . . Bouquets Finos
Caney . . . . Delgados
Cifuentes . . . . Vegueritos
La Flor de Cano . . . . Preferidos
Por Larrañaga . . . . Panetelas
Quintero . . . . Panetelas

A Few Legendary Brands

Montecristo, A COUNT AMONG CUBAN CIGARS

Toward the end of the nineteenth century a rich Spaniard living in New York brought over from Spain his nephew, Benjamín Menéndez García, to set him up in business. Hired by Cullman, the head of Philip Morris and General Cigar, Benjamín Menéndez was sent to Cuba and, with his brother Félix, took over the direction of the Pierra Company, which he refounded as Menéndez y Cía around 1913.

At the time, this thriving enterprise was not yet involved in cigar manufacturing strictly speaking, but the two brothers were successful in producing cigarettes and trading in cooking oil. In 1923, thanks to the arrival of Benjamín and Félix's uncle, Alonso Menéndez, and a renowned master cigar maker, Pepe García, the company tossed its hat in the cigar-smoke ring (as it were) and turned to cigar manufacturing, initially courting Cuban consumers.

Menéndez y Cía next bought out a brand that enjoyed a solid reputation, Particulares, and in 1935 launched a new brand for sale abroad, the Montecristo. Several versions of how the name was coined continue to circulate, including among them an attribution to Aléxandre Dumas's novel. The following year the venture was such a success the company sold Particulares in order to buy H. Upmann. Menéndez y Cía quickly became the most important cigar manufacturer in Havana, with 25 million cigars sold each year. Today, the Montecristo No. 4 is still the best-selling Havana in the world.

Partagás, THE BRAND THAT BOASTED A THOUSAND "VITOLAS"

Jaime Partagás owned a number of plantations in the Pinar del Río region. Opened in 1845, his cigar factory prospered, but Jaime was murdered in 1864. His son and successor José did not share his father's savvy at running the business, except to run it—rapidly—into the ground and bankruptcy.

Partagás was then bought up by José Bances, and subsequently, in 1900, by Ramón Cifuentes and José Fernández. The Cifuentes family formed a cigar empire in those days, with brands like La Intimidad and Ramón Allones. Driven from Cuba by the Socialist revolution, these industrialists emigrated to Florida and turned to trading in wrapper leaves. They launched a second Partagás brand with the backing of General Cigar, which explains the coexistence today of Partagás cigars made in both Cuba and the Dominican Republic.

Hoyo de Monterrey

The founders of this brand, which dates back to the early nineteenth century, were two Catalans, Miguel Jané y Gener and Juan Conill y Pi. Their first cigar business was called La Majagua. But the man to leave the greatest mark on this brand was José Gener, Miguel's nephew, who bought up several plantations and opened a raw tobacco trading company in Havana in 1831. It was an especially prosperous period because King Ferdinand VII of Spain had abolished the Spanish tobacco monopoly at this time.

Very authoritarian but also very effective, José Gener set up a cigar factory, La Escepción (for Excepción, a spelling error that has become famous), and married Panchita, a rich Cuban heiress. In 1867 he founded first José Gener y Miguel with his uncle, then José Gener y Cía with his brothers, and finally José Gener y Batet, which he directed alone. After his death in 1900, the company was sold to Ramón Fernández and Fernando Palicio, who transformed it into the basis of a new industrial conglomeration.

La Escepción and Hoyo de Monterrey cigars quickly became classics, personalized with the initials of the manufacturer's clients. Early in this century they began to appear in non-banded bundles: Hoyo des Dieux, Hoyo du Roi, Hoyo du Prince, and so on. Distributed for a time by Davidoff, this brand has maintained its prestige over the years, even in postrevolutionary Cuba.

Romeo y Julieta, THE CIGAR LOVERS' CIGAR

Founded in 1850, this brand eventually made a name for itself thanks to the unprecedented advertising campaign of the eccentric millionaire "Pepín" Fernández Rodríguez, who had bought up the manufacturer in 1903. Pepín handed out cigars at race tracks the world over, wherever his mare Julieta was running. Every puff of his free cigars became a free puff for his brand. Later he became famous for attempting to buy, though always unsuccessfully, the Capulet family's ancestral mansion in Verona. He eventually had to settle with opening a cigar shop there. Whatever Shakespeare might have thought, Romeo y Julieta cigars are among the best-loved Havanas in the world.

Punch, THE DYNAMIC BRAND

Inspired by the British humor magazine *Punch,* this manufacturer was founded by a German named Stockmann and counted a number of secondary brands for local consumption. Punch was an immediate hit with cigar enthusiasts and the happy owner sold his concern to other cigar makers. In 1875 Punch was in the hands of Buenaventura Parera and later, in 1884, became the property of Fernando López Fernández, the same cigar maker who was then head of Juan Valle y Cía. But it was in fact Manuel López, Fernando's brother, who ran Punch until his death in 1925 and had his name printed on the bands decorating the cigars. The stock market crash of 1929 and subsequent economic mess led to the merger of a great number of manufacturers, including Punch, under the direction of the Fernandez y Palicio group, although Punch cigars would continue to be produced right up to the revolution.

Cohiba, THE KING OF CIGARS

The father of the Cohiba brand, Eduardo Rivero, is still alive and continues to roll cigars in his *galera* in Havana. First engaged by a small manufacturer in Palma Soriano (Santiago province), he became a *torcedor* in 1957 at Por Larrañaga, whose product was famous then for its triple fermentation. With Castro's revolution Eduardo was conscripted and served for a few years, but he eventually returned to his position and *chaveta.* At this time, while respecting regulations, he started to roll for his own consumption, over and above his professional quotas, extraordinarily small cigars in an unheard-of *vitola* ($5/8$ inches in diameter and $7^1/2$ inches long [15×192 mm]) that gave off a very subtle aroma, the future Lanceros.

It was through Bienvenido "Chicho" Pérez, a friend of Eduardo's and the *líder máximo's* personal bodyguard, that Castro discovered the Lanceros and, won over by their taste, decided to launch their production in a new factory. The new cigar was named Cohiba, a reference to the tobacco ceremony practiced in pre-Columbian civilizations. The brand's emblem is a portrait of the brave Taino warrior Hatuey, who is seen as a precursor of Cuban independence. Cohiba remains the symbol of the Havana cigar industry's rebirth under Castro's regime.

Eduardo Rivero oversaw the top-secret foundation of this new manufacturer, just as he guaranteed the head of the Cuban revolution his own personal supply of cigars, naturally under wraps as well. Carried out by a small team of workers, production of the Cohiba held to one guiding principle only, quality: from the selection of the *vegas,* to the excellence of the leaves, to the strict control of the fermentation process. Aficionados recognize Eduardo Rivero's cigars by their signal light wrappers. The manufacturer took the name El Laguito and initially turned out cigars in three *vitolas,* lancero, corona especiales, and panatelas.

Following the Davidoff negotiations (1967–70), after which the El Laguito production was marketed under the Swiss cigar seller's name, Cubatabaco took over the direction of the manufacturer. Cohiba was sold directly by the state, beginning in 1982, as a way of defending the brand from the numerous counterfeit makes that had invaded the market. That decision marked the end of the manufacturer's collaboration with Davidoff, who lost exclusive rights to distributing Eduardo Rivero's cigars.

Other *vitolas* were introduced, filling out the range of Cohiba cigars: linea clasica in 1989, and the 1492 line to commemorate the five-hundredth anniversary of Columbus's landing in America.

Finally, it seems that El Laguito produces an exceptional vitola in absolute secrecy that has been baptized Trinidad. Asked about it in 1994, Castro himself admitted that he knew nothing of the super-secret cigar—and the question no doubt put the *líder máximo* in high dudgeon. Still, there is no proof that this phantom production has been curtailed.

Yesterday's Manufacturers, Today's Brands

*Since the 1940s some thirty manufacturers have disappeared;
now only a few brands carry on the tradition.*

Today there are nine cigar factories in Havana producing thirty-six brands. The different *vitolas* of a single brand may actually be rolled at several different factories. In 1940 there were forty cigar manufacturers (listed below) which turned out 309 different brands solely for markets abroad. Many of the names of these brands were borrowed from well-known operas like *La Tosca, La Traviata, Rigoletto,* and so on, or referred to famous writers such as Shakespeare and Victor Hugo, or simply proclaimed the supposed qualities of the cigar in question, for example *La Inmejorable* (cannot be improved), or *La Insuperable* (the invincible).

Brand names italicized below are still sold.

Name: Martinez y Cia.
Address: Calle Real no. 200, Marianoa, Habana, Cuba
Brands: Antilla Cubana / C. E. Beck y Cia. / Fine / Flor de Miramar / Frank Halls / Kings of Havana / La Devesa de Murias / La Feriada / La Flor de Dascall / La Flor de Pedro Miro y Cia. / La Flor de Zavo / La Imperiosa / La Ranesa / *Los Statos de Luxe* / Mapa Mundi / Ricoro / Santa Rosalia / Sol / *Troya*

Name: Fernandez, Palacio y Cia, S. en C.
Address: Maximo Gomez 51, Habana, Cuba
Brands: *Belinda* / El Vinyet / Flor de Fernandez Garcia / Gener / Gioconda / Gladstone Habanos / *Hoyo de Monterrey* / La Emperatriz de India / *La Escepcion* / La Gloria de Inglaterra / La Iberia / La Sin Par / Las Perlas / Palacio / *Punch* / Santa Felipa / Smart Set / Vuelta Abajo

Name: Por Larrañaga, Fabrica de tabacos S.A.
Address: Carlos III no. 713, Habana, Cuba
Brands: El Torcillo / Flor de Cimiente / Flor de Zavo / Habanos 1834 / La Atlanta / La Flor de Alvarez / La Gloria / La Legitimidad / Petronio / *Por Larrañaga*

Name: Calixto Lopez y Cia.
Address: Agramonte no. 702, Habana, Cuba
Brands: Calixto Lopez / Edèn / Flor de Lopez Hermanos / Francisco C. Banes / Lo Mejor / Lopez Hermanos / Los Reyes de Espagitimidad / Petron

Name: Menendez, Garcia y Cia. Ltda
Address: Virtudes no. 609, Habana, Cuba
Brands: El Patio / *H. Upmann* / *Monte Cristo* / Particulares

Name: Rey del Mundo Cigar Company
Address: Padre Varela no. 852, Habana, Cuba
Brands: Casamontez / Cuesta Rey / Don Candido / Don Ricardo / El Collado / El Uruguay / Fausto / Flor de Allones / Flor de Marqués / Flor de Milamores / *Flor de Rafael Gonzalez* / Fragus de Cuba / La Confederacion Suiza / La Seductiva / La Solera / *Rey del Mundo* / *Sancho Panza* / San Sebatian

Name: Romeo y Julieta, Fabrica de Tabacos S. A.
Address: Padre Valera no. 152, Habana, Cuba
Brands: Don Pepin / Falman / Flor de Rodriguez, Argüelles y Cia. / His Majesty / La Mar / *Maria Guerrero* / *Romeo y Julieta*

Name: Castañeda-Montero-Fonseca, S.A.
Address: Galiano no. 466, Habana, Cuba
Brands: Castañeda / El Genio / Filoteo / *Fonseca* / Hamlet / J. Montero y Cia. Lurline / Para Mi / Real Carmen / Rotario

Name: Fabrica de Tabacos F. Solaun, S. A.
Address: Figueras no. 106, Habana, Cuba
Brands: Baire / Boccacio / Figaro / Flor de Solaùn / La Nacional

Name: Cifuentes, Pego y Cia.
Address: Industria no. 529, Habana, Cuba
Brands: Caruncho / *Cifuentes* / Corojo / El Cambio Real / El Marqués de Caxias Flor de Alma / Flor de Caruncho / Flor de F. Pego Pita / Flor de P. Rabell Flor de Tabacos / Flor de Tabacos de Partagas y Cia. / Gayarre / La Eminencia / La Flor de J. A. Bances / La Inmejorable / La Insuperable / La Intimidad / La Lealtad / La Tropical / Marqués de Rabell / Mi Necha Modelo de Cuba / Nada Mas / Osceola / Partagas / Partagas & Co. / Partagas y Cia. / Prudencio Rabell / Rallones / *Ramon Allones*

Name: Zamora y Guerra.
Address: Gomez no. 810, Habana, Cuba
Brands: Belanza / Coranto / La Flor de Santa Gertruda / La Loma / La Noble Habana / Landsdown / La Zona / Lions / *Saint Luis Rey*

Name: Eduardo Suarez Murias y Cia.
Address: Luz no. 3, Arroyo Naranjo, Habana, Cuba
Brands: La Radiante / Reva

Name: Manuel Fernandez Argudin.
Address: Norte no. 25, Marianao, Habana, Cuba
Brands: Argudin / Esclava / La Cordialidad / Macabeus / Manuel Fernandez

Name: J. F. Rocha y Cia., S. en C.
Address: San Miguel no. 364, Habana, Cuba
Brands: *Bolivar* / Flor de Ambrosio / El Crepùsculo / La Gloria Cubana / *La Glorieta Cubana* / La Navarra / La Petenera / Nene

Name: Tabacalera Cubana, S. A.
Address: Agramonte no. 106, Habana, Cuba
Brands: A. de Villar y Villar / Antonio y Cleopatra / Arlington / Balmoral / Bock & Co / Cayos de San Felipe / Clara Maria / Cortina Mora / Cuba / Cubanola / Delmonico's / Don Quijote de la Macha / *Don Caba* / *Don Cabañas* / El Aguila de Oro / El Aguila Imperial / El Fénix / El Pueble / *El Siboney* / Estella / Eureka / Flor de Cortina / Flor de F. de P. Alvarez / Flor de Garcia / Flor de Gumersindo / Flor de J. S. Murias y Cia. / Flor de M. Lopez y Cia. / Flor de Monte Carlo / Flor de Pedro Roger / Flor de Segundo Alvarez / General R. E. Lee / Habana Club / Hamilton Club / H. de Cabañas y Carbajal / José Domingo / Joya de San Luis / Justicia al Mérito / Kathérine & Petruchio / La Africana / La Alhambra / La Antigüedad / La Aristocratica / La California / La Capitana / La Carolina / La Comercial / La Corona / La Coronilla / La Crema de Cuba / La Espa Alvarez / Flor de Garcia / Flor de Gumersindo / Flor de J. S. Murias y Cia. / Flor de M. Lopez y Cia. / Flor de Monte Carlo / Flor de Pedro Roger / Flor de Segundo Alvarez Meridiana / La Opulencia / La Paz de China / La Perfeccion / La Perla de Cuba / La Princesa de Gales / La Prominente / La Prosperidad / La Reina del Oriente / La Reserva / La Rosa Aromatica / La Rosa de Santiago / La Savoie / La Selecta / La Tosca / La Traviata / La Vencedora / La Ventana / La Virtud / L. Carbajal / Lincoln / Lords of England / Manuel Garcia Alonso / Manuel Lopez y Cia. / Pedro Murias y Ca. / Privilegio / Puck / Santa Damiana / Sheakespeare / The Derby / Victor Hugo / Waldorf / Waldorf Astoria / Walter Scott

Name: The Fernandez-Havana Cigar Co.
Address: Marti 64, Guanabacoa, Habana, Cuba
Brands: Amor de Cuba / Casco de Oro / Don Alfonso / El Bataclan / Flor de Todo / José Jiménez Pérez / La Bonita / La Democracia / Lord Beaconsfield / Mascota

Name: José L.Piedra
Address: Reina no. 404, Habana, Cuba
Brands: José L. Piedra / Ovalo Rojo / Piedra

Name: Lomez y Cia., S. en C.
Address: Maximo Gomez 466, Habana, Cuba
Brands: Casin / Flor de Lobeto

Name: Rogelio Cuervo y Aguirre
Address: E. Barnet no. 318, Habana, Cuba
Brands: La Diosa / Magnolia / Rigoletto

Name: B. Menendez y Hno.
Address: Habana no. 906, Habana, Cuba
Brands: El Rico Habano / Flor de R. Barcia / La Prueba

Name: C. del Peso y Cia.
Address: San Ignacio no. 314, Habana, Cuba
Brands: Flor de Juan Lopez / Flor de Tomas Gutiérrez / La Igualdad / Pierrot

Name: Pita Hnos.
Address: Estévez nos. 67 y 69, Habana, Cuba
Brands: Caribe / Pita / Pita Hnos

Name: Augustin Quintero y Cia.
Address: D'Clouet no. 16, Cienfuegos, Santa Clara, Cuba
Brands: El Cañon Rayado / La Riqueza / *Quintero y Hnos*

Name: Juan Cano Sainz
Address: Manrique no. 615, Habana, Cuba
Brands: Caracol / *La Flor de Cano* / La Rica Hoja / Trocadero

Name: Oliver y Hno.
Address: Segunda del Sur y Marti, Santa Clara, Cuba
Brands: La Cachimba / Oliver

Name: José Sixto Valdés
Address: Vélez Caviedes no. 34, Pinar del Rio, Cuba
Brand: Figueras

Name: Simon Vela Pelaez
Address: Juan del Haya s/n, Pinar del Rio, Cuba
Brands: *Gispert*

Name: Rodriguez, Montero y Cia
Address: Encarnacion no. 163, Santos Suarez, Habana, Cuba
Brands: El Trio / La Primavera

Name: Daniel Blanco y Cia
Address: San Miguel 463, Habana, Cuba
Brands: Konuko / Mundial

Name: Francisco Farach
Address: Marti no. 24, Caibarién, Santa Clara, Cuba
Brand: Flor de Farach

Name: Pardo, Hno. y Cia
Address: Serafines 164, Habana, Cuba
Brand: El Crédito

Name: Julio Gonzalez
Address: Salud no. 113, Habana, Cuba
Brand: Minerv

Name: Estrada y Cia., Soc. Ltda.
Address: Habana no. 66, Cienfuegos, Santa Clara, Cuba
Brand: Estrada

Name: Compañia Industrial Tabacalera S.A.
Address: Cuba no. 801, Habana, Cuba
Brands: Daiquiri / Eloisa / La Bayadera / Pirata / William

Name: C. Rivero Alvarez
Address: Calle 8 no. 92, Santiago de las Vegas, Provincia de La Habana, Cuba
Brands: Fedia / Mi Ideal / Santos Suarez

Name: Andrés Rodriguez Velazquez
Address: Ajiconal, barrio Paso Viejo, Pinar del Rio, Cuba
Brand: La Dulzura

Name: Manuel Hernandez Garcia
Address: Vélez Caviedes no. 55, Pinar de Rio, Cuba
Brand: El Campesino

Name: Roberts & Co.
Address: Neptuno no. 167, Habana, Cuba
Brands: Almendares / La Exportadora / Perla del Océano

Name: Gabino Campos Beltran
Address: 10 de Octubre no. 1255, Jesus del Monte, Habana, Cuba
Brand: Gabino Campos

Name: Desiderio M. Camacho
Address: Reparto Camacho s/n., Santa Clara, Cuba
Brand: La Flor de Lis

The Artisans Behind the Cigar

With know-how that has been transmitted from generation to generation over many years, the *tabacaleros* are individual links in a complex chain of operations. Three hundred and sixteen manipulations of the tobacco make up the indispensable steps that go into producing one Havana cigar. While the label *tabacalero* designates any employee of the cigar industry, most workers have an official title that is supposed to describe the task they fulfill. The names given below are arranged in chronological order following the process of creating the Havana cigar. Certain terms appearing more than once refer to the same task performed at different stages of production.

AGRICULTURAL PHASE

veguero Grows the tobacco.

semillerero Responsible for watering the *canteros*.

tendedor Spreads the cheesecloth coverings for the *zanqueros*.

zanquero Fixes the cheesecloth coverings in place over shade-grown tobacco.

recolector Responsible for harvesting the leaves.

sacador Carries the harvested leaves to the *llenador de cesto*.

llenador de cesto Checks the quality of the leaves and fills the baskets sent to the *casa de tabaco*.

cestero Transports the baskets of leaves to the *casa de tabaco*.

TREATMENT PHASE, *CASA DE TABACO*

descargador Unloads the baskets from the trucks.

ensartador Attaches the tobacco leaves at the base of their midrib to the drying bars.

zafador Unties the leaves from the drying bars.

curador Makes sure that drying and fermentation of the leaves takes place correctly.

engavillador Prepares the *gavillas,* i.e., the bunches of tobacco leaves.

manojeador Prepares the *manojos,* or hands of tobacco leaves, made up of four *gavillas*.

enterciador Packs the *manojos* in bundles for their journey to the *casa de escogida*.

TREATMENT PHASE, *CASA DE ESCOGIDA*

zafador Undoes the bunches of tobacco to enable workers to handle the leaves.

mojador Moistens tobacco leaves to avoid damage in handling.

rezagador Classifies the tobacco leaves by size, texture, and color.

revisador de tarea Supervises the *rezagador*'s work.

engavillador Prepares the *gavillas*.

manojeador Prepares the manojos of four *gavillas*.

enterciador Packs the *manojos* in bundles for their transfer to the manufacturer's storerooms.

dependiente Oversees the storerooms, regularly shifting the bales of tobacco around in order to aerate them and hinder fermentation.

TREATMENT PHASE, *CASA DE DESPALILLO*

zafador Undoes the *sol ensartado* leaves and moistens them for stripping.

despalillador Removes part of the leaf's midrib.

engavillador Prepares the *gavillas*.

manojeador Prepares the *manojos*.

enterciador Packs the *manojos* in bundles for their transfer to the manufacturer's storerooms.

dependiente Oversees the storerooms, regularly shifting the bales of tobacco around in order to aerate them and hinder fermentation.

ASSEMBLY PHASE, THE HAVANA MANUFACTURER

zafador Unties the bunches of leaves for moistening.

mojador Moistens tobacco leaves to avoid damage in handling.

sacudidor Shakes the moistened leaves to eliminate excess water.

despalillador Removes the midrib of wrapper leaves.

rezagador Classifies wrapper leaves by size and color.

ligador Prepares the *ligas,* i.e., the filler leaves that make up the body of the cigar.

torcedor Rolls the cigars. Cigar manufacturers have their own school for training workers to roll cigars correctly. *Torcedores* nowadays take between six and nine months to learn their craft.

tasador Tastes the newly rolled cigars to verify their overall quality.

controlador Checks to make sure the cigars are rolled correctly and correspond to set standards.

escogedor Classifies the cigars of the same *vitola* according to color.

fileteador Decorates cigar boxes with lithographed labels.

envasador Separates cigars into two groups, one each for upper and lower layer of the cigar box.

encajetillador Puts the cigars in their boxes.

anillador Places a cigar band on each cigar.

controlador Verifies the cigar boxes' appearance and makes a final check of the quality of the Havanas inside.

Glossary

abertura (opening) in the *casas de escogida,* or grading and sorting houses, of Vuelta Abajo, this operation consists of opening, classifying, and piling the leaves. It is performed solely by women.

abono (fertilizer) replaces, if necessary, nutritive elements; amounts are progressively increased to improve yield. The amount of fertilizer used is established following soil analysis. Fertilizers may be organic (animal, vegetable, or both) or inorganic (mineral or chemical). They are subdivided into nitrates, phosphates, calcites, and stimulants.

PRINCIPAL NUTRITIVE ELEMENTS OF TOBACCO

Nitrogen (N) is essential to the overall development of the plant, especially its leaves. Regulates chlorophyll, proteins, and nicotine. A tobacco leaf contains from 2 to 5 percent nitrogen; a level below 1.5 percent is considered insufficient. The height at which the leaf is growing, the age of the plant, and fertilization affect these percentages. A plant that is deficient in nitrogen grows less, has smaller leaves, and appears a pale green due to a reduction in chlorophyll levels. The lower leaves turn yellow and dry out prematurely. The plant blooms later, and the tobacco, when smoked, has no taste. An overabundance of nitrogen slows down maturation of

the standing plants. Leaves have a dark color and exaggerated growth. Such tobacco has a harsh, bitter, biting flavor and burns with greater difficulty.

Phosphorous (P), very important to tobacco, is applied in greater quantities than naturally required by the plant. It hastens maturation in conjunction with photosynthesis and the increase of the amounts of carbohydrate. Its absorption by the plant depends upon soil temperature (57–70°F [14–21°C]) and pH level (5.0–6.0).

The plant starts to absorb phosphorous very early in its development. This element's mobility in the soil is limited and many soils fix phosphorous in forms that are inaccessible to the plant. A careful application of phosphorous before or just after transplanting tobacco seedlings improves results. Phosphorous deficiency produces very dark, atrophied leaves that tend to grow horizontally; the plant has an open, flat aspect, and takes longer to mature. The dried leaf is lackluster and the plant's lower regions show small maroon spots. The ash it produces is dark black.

Potassium (K), absorbed in large quantities, can make up as much as 10 percent of the leaves' dry matter, while levels below 3 percent indicate a deficiency of this element. Potassium greatly influences the tobacco's

color, aroma, and the flameless combustion of the leaf. It is also the principal element in the ash of a cigar. It can neutralize the harmful effects of other elements like chlorine and makes the leaves more resistant to certain parasitic diseases and drought. A lack of potassium inhibits the plant's development; leaves take on a dark color while yellow spots begin to appear at the tips and along the edges, gradually moving toward the midrib. In the worst cases, the leaves dry out totally. Potassium is quite mobile within the plant and a deficiency is initially felt in the lower leaves. If the plant's growth is well advanced, the upper leaves deteriorate in turn.

Calcium (Ca) is one of the chief elements in the ash of a cigar. A deficiency of this element leads to a malformation of the smaller leaves, which seem damaged by insects as they start to sprout. The tips disappear and the edges are rough. An overabundance of calcium is also harmful to the plant: the leaves become strawy, undulate, and pale. The tobacco takes longer to mature and burns with greater difficulty.

Magnesium (Mg) is important to combustion. Its presence in moderate amounts whitens ash, whereas an overabundance produces a scaly ash. Tobacco leaf contains significantly less magnesium than potassium or calcium, from 0.4 to 1.5 percent only.

Magnesium deficiency produces a loss of carotene and xanthophyll as well as an absence of chlorophyll, the molecule which contains magnesium. The leaf loses its natural color progressively from the edge toward the midrib, beginning with the oldest and highest along the stalk and eventually reaching the lowest.

Chlorine (Cl) is better known for its harmful effects when overabundant than for its benefits as a nutritive element. Yet it is clearly important; when present at levels of 0.5 percent in dry tobacco it improves the leaf's texture and suppleness, enabling workers to handle it without problem. Chlorine is quickly absorbed, however, and its abundance in certain soils leads to an overconcentration in the tobacco plant. Such leaf is termed "chlorinated tobacco."

ahuevado (egg-shaped, i.e., spindle-shaped) misshaped cigar that bulges in the middle. A *figurado,* also incorrectly rolled, is one that is pointed.

almacenaje (storage) *tercios,* or bales, generally remain in storage for from one to two years before being sent to the manufacturers or the *despalillo.* These warehouses are clean, dry, and protected from the sun, like the manufacturers' storerooms.

Tercios are stacked according to

the type of tobacco in question, *tapado* or *sol ensartado*. Bales of *tapado* are placed in refrigerated rooms (60–64°F [16–18°C]) whose relative humidity varies between 80 and 90 percent, two vertical bales upholding a third horizontal one. Bales of *sol ensartado* are piled three vertical bales high topped by a horizontal one.

The *tercios* are stacked four inches (10 cm) from the ground, two feet (60 cm) from the walls, and three feet (1 m) from the ceiling. The warehouse hands shuffle the bales around following the first fumigation, that is, fifteen days after baling, then every thirty days. The slow fermentation that is taking place at this stage allows aging, *añejamiento*, of the tobacco.

amarrador instrument used to hold the cigars fast while forming a bundle, or *mazo*. It consists of a small wooden board fitted with four wooden rods slanting outward, like two V's. A second, smaller, wooden panel at the end enables a worker to make cigars of the same height.

ancho (wide, broad) central or widest part of the wrapper.

anillado (banding) department where the "ring," or cigar band, is put on.

anillo (band) lithographed paper band affixed to the cigar to identify the brand.

anillo de combustión (combustion ring) area between the ash and the rest of the tobacco that forms when a cigar is being smoked. It should remain even.

apagón (extinguisher) a cigar that burns poorly.

aporque, aporcadura (banking of soil, earthing over) the process that occurs twenty days after transplanting, when the feet of seedlings are banked with soil from the furrows.

aposento (section) division of a tobacco curing barn in which the drying bars are stacked top to bottom. The spaces between compartments are called *falsos*.

apuyarse (to droop) tobacco plant that is defective, sickly, grows from a weak seedling.

arder (to burn) combustibility, an essential quality of any cigar.

arder a la vela (to burn perfectly) to check the combustibility of tobacco, workers used to touch the leaf with a lighted cigar and observe how it burned. If it burned perfectly, the tobacco was said to *arder a la vela* (*a la vela* is an idiomatic expression meaning "prepared, equipped, ready").

ardido (burned up, irritated) moldy tobacco, due to overheating in the *pilón*, or bulk.

arique (small cord) small cord of *yagua* used to tie the hands (*manojos*) of tobacco.

aroma a cigar's aroma is not its "strength"; a smoker's sense of smell and taste appreciate the aroma, whereas the strength is felt in the throat.

arpillera (burlap) coarse jute fabric used to bale the tobacco.

babosa (*Veronicella floridana*) a small slug harmful to tobacco. It can cause serious damage by perforating the plant's leaves.

bajar el surco (to lower the furrow) initial turn given to the soil with a spade or plow to ready it for planting the tobacco.

banda (band) half-leaf of a wrapper or binder leaf, in which the filler leaves are rolled. Two half-leaves are obtained when the leaf is stemmed.

bandera (flag) a cigar whose wrapper does not present a uniform color.

barbacoa (*galetas*, drying room) department at the factory where the filler leaf is dried and the *ligas*, the blended bunches of leaves, are prepared.

barredera (tier poles) lumber placed horizontally and on which the ends of the tobacco poles, or drying bars, rest in the curing barn.

barril (barrel) in the stemming department, the worktable at which the leaf is stripped of its midrib. In requesting a job, workers used to ask for "a barrel." This is also where the filler leaf is kept at the manufacturers.

besana (half-furrow) furrows are divided in two to make work easier in the fields.

blandura (suppleness) a necessary attribute of the leaves when they are tied in bunches after drying.

bofetón loose lithographed sheet of paper that covers the cigars in their box.

boîte nature (plain box) plain wooden cigar box without decorations.

boîte semi-nature (semi-plain box) varnished wooden cigar box without decorations.

bonche (bunch) the body of the cigar made up of the core, i.e., the filler rolled in the binder.

boquilla (tuck, lit. "small mouth") the end that is lighted.

burro, dar el burro the process of bulking leaves when fermenting the tobacco. The operation is repeated until the odor and other desired characteristics of fermented tobacco are obtained.

The *burro* and the *casilla* (cf.) reduce the strength of the tobacco when the harvest is too heavy (i.e., the leaves are thick) or fermentation is incomplete. These operations are essential to controlling the odor, flavor, and combustion of the cigar.

The *gavillas* are arranged in a circle with their tops facing outward on a piece of cloth laid directly on the ground. Each layer is dampened, and the pile is built up in this manner, then covered with cloth. The temperature at which the leaves ferment is carefully controlled and is not allowed to exceed 104°F (40°C).

cabacear (to assemble, lit. "to head") to arrange the tobacco leaves so that the base of their midribs coincide.

cabeza (head) another name given to the end of the cigar that goes into the smoker's mouth (also *perilla*).

cabinet cedar box in which *mazos* (bundles) of cigars are kept.

cabo, colilla (stub) the butt of the cigar.

cachazudo (*Feltia annexa, Feltia malefida*) cutworm harmful to tobacco, especially seedlings. Hiding during the day in the upper layer of the soil, this pest comes out at night and eats the stem of young plants; it also cuts off higher leaves to eat them on the ground.

cachimba tobacco pipe or even certain type of cigarette rolled in the shape of a pipe.

caja de galera (cigar room box) wooden box or drawer in which the ligas of tobacco are stored. The *torcedor* uses the tobacco from this drawer to roll his cigars.

caja de liga (blend box) large amounts of tobacco that have been formed into *ligas* are stored in these crates or chests.

caja de tercio (baling box) hardwood frame used for baling tobacco.

cajón (box) wooden box for selling cigars retail. These boxes generally hold from twenty-five to fifty cigars.

calidad (quality) for unprocessed tobacco *calidad* varies with the quantity of juice in the leaf, its gumminess. For rolled tobacco, quality is determined by assessing any number of characteristics.

camellón ridge of a furrow.

candelilla (*Phthorimaea operculella*) tobacco leaf borer, a caterpillar of a small moth that is relatively rare in Cuba. Attacks the lower leaves of the tobacco plant without causing much damage.

canasta (basket) shallow, though quite broad rattan basket used for carrying tobacco leaves in the *vegas* and bunches of tobacco at the curing barns and manufacturers.

cantero (parcel of land, bed) a division of the nursery allowing the *vegueros* to circulate more freely. Each *cantero* measures 59 feet long by 3 feet (18 × 1 m) wide; a 16-inch (40-cm) strip of land separates one seed bed from the next.

cañón (tube) the body of the cigar, or *bonche,* with unfinished head and tuck.

capa (wrapper) the outer leaf in which the cigar is rolled.

caperos (wrapper leaves) tobacco leaf used for wrappers.

capote (binder) leaf enveloping the filler that is in turn rolled in the wrapper.

casa de tabaco (curing barn) barn where the cut tobacco leaf is dried.

casilla (compartment) chests or compartments in which the tobacco leaves are stocked once they have been classified and gathered into bunches. The length of time spent in the *casillas* depends upon the quality of the tobacco.

cedro (cedar) indigenous tree of the order Meliaceae growing wild in Cuba where it is commonly found in hilly and chalky terrains. The cedar yields a light, flexible, porous wood that is too bitter for insects and easy to work. These qualities have made it the ideal material for cigar boxes.

celofán (cellophane) transparent film covering certain cigars or cigar boxes.

centésimos (hundredths, 1/100) containers holding ten cigars; there are one hundred boxes per one thousand cigars.

centro (center) part of the cigar body equidistant from the *perilla* and the *boquilla.*

centros (middle leaves) leaves situated at the center of the tobacco stalk between the *libre de pie* and the *corona.*

cepo (standard, gauge) instrument for measuring the length of the cigar. At its center is a hole indicating the diameter of the *vitola*. A *cepo* value of 1 indicates a diameter of 1/64 of an inch. The *cepo* itself also lists for the *torcedor* other necessary measurements for rolling the correct type of cigar.

cigarro (cigarette) in Cuba *cigarros* are cigarettes while cigars are called *tabaco torcido* or *tabaco.*

clasificación (classification), apartura or escogida sorting and grading tobacco leaves by color, size, texture, and so on.

cobertor (cover) straw or cheese-cloth laid over the newly sown seed during germination to protect it from the elements.

cogollero *(Heliothis virescens)* tobacco budworm, a small green worm common to Cuba and very harmful to tobacco, attacking the plant throughout its growth. It perforates the plant's leaves, rendering them useless as wrappers, and can also damage sprouts and blossoms.

cohoyo de palma (palma cord) small cord made from dried royal palm leaves.

combustibilidad (combustibility) the burning qualities of the leaf, whether it kindles easily or not. A tobacco that does not burn well is called *jorro* or *horro* (miser).

condición (condition) "to condition the tobacco" means to carefully follow all leaf fermentation and preparation procedures right up to rolling the cigar.

conuco small tobacco field, generally cultivated for family use.

corojo variety of tobacco used for the Havana's wrappers.

corona (crown) leaves growing at the top of the plant.

corte (cut) harvesting the tobacco by stages at intervals of about one week.

Costa Norte subdistrict of Vuelta Abajo which includes parts of the municipalities of Consolación del Sur, Mantua, Pinar del Río, and San Luis.

Costa Sur subdistrict of Vuelta Abajo which includes parts of the municipalities of Consolación del Sur, Pinar del Río, and San Luis.

costillas (ribs) network of fine veins that branch from the midrib of the tobacco leaf. The fineness of these veins is a determining factor in selection of wrappers. Wrappers should be cut so that these side veins run straight up and down the length of the cigar. If not, the cigar is poorly rolled.

criollo variety of tobacco used in the Havana as filler and binder.

crudo (raw, unfinished) tobacco that has not had all of its juice eliminated.

cuadragésimos (fortieths, 1/40) containers holding twenty-five cigars; there are forty boxes per one thousand cigars.

cubierta (covering) label pasted on the cover of the cigar box.

cuje (tobacco pole, drying bar) wooden bar from which tobacco is hung to dry. There are strict rules to follow for producing a cuje: the cut wood must be soaked in salt water for fifty days to strip off its bark so that it does not transmit its odor to the tobacco. The wooden bar is sanded until smooth and all knots are removed to avoid any possible damage to the leaves. The term *cuje* also signifies the number of tobacco leaves placed on an individual bar.

curación (curing) operations concerning the tobacco after it is harvested; carried out in the curing barns and at the manufacturers.

chapucero (bungler) cigar maker who does not do his work well.

chaveta short, broad, handleless blade used by the *torcedor* to trim the tobacco leaves and work the cigar.

cheesecloth used to cover the fields of tapado tobacco as a way of attenuating the effects of the sun. It was introduced by Don Luis Marx.

chinchal small cigar shop or factory which sells its products at retail.

décimos (tenths, 1/10) containers holding one hundred cigars; there are ten boxes per thousand cigars.

desangrar (preliminary dressing) cutting the thickest part of the leaf so that the veins do not stand out in the finished cigar.

desbotonar, desbotonar a la caja (to top, to top in the sheath) pinching off the buds that appear at the top of the tobacco plants and consume nutritive elements. Buds are removed as soon as they appear to force the plant to grow broader rather than taller.

desbotonar alto (to top high) procedure in which buds are removed after they have already started to develop. A plant that has the bud removed at this stage is taller than one from which the bud is removed as soon as it appears.

desecado (drying) drying the tobacco begins when the leaves are hung from the *cujes* in the drying barns. Two steps are involved: first, the gradual loss of moisture contained in the leaf; and secondly, the change of color due to oxidation. When the leaves have turned a dark golden brown, the midrib is dry and the process is complete.

deshijar removing the suckers and shoots that appear after the plant has been topped, *desbotonado.* This operation is repeated as many times as necessary. The suckers should not be allowed to grow beyond one inch. The process is also called *repasar,* to go over again.

deshile y selección (removal of threads and selection) untying the *gavillas* in the *casas de escogida.* The leaves are then brought to the *abridoras* (women workers) who unfold them and arrange them in uniform piles (*planchas*). They set aside any leaves that are too small or defective (checking the size of the veins, elasticity, spots, etc.), which are then used as *tripas de la capa* or *tripas de banco* in the production of cigars for consumption within Cuba.

despalillo (stemming) department where the leaf is stemmed, that is, stripped of its midrib.

despunte (eradication) elimination of tobacco seedlings that are over-developed.

desvenar stemming or removing the large veins of binder leaves.

elasticidad (elasticity) leaf's capacity to stretch without breaking, an essential quality for wrapper leaves.

emboquillar first turn given by the cigar maker to the filler when he begins to enclose it in the wrapper as he fashions the cigar.

empacar (to pack) putting the tobacco into bales before classification.

empilonar (to pile) arranging the bundles of leaves atop one another to start the process of fermentation.

encentrar la hoja (to center the leaf) to make the necessary cuts in the wrapper leaf to remove damaged parts.

engavillar (to bunch, sheave) at the *casas de escogida,* arranging the tobacco bunches with the stems together and tying them at the top, i.e., near the base of the stems. For wrapper leaves, the *engavilladores* attach the graded leaves according to their *tiempo* in *gavillas* of forty to sixty leaves (forty for classes 11 to 14; fifty for classes 14a, 15, 16, 18a, 19a, E; sixty for classes 15a and 16a). For filler leaves, each bunch of four gavillas is assembled according to a certain predetermined weight and not the number of leaves.

ensartar (to string) stringing a cotton thread through the leaves before suspending them from the tobacco poles.

enterceo (baling) baling wrapper and filler leaves in the grading houses. Wrapper leaves travel in collapsible wooden crates, caja de tercio ("third crates"). The name apparently comes from the fact that three men were needed for this operation. The mounted tercio measures 28 inches long, 24 inches wide, and 22 inches high ($70 \times 60 \times 55$ cm). For filler leaves, the tercio, or paca, is put together with the help of a wooden crate with a sliding bottom that measures about 35 cubic feet (1 m^3). A paca contains 110 pounds (55 kg) of fortaleza no. 1 or capote, 120 pounds (60 kg) of fortaleza no. 2, or 130 pounds (65 kg) of fortaleza nos. 3 or 4.

escaparate (display cabinet) air-conditioned room containing wooden cabinets in which the finished cigars are stocked before being placed in their boxes.

escogida (grading) at the manufacturer, the department where the finished cigars are classified by color and put into boxes. In the *casas de escogida* the wrappers are classified by the *escogedores,* also called *rezagadoras,* according to the leaves' size.

evaluación sensorial (sensory evaluation) taste-testing cigars to ensure their quality before they are put into boxes.

fábrica de tabaco cigar manufacturer.

falso (lit. "false") aisle separating two *aposentos* in a curing barn.

fermentacing (fermentation) chemical transformation of the tobacco leaf that enables it to acquire its aroma.

filete (fillet, ornamental edge) paper ribbon decorating the edges of cigar boxes.

fileteado (decorating) department where cigar boxes are "dressed," i.e., decorated with lithographed labels and such. The verb is *filetear.*

fortaleza (strength) a unit of measure for grading filler tobacco.

fumas cigars that *torcedores* may smoke or take home with them.

fumigación (fumigation) disinfecting by fumigation in order to eliminate insect pests and parasites that are harmful to tobacco.

galera (lit. "galley") department of cigar manufacturers where their product is rolled; so called because of the systematic use of convicts for this job in the nineteenth century. The term is still employed today.

gavilla (sheaf) tobacco leaves are bound into sheaves after they have been classified.

guano dried leaves of the royal palm still used for thatching in farmers' houses.

guillotina (standard cigar guillotine) cuts the finished cigars to the correct length for the *vitola* in question.

Habana Havana, Cuba.

Habano (Havana) cigar produced by Cuban manufacturers using Cuban tobacco from the Vuelta Abajo region and guaranteed with the official seal of the Cuban government.

habilitación (decorating) the lithographed labels used to decorate a cigar box.

largueros (sides) front and back sides of the cigar box.

lector (reader) employee of the manufacturers who, seated on a special platform or rostrum provided for this purpose, reads to the other cigar workers while they perform their tasks. The official government review is read in the morning, and a novel of the employees' choosing in the afternoon.

libre de pie (foot leaves, lit. "free footed") the first leaves at the base of the tobacco plant.

liga (blend) blend of leaves that give the finished cigar its characteristic taste and aroma.

ligero (light) one of the *tiempos* in grading tobacco.

Lomas subdistrict of Vuelta Abajo that includes parts of the municipalities of Guane, Mantua, Pinar del Río, San Juan y Martínez, and Viñales.

Llano subdistrict of Vuelta Abajo that includes parts of the municipalities of Consolaciities of Guane, Mantua, Pinar del Río, San Juan y Martínez, and San Luis.

macho (mosaic) a widespread viral disease affecting Cuban tobacco. Affected leaves turn yellowish or pale green and some become rough, interrupting the plant's growth.

maduro (mature) tobacco that has reached its optimum growth. This is also one of the classifications of tobacco leaf.

manojear (to put into hands) action of forming a hand of tobacco.

manojeo (assembling) in the *casa de escogida,* four sheaves of wrapper leaves are tied together using a length of vegetable fiber, usually dried royal palm leaves, that measures about a quarter of an inch thick. Any leaves that stick out are placed back in the *manojos.* Before binding the *manojos,* they are placed in compartments set against the wall called *casillas* and covered. The sheaves remain there until the strength of the tobacco is sufficiently diminished.

manojo (hand) four bound *gavillas,* the result of the *manojeo.*

mazo (bunch) a bunch of either tobacco seedlings or cigars.

media rueda (half wheel) a bundle of fifty cigars.

meluza oily liquid secreted by tobacco leaf that greatly influences the quality of the tobacco.

medio tiempo a classification of tobacco leaves.

milésimos (thousandths, $1/1,000$) individual cigar containers; there are one thousand boxes per thousand cigars.

molde (mold) wooden mold used since the 1950s to assist the *torcedor* in forming the core of the Havana. Before the introduction of the *molde,* torcedores alone guaranteed consistency in the diameter and density of the cigar.

moja (dampening) department of the *casas de escogida* where the leaves are dampened with pressurized water vapor (for wrappers) or moistened with a sponge (for filler) to make classification and handling easier.

oreo (airing) in the *casas de escogida,* damp wrapper leaves are allowed to air to eliminate excess water.

paca (bale) bale of ungraded tobacco or stemmed filler leaves.

pajizo (straw) low-grade, dry tobacco.

palito (stem) midrib of the tobacco leaf.

paño (texture) the leaf's texture or body. When a leaf is flexible and appears to be of high quality, it is said to have a good *pait.*

papeleta (bill) lithograph of the trademark or emblem of the cigar manufacturer pasted to the side of the cigar box.

parejo (smooth, even) said complimentarily of a cigar with a regular thickness throughout its entire length.

parillas (racks) wooden stands or platforms on which stemmed tobacco leaves are laid to eliminate excess moisture.

perforador del tabaco *(Lasioderma serricorne)* tobacco borer, an insect that is harmful to tobacco in all its forms. This pest bores minuscule holes or burrows in the plant.

perilla (head, lit. "little pear") the tip of the cigar that goes into the smoker's mouth.

pesada (heavy) a leaf that is quite gummy or of excellent quality.

petaca cigar holder.

picadero room in the *casa de escogida* in which all the categories of graded tobacco are brought together before being put into bunches.

picadura shredded tobacco.

pilón (fermentation pile, loaf) bulk of dried tobacco that starts the fermentation process.

preparación de terreno (preparation of the soil) the most widespread technique for preparing the soil consists of a ninety-day cycle leading up to the transplantation of the tobacco seedlings.

A plow is run through the ground twice to break up the soil cover and make the succeeding phases easier.

Roturación (clearing of the ground) occurs as soon after plowing as possible. The green ground cover is turned under to a depth of about six to eight inches (15–20 cm) to aid decomposition. In sandy soils this is done with an *arado de vertedera* (moldboard plow) and in clayey soils with an *arado de disco* (disc plow). A *grada* (harrow) then smoothes out the soil. Five to ten days later, *cruce* (crossing) breaks up those areas that have gone untilled. This operation loosens the soil to the required depth. Fifteen days after *cruce,* the *grada* is passed over the soil once again to loosen it and eliminate any unwanted plants. The *tiller* (plow) then leaves the soil supple and well aerated to a depth of 10 to 12 inches (25–30 cm), aiding both surface and internal drainage.

The fields are plowed to maximize the effectiveness of irrigation and drainage. To avoid erosion, furrows run parallel to the slope of the land (preferably in a north-south direction). They go to a depth of 4 to 5 inches (10–12 cm) and are divided by the *vegueros* into *besanas* measuring 66 feet (20 m) in length. For *tapado* tobacco, a distance of 33 inches (82.5 cm) is maintained between furrows, for *sol ensartado,* that distance is reduced to 30 inches (75 cm).

punta (point, tip) the narrowest distal part of the leaf.

puntal (pillar) support pillar in the curing barns.

rama (leaf or unmanufactured tobacco) tobacco that is not subjected to industrial processing.

rapé (rappee) tobacco taken as snuff.

reata cord used to tie up bales.

recortes (trimmings) scraps of leaves left after constructing the cigar.

regalía deluxe *vitolas.*

rezagado (selection) selection and classification of wrapper leaves by size and color.

rezagos de escogida cigars considered defective because of their color or other flaws.

rueda (wheel) a bundle of one hundred cigars.

sahorno (chafing) rot caused by excess moisture on the leaves during drying.

sazón (season) said of soils whose moisture content at a depth of one foot (30 cm) lies between 15 and 23 percent.

seco (dry) one of the *tiempos* in grading tobacco.

semillero (seedbed) field in which the tobacco seeds are sown and the seedlings are raised until ready for transplanting in the *vegas. Semilleros* have a maximum area of thirty-three acres (13.5 ha), and are characterized by sandy, light earth that provides good drainage. They always lie near a fresh water spring to lessen the risk of contamination by other plants.

tabaco de sol (sun-grown tobacco) tobacco raised directly in the sun.

tabaco tapado (shade tobacco, lit. "covered") tobacco raised out of direct sunlight beneath a cheesecloth canopy.

tabla (board) square wooden board on which the *torcedor* rolls his cigars.

tercio (bale, lit. "third") curing the hands of tobacco (*manojos*).

tiempos degrees used in grading tobacco leaves, referring to texture, thickness, etc.

torcer (to roll) the action of rolling a cigar.

trasplante (transplanting) replanting seedlings.

tripa (filler) the main content of the cigar's core, comprising one, two, or three classes of tobacco leaf.

tripa empalmada filler that has been incorrectly fashioned such that the leaves hinder the flow of air, resulting in poor combustion.

vega tobacco field or plantation.

vicentésimos (two-hundredths, 1/200) containers holding five cigars; there are two hundred boxes per one thousand cigars.

viso one of the *tiempos* in grading tobacco.

vista (view) lithographed label pasted on the inside of the cigar box cover.

vitola (type) type or shape of cigar; an umbrella term that encompasses a cigar's specific dimensions (length, diameter, weight).

volado class of tobacco.

yagua leaf of the royal palm that is subjected to a number of complex treatments before being used in baling tobacco leaves. *Yagua* acts as tobacco's thermometer; it protects the leaf and regulates its moisture content, serving as a kind of buffer and blotter.

yema terminal (also *botón*) blossom located at the top of the plant.

zafado (loosening) separating the sheaves of wrappers before dampening.

Bibliography

PERIODICALS

Arts Graphiques, October-December 1974, Cuba.

Cigar Aficionado, summer 1994.

Cubatabaco International, first quarter 1985, Cuba.

El Tabaco, no. 19, Cuba.

Habano, November 1936, Cuba.

BOOKS

Abdallah, Fawky. *Se puede medir la calidad del tabaco.* Havana: Cuban Book Institute, 1970.

Akehurst, B. C. *El tabaco.* Havana: Cuban Book Institute, 1973.

Casado, Ricardo A. *Nuestro tabaco.* Havana, 1939.

Claussell, Pablo Medina, and Juan Francisco Valdéz Valdéz. *Agrotecnica del tabaco.* Havana: Ministerio de Agricultura, 1986.

Cortina, Humberto. *Tabaco, historia y psicología.* Havana: Editions Fernandez, 1939.

Davidoff, Zino. *L'Histoire du Havane.* Paris: Éditions Daniel Briand, 1981.

Espino, Eumelio. *Variedades del tabaco.* Havana: Ministerio de Agricultura, 1989.

Felipe, Pedro Alfonso. *Estudios agroedafologicos de las zonas tabacaleras de Cuba.* Havana: Ministerio de Agricultura, 1989.

Galló, Gaspar Jorge Garcia. *Biografia del Habano.* Havana: Comision nacionale del Habano, 1961.

Infante, G. Cabrera. *Holy Smoke.* Boston: Faber & Faber, 1985.

Jiménez, Antonio Núñez. *The Journey of the Havana Cigar.* Neptune City, N.J.: T.F.H. Publications, 1988.

Muñiz, José Rivero. *Tabaco, su historia en Cuba.* Havana: Cuban Historical Institute, 1992.

Ortiz, Fernando. *Cuban Counterpoint: Tobacco and Sugar.* Durham, N.C.: Duke University Press, 1995.

Ramos, Manuel Rodriguez. *Siembra, fabricacion e historia del tabaca.* Havana: Librairie del Monte, 1905.

Voges, Ernst, ed. *Tobacco Encyclopedia.* Mainz, Germany: T.J.I., 1984.

Acknowledgments

The photographer would like to thank Marinette for her patience and constant help, without which none of these photographs would have seen the light of day; the team at Studio Patrick in Villars, always on the ball when their director is on the road; and Tabashop in Montreux, for their assistance with the glossary. In Cuba, thanks go to Jean-Yves and José, who provided help and handled logistics for the entire content of this book; and Yvenka, ever ready to answer questions and act as our guide.

The author would like to thank Kiko for her help, understanding, and enthusiasm; and, in Cuba, Katia, Raphaël, Bernardo, Arsenio, Enrique, Ana Isis, and Juan Carlos, for their kindness and unfailing willingness to help.

Photos on pages 26–27, 31, 33, and 34–35 by Charles Del Todesco

Index

Page numbers in *italic* refer to illustrations.

grading tobacco leaves, 60–63
gran coronas, 124, 211
Grant, Ulysses S., 18
Guevara, Ernesto "Che," 19, *72–73*

H

harvesting tobacco, *20, 43,* 45
Havana, *66–69, 127;* before
　revolution, 18
Havana cigars: classification of, 110;
　classifying tobacco for, 13, 60–63,
　80–81; cultivating tobacco for, 13,
　23, 24–45, *25–28, 31, 33, 34,*
　40–42; curing tobacco for, 13,
　50–60, *51–55, 58–59;* early
　manufacturers of, 13; fumigation
　of, 106, 111; humidity control
　and, 120–24; making, *16–17,*
　82–116, *83, 89–97, 100;* nicotine
　content of, 128; origin of term, 13;
　packaging of, 14, 110–11, 120;
　paper bands or rings on, 14, 110,
　111–16, 124; physical inspection
　of, 102–6, 116; popularity of,
　14–18; shipping of, 13–14, 120;
　smok-ing, 124–28; taste testing of,
　101–2, *110*
Havana Commercial Co. ("American
　trust"), 14, 18
Hemingway, Ernest, 18
Henry Clay, 14, 19
Henry Clay and Block Company
　Ltd., 14
Hermosos No. 4, 211
Holy Smoke (Cabrera Infante), 101
Hoyo de Monterrey, 82, 150–54,
　203, 216, 218

I

infantes, 212
La Intimidad, 14, 216

J

Jané y Gener, Miguel, 216
José Gener, 14, 155, 204
José L. Piedra, 155, 203, 219
Joyce, James, 101
Juan Valle y Cía, 217
Julieta 2, 124, 212

K

Kennedy, John F., 19
Key West, Fla., offshoot of Cuban
　tobacco industry in, 14
Khrushchev, Nikita, 22
Kipling, Rudyard, 22

L

El Laguito, 22, 217
lanceros, 217

libre de pie leaves, 13, 29, 45, 60, 63
ligero leaves, 63, 64, 74, 88, 101
Lincoln, Abraham, 18
Londres, 212
López, Manuel, 217
López Fernández, Fernando, 217

L

La Majagua, 216
Mao Zedong, 22
marevas, 212
Maria Guerrero, 204, 218
Martí, José, 14, 19
Médicis, Catherine de, 9
medio tiempo tobacco, 63, 64, 74
Menéndez, Dina, 19
Menéndez y Cía, 216
minutos, 212
Montecristo, 18–19, 82, 156–57,
　204, 216, 218
Murias, 19

N

nacionales, 212
Napoleonic Wars, 12
naturales, 213
Nicot, Jean, 9
Nicotiana, 9
nicotine, 128
ninfas, 124, 213
Nueva Marca, 204

O

Ortiz, Fernando, 6

P

Palicio, Fernando, 216
palmas, 213
palmitas, 213
panetelas, 213
panetelas largas, 213
parejos, 213
Parera, Buenaventura, 217
Partagás, 13, 14, *72–73,* 82, 158–65,
　204, 216, 218
Particulares, 216
Pérez, Bienvenido "Chicho," 22, 217
Pérez, Francisco, *72–73*
perfectos, 213
perillas: cutting off, 124; fashioning,
　100, 101
perlas, 124, 213
petit cetros, 214
petit coronas, 214
petits, 124, 214
Picasso, Pablo, 13
piramides, 214
placeras, 214
Por Larrañaga, 13, 14, 166–67, 205,
　217, 218

pre-Columbian civilizations, 6–9
preferidos, 214
prefermentation, 64
pregermination, 30
prominentes, 124, 214
Punch, 13, 82, 168–73, 205, 217,
　218

Q

Quai d'Orsay, 174, 205
quality control, 101–6, *108–10,* 116
Quintero, 175–76, 205, 219

R

Rafaël Gonzales, 177–78, 205, 218
Ramón Allones, 14, 120, 179–80,
　205, 216, 218
El Rey Del Mundo, 13, 181–83,
　206, 218
rezago class, 63
rezagos, 106
Rivero, Eduardo, 22, 217
robustos, 214
rolling cigars, *16–17,* 88–101,
　89–97, 100
Romeo y Julieta, 13, 14, 82, 184–90,
　206, 216–17, 218

S

Sancho Panza, 191–92, 206, 218
San Luis Rey, 193, 206, 218
seco leaves, 63, 64, 74, 88, 101
seed. *See* tobacco seed
seoanes, 214
Sibelius, Jean, 18
Siboney, 206, 219
sol ensartado tobacco, 60; classifica-
　tion of, 60–63; cultivation of, 38;
　prefermentation of, 64
Spanish-American War, 14
sports, 214
standards, 215
Statos De Luxe, 194, 206, 218
stemming, *19,* 64–74, 87
superiores, 124, 215

T

Tabacalera Cubana S. A., 18, 219
tacos, 215
Taino people, 6, 24
tapado tobacco, 60; classification of,
　60–63; cultivation of, 38
taste testing, 101–2, *110*
tiempos, 60–63
tobacco: classification of, *13,* 60–63,
　80–81; cultivation of, 9–12, 13,
　23, 24–45, *25–28, 31, 33, 34,*
　40–42; curative properties of, 9,
　13; curing of, 13, 50–60, *51–55,*
　58–59; denounced by Catholic

priests, 9; fermentation of, *54–55,*
　58–59, 60, 74; fumigation of, 106,
　111; growth habit of, 13; in pre-
　Columbian civilizations, 6–9;
　quality standards established for,
　13; research on, 30; stemming,
　19, 64–74, 87; taxonomy of, 9;
　trade in, 9, 12–13
tobacco flowers, 13, *40–42;* disbud-
　ding and, 30, 43; gathering seed
　from, 30–31, *46–47*
tobacco seed, 13, *44, 48–49;*
　categories of, 24–30; gathering
　for future crops, 30–31, *46–47;*
　pregermination of, 30; preparing
　nursery beds for, 31–32; sowing
　of, 32–38, *33*
tobacco seedlings: replanting of, *25,*
　38–43; tending of, 38
toppers, 215
Torres, Luis de, 6, 24
trabucos, 215
Trinidad, 217
Troya, 194, 206, 218

U

Ulysses (Joyce), 101
universales, 215
uno y media leaves, 13, 29, 45, 60,
　63
H. Upmann, 13, 14, 195–200,
　206–7, 216, 218

V

vegueritos, 215
Velázquez, Diego, 9
Villar y Villar, 19
vitolas: commercial (table), 202–7;
　distinctive blends in, 88; meaning
　of, 101; origin of word, 101;
　production (table), 208–15
volado leaves, 63, 64, 74, 88, 101

W

Wagner, Richard, 18
women: in cigar factories, 22
World War I, 18
wrapper leaves, 13, *75,* 82–88, *86;*
　best leaves for, 29; change in
　appearance of, 110; classification
　of, *18, 21,* 60–63, 87; physical
　inspection of, 106; in rolling
　process, 101; stemming, 87.
　See also corojo tobacco

X

Xerex, Rodrigo de, 6, 9, 24

Z

zurdos, 101